Mike McGrath

HTML

In easy steps is an imprint of In Easy Steps Limited
Southfield Road · Southam
Warwickshire CV47 0FB · United Kingdom
www.ineasysteps.com

6th Edition

Notice of Liability

Every effort has been made to ensure that this book contains accurate and current information. However, In Easy Steps Limited and the author shall not be liable for any loss or damage suffered by readers as a result of any information contained herein.

Trademarks

All trademarks are acknowledged as belonging to their respective companies.

Printed and bound in the United Kingdom

ISBN-13 978-1-84078-359-9
ISBN-10 1-84078-359-1

Contents

8 Inserting hyperlinks 129

9 Using frames 145

10 Building forms 159

Index 187

Foreword

The examples in this book have been carefully prepared to demonstrate features of the HyperText Markup Language (HTML). You are encouraged to try out the examples on your own computer to discover the exciting possibilities offered by HTML. The straightforward descriptions should allow you to easily recreate the examples manually or, if you prefer, you can download an archive containing all the source code by following these simple steps:

1. Open your browser and visit our website at **http://www.ineasysteps.com**
2. Navigate to the "Resource center" and choose the "Downloads" section
3. Find the "From HTML in easy steps, 6th edition" item in the "Source code" list, then click on the hyperlink entitled "All code examples" to download the ZIP archive
4. Extract the contents of the ZIP archive to any convenient location on your computer – for easy reference these are arranged in sub-folders whose names match each chapter title of this book. The documents are named as described in the book and are located in the appropriate chapter folder of the archive. For example, the **body.html** document, described in the third chapter, is located in the folder named **3-Creating body content**

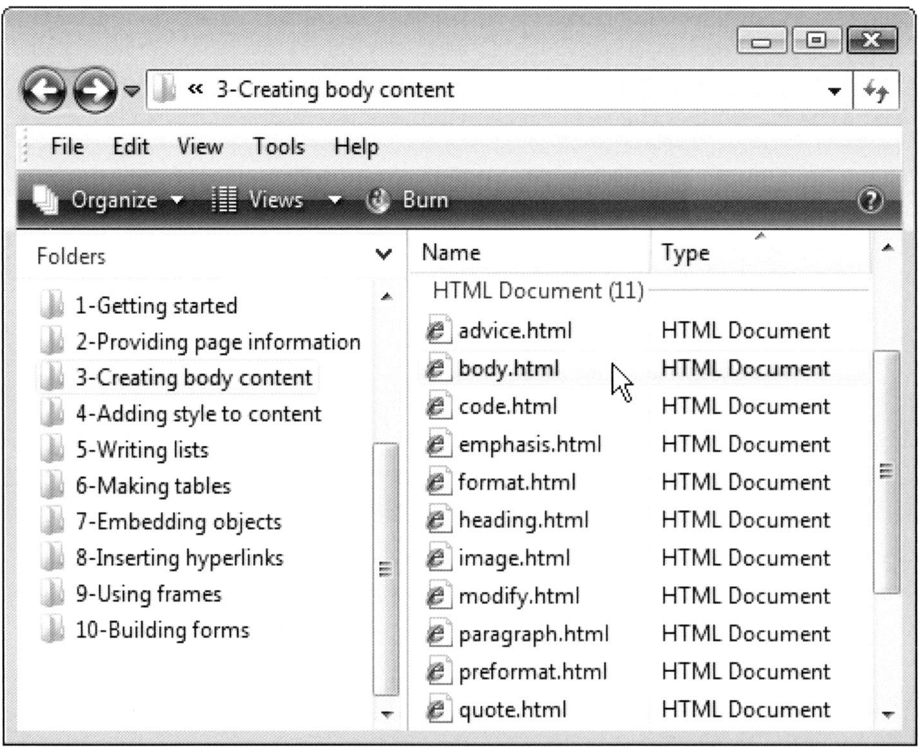

1 Getting started

Welcome to the exciting world of HTML. This chapter introduces HTML and demonstrates how to create a "barebones" HTML document.

Introduction

Historically, the desire to have text printed in specific formats meant that original manuscripts were "marked up" with annotation to indicate to the book-printer how the author would like sections of text laid out. This annotation had to be concise and needed to be understood both by the printer and the text originator. A series of commonly recognized abbreviations therefore formed the basis of a standard markup language.

The W3C is the recognized body that oversees standards on the web. See the latest developments on their informative website at **www.w3.org**.

HyperText Markup Language (HTML) is a modern standard markup language that uses common abbreviations called "tags" to indicate to the web browser how the author would like to have sections of a web page laid out. It was first devised in March 1989 by a British physicist named Tim Berners-Lee while he was working at CERN in Switzerland – the European Organization for Nuclear Research. His proposal showed how information could be easily transferred over the Internet using hypertext to provide the, now familiar, point-and-click navigation system. Connecting personal computers to the Internet using hypertext would create a single information network, allowing CERN physicists to share all computer-stored information at the laboratory. Berners-Lee created a text browser and in May 1990 the system was named the World Wide Web.

The simplicity of HTML led it to become popular in the early days of the Internet with text-based web browsers. A major development with HTML came in 1993 when a college student named Marc Andreessen added an image tag so that HTML could display images in addition to text. This version was then included in the Mosaic web browser from the National Center for Supercomputing Applications (NCSA) and became very successful. Marc went on to establish the Netscape web browser.

Sir Tim Berners-Lee, creator of the World Wide Web

During the "browser wars" of the mid 1990s the various web browsers that were fighting for market share began to add proprietary tags to effectively create their own versions of HTML. The World Wide Web Consortium (W3C) standards organization recognized the danger that HTML could become fragmented and acted to create a standard to which all web browsers should adhere. Today Sir Tim Berners-Lee is a director of the W3C.

The latest recommended version of the W3C HTML standard is HTML 4.01. This version is covered throughout the book, but is generically referred to as "HTML 4" or just plain "HTML".

What's new in HTML 4?

The features in the earlier standard of HTML 3.2 are updated in HTML 4 to provide more flexibility for current and future development of the Internet. Most importantly HTML 4 separates document structure from document presentation. While HTML markup tags are still used to define document structure, controlling the layout of content, Cascading Style Sheets (CSS) are now used to define document presentation, controlling the appearance of content. Consequently many presentational tags have been made obsolete (deprecated) in favor of style sheets:

- The **<center>** tag that was used to center blocks is deprecated
- The **<font>** and **<basefont>** tags that were used to specify fonts are deprecated
- The **<strike>**, **<s>**, and **<u>** tags that were used to decorate character appearance are deprecated
- The **<applet>** tag that was used to embed Java applets is now deprecated in favor of an **<object>** tag
- The **<dir>** and **<menu>** tags that were used for lists are deprecated in favor of a **<ul>** tag
- The **<isindex>** tag that was used to denote an input prompt is deprecated in favor of an **<input>** tag

HTML 4 introduces new tags to extend the precision of how document content may be defined and support has been added for languages written right-to-left to increase global utilization. Additionally a new model for table layout allows the browser to start rendering a table even before the entire table is downloaded.

HTML 4 has been designed to make web pages more accessible to those with physical limitations and greater scripting possibilities are provided by the addition of more page "events". Further new tags allow the creation of compound web documents by the inclusion of resources from a variety of sources.

Deprecated features are still supported by "HTML 4 Transitional" and "HTML 4 Frameset" specifications for backward compatability but not by the modern "HTML 4 Strict" specification described in this book.

Addressing web pages

The World Wide Web comprises a series of large-capacity computers, known as "web servers", which are connected to the Internet via telephone line and satellite. The web servers each use the HyperText Transfer Protocol (HTTP) as a common communication standard to allow any computer connected to any web server access to all files across the web.

Beware

A web page address (URL) cannot contain any blank spaces.

HTML web pages are merely plain text files that have been saved with a file extension of ".htm" or ".html" – for instance **index.html**.

In order to access a file across the web its web address must be entered into the address field of a web browser. The web address is formally known as its "Uniform Resource Locator" (URL) and typically has three parts:

- **Protocol** – any URL using the HTTP protocol begins by specifying the protocol as **http://**
- **Domain** – the host name of the computer from which the file can be downloaded. For instance **www.example.com**
- **Path** – the virtual path to the file on the named domain, including any parent directory names where applicable. For instance **/htdocs/index.html**

Hot tip

Where an address states only the HTTP protocol and a domain name most web servers are configured to seek a file named as **index.html** in their default directory.

A URL describing the location of a file by protocol, domain, and path is stating its "absolute" address. So the absolute address of the file described by the protocol, domain, and path components above is **http://www.example.com/htdocs/index.html**.

Code contained within a HTML web page can reference other HTML files in any domain by their absolute address. HTML files resident within the same domain can also be referenced by their absolute address or more simply by their "relative" address. This means that files located within the same directory can be referenced in another file just by their file name. For instance, a file named "adjacent.html" can be referenced as **adjacent.html**.

Additionally, a relative address can reference a file located within a parent directory by prefixing its file name with the syntax "../". For instance, a file named "higher.html" in the parent directory can be referenced from the current directory as **../higher.html**.

How do web servers work?

When you enter a URL into the browser address field the browser first examines the specified protocol. Where the protocol is HTTP it recognizes that a file is being sought from a web server so then contacts a Domain Name Server (DNS) to look up the numerical Internet Protocol (IP) address of the specified domain. Next a connection is established with the web server at that IP address to request the file at the specified path. When the file is successfully located it is sent back to the web browser, otherwise the web server sends an error code such as "404 – Page Not Found".

The Domain Name Server is typically run by your Internet Service Provider or by your company.

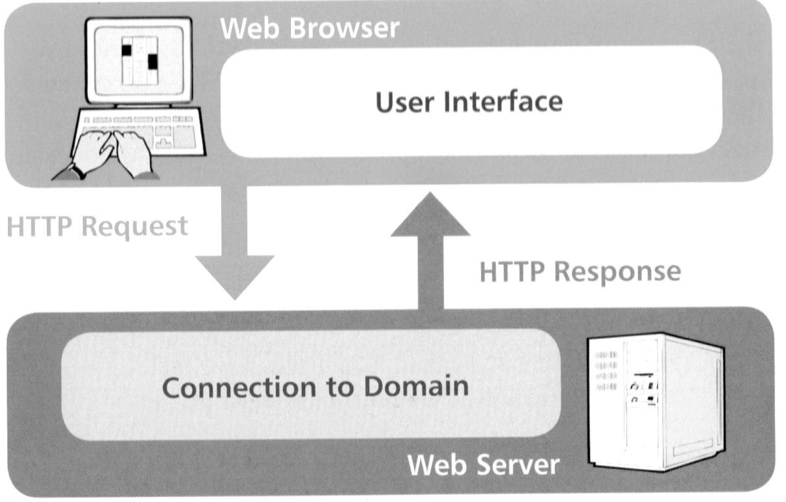

A successful response sends HTTP "headers" to the web browser, describing the nature of the response, along with the requested file. The headers are not normally visible but can be seen using special software, like the "ieHTTPHeaders" plugin for Internet Explorer:

```
HTTP/1.1 200 OK
Content-type: text/html
Connection: Keep-Alive
Keep-Alive: timeout=150000, max=10
Transfer-Encoding: Chunked
Date: Mon, 18 Feb 2010 15:33:39 GMT
Server: Abyss/2.5.0.0-X1-Win32 AbyssLib/2.5.0.0
```

Here the web server identifies the protocol as HTTP/1.1 and sends the success code "200 - OK".

You can learn more about the ieHTTPHeaders plugin at **www.blunck.se** or Linux users can invoke the **-i** option with **curl** to see the HTTP headers.

Notice that the HTTP Content-type is described as "text/html". This is the universally recognized unique MIME type that is used by all web servers to identify regular plain text HTML files.

Defining document structure

The structure of a HTML 4 document has these three parts:

- **Document Type Definition (DTD)** – defining precisely which HTML version type the document conforms to
- **Head section** – containing descriptive data about the document itself, such as the document's title and character set
- **Body section** – containing the content that is to appear when the document gets loaded into a web browser

Beware

The Document Type Definition may appear on a single line if space permits but should otherwise be copied precisely as listed here.

Document Type Definition

The Document Type Definition is a non-HTML tag that must appear at the start of the first line of every HTML 4 document. The DTD is just a piece of code, specified in the HTML standard, that can be pasted into the top of each page. It states an address containing the language rules for that version of HTML.

The standard DTD is called "Strict" and should be used for a HTML document that uses only valid HTML 4 markup. For instance, the DTD using HTML version 4.01 looks like this:

```
<!DOCTYPE HTML PUBLIC "-//W3C//DTD HTML 4.01//EN"
              "http://www.w3.org/TR/html4/strict.dtd" >
```

The specification also provides a "Transitional" DTD for backward compatibility. This should only be used where the HTML document contains some obsolete deprecated markup:

```
<!DOCTYPE HTML PUBLIC
        "-//W3C//DTD HTML 4.01 Transitional//EN"
        "http://www.w3.org/TR/html4/loose.dtd" >
```

Don't forget

The web browser can use the address in the DTD to validate the HTML code contained in that HTML document.

Finally there is a special DTD that is only to be used for a HTML "Frameset" document that specifies the frames to be used in a multi-document web page:

```
<!DOCTYPE HTML PUBLIC
        "-//W3C//DTD HTML 4.01 Frameset//EN"
        "http://www.w3.org/TR/html4/frameset.dtd" >
```

As the example code given in this book does not use any obsolete deprecated markup the Strict DTD is used in all example HTML documents except the special frameset examples in chapter nine.

The entire head section and body section can be enclosed within a pair of **<html> </html>** tags to contain all HTML markup. The W3C HTML 4.01 specification actually states that these are optional but it is logical to provide a single "root" element. Most HTML tags are used in pairs like this to act as "containers" with the syntax **< *tagname* > *data* < /*tagname* >**

Hot tip

A HTML "element" is any matching pair of opening and closing tags, or any single tag not requiring a closing tag – as described in the HTML element tags list on the inside front cover of this book.

Head section

The document's head section begins with a HTML opening **<head>** tag and ends with a corresponding closing **</head>** tag. Data describing the document can be added later between these two tags to complete the HTML document's head section.

Body section

The document's body section starts with an opening **<body>** tag and ends with a corresponding closing **</body>** tag. Actual document content that is to appear in the web browser can be added later between these two tags to complete the HTML document's body section.

Code comments can be added at any point within both the head and body sections between a pair of **<!--** and **-->** tags. Anything that appears between these special comment tags is completely ignored by the web browser.

So the markup tags that create the fundamental document structure of a Strict HTML 4 document look like this:

```
<!DOCTYPE HTML PUBLIC "-//W3C//DTD HTML 4.01//EN"
                     "http://www.w3.org/TR/html4/strict.dtd" >
<html>

    <head>
         <!-- Data describing the document to be added here. -->
    </head>

      <body>
         <!-- Actual document content to be added here. -->
      </body>

</html>
```

Hot tip

The "invisible" characters that represent tabs, newlines, carriage returns, and spaces are collectively known as "whitespace". They may optionally be used to inset the tags for clarity.

Note that HTML 4 tag names may appear in either uppercase or lowercase but future specifications may allow lowercase only – so only lowercase tag names are used throughout this book.

Creating a HTML document

The fundamental HTML document structure, described on the previous page, can be used to create a simple HTML document in any plain text editor such as Notepad on Windows systems. In order to create a valid "barebones" HTML document two tags need to be added to the head section – describing the document's title, and the character set in which the document is written.

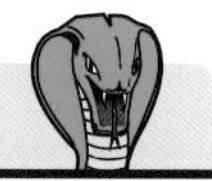

Beware

HTML documents should not be created in Word processors, such as Word, as they include additional information in their file formats.

The document title is defined between **<title>** and **</title>** tags. Defining the character set requires values to be specified to two "attributes" within a HTML **<meta>** tag. The **http-equiv** attribute represents the equivalent of the HTTP Content-type header with the statement **http-equiv="Content-type"**. The **content** attribute defines the MIME type as "text/html" and the encoding (**charset**) character set. Where the document is created in ANSI format for Western languages the encoding is "ISO-8859-1".

Follow these steps to create a valid "barebones" HTML document :

hello.html

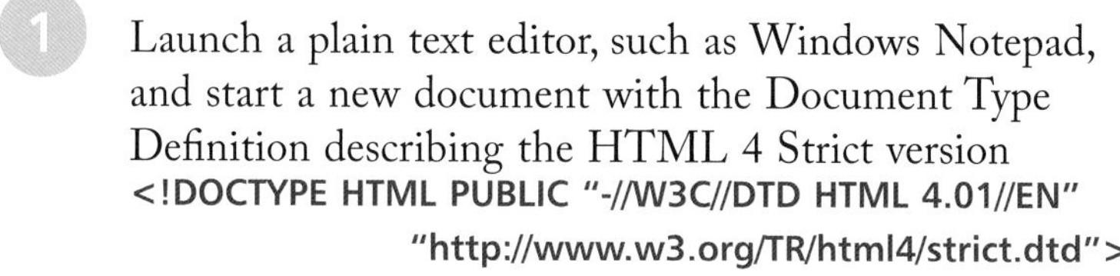

1. Launch a plain text editor, such as Windows Notepad, and start a new document with the Document Type Definition describing the HTML 4 Strict version

```
<!DOCTYPE HTML PUBLIC "-//W3C//DTD HTML 4.01//EN"
                "http://www.w3.org/TR/html4/strict.dtd">
```

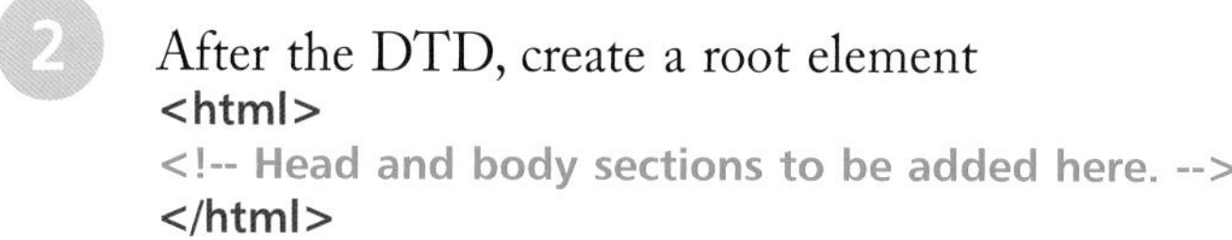

2. After the DTD, create a root element

```
<html>
<!-- Head and body sections to be added here. -->
</html>
```

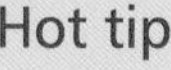

Hot tip

The **<meta>** tag is a single tag – it does not need a matching closing tag. See the element tag list on the inside front cover of this book to find other single tags.

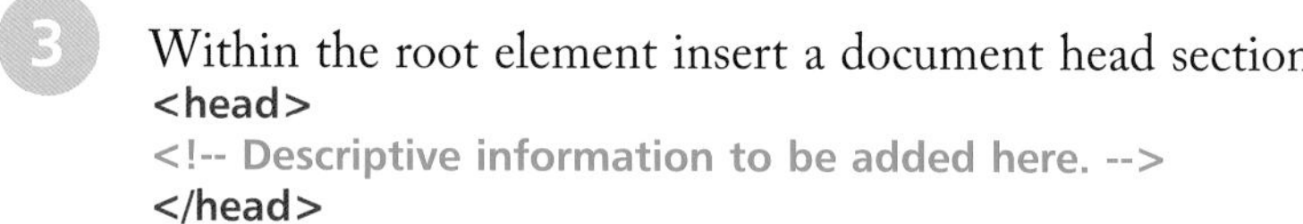

3. Within the root element insert a document head section

```
<head>
<!-- Descriptive information to be added here. -->
</head>
```

4. Within the head section, insert tags describing the document's title

```
<title>Getting Started with HTML</title>
```

5. Within the head section, insert a tag describing the document's character set

```
<meta http-equiv="Content-type"
        content="text/html; charset=ISO-8859-1" >
```

6. After the head section, insert a document body section

```
<body>
<!-- Actual document content to be added here. -->
</body>
```

7. Within the body section, insert a size one large heading

```
<h1>Hello World!</h1>
```

```
<!DOCTYPE HTML PUBLIC "-//W3C//DTD HTML 4.01//EN"
                "http://www.w3.org/TR/html4/strict.dtd" >
<html>
  <head>
    <title>Getting Started with HTML</title>
    <meta http-equiv="Content-Type"
        content="text/html; charset=ISO-8859-1">
  </head>
  <body>
    <h1>Hello World!</h1>
  </body>
</html>
```

8. Save the document as "hello.html" being sure to set the encoding to ANSI

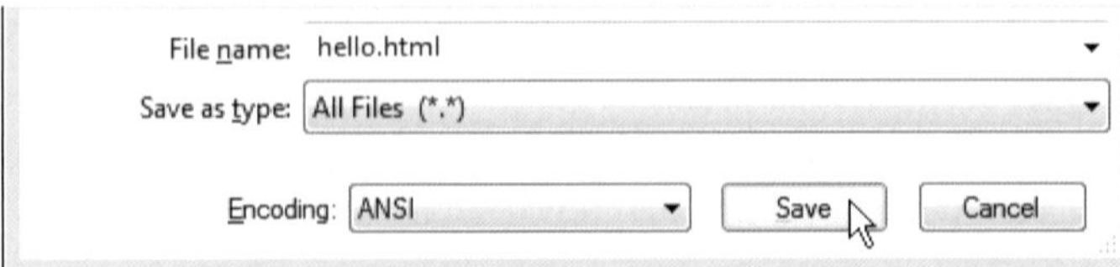

9. Now open the HTML document in a web browser to see the document title displayed on the title bar or tab and to see the document content displayed as a large heading

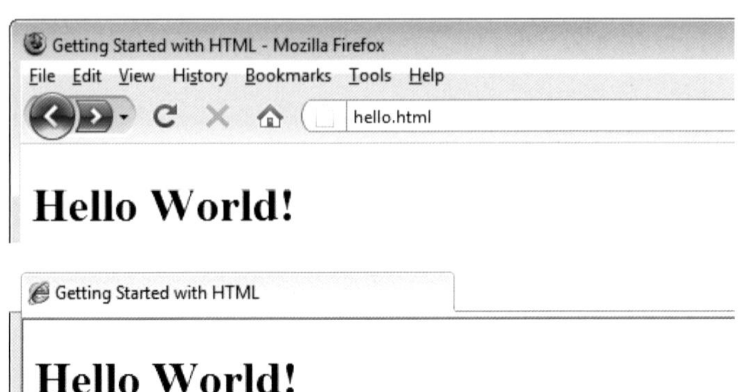

Don't forget

Attribute values must always be enclosed within quotes.

Hot tip

ANSI (American National Standards Institute) encoding is the "Latin 1" character set defined in the ISO-8859-1 standard.

Validating documents

Just as text documents may contain spelling and grammar errors HTML documents may contain various errors that prevent them from conforming to the specification rules. In order to verify that a HTML document does indeed conform to the rules of its specified Document Type Definition it can be tested by a validator tool. Only HTML documents that pass the validation test successfully are sure to be valid documents.

The W3C's online HTML validator can be found at **http://validator.w3.org**.

Web browsers make no attempt at validation so it is well worth verifying every HTML document with a validator tool before it is published, even when the content looks fine in your web browser. When the browser encounters HTML errors it will make a guess at what is intended – but different browsers can make different interpretations so may display the document incorrectly. Conversely, valid HTML documents should always appear correctly in any standards-compliant browser.

The World Wide Web Consortium (W3C) provide a free online validator tool that checks the syntax of web documents. It allows HTML documents that are found to be valid to include an icon demonstrating that you have taken the care to create a standards-compliant web page.

1. With an Internet connection, open your web browser and navigate to the W3C Validator Tool at **validator.w3.org** then click on the "Validate by File Upload" tab

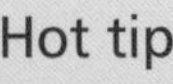

Hot tip

Other tabs in the validator allow you to enter the web address of a HTML document located on a web server to "Validate by URI" or copy'n'paste all code from a document to "Validate by Direct Input".

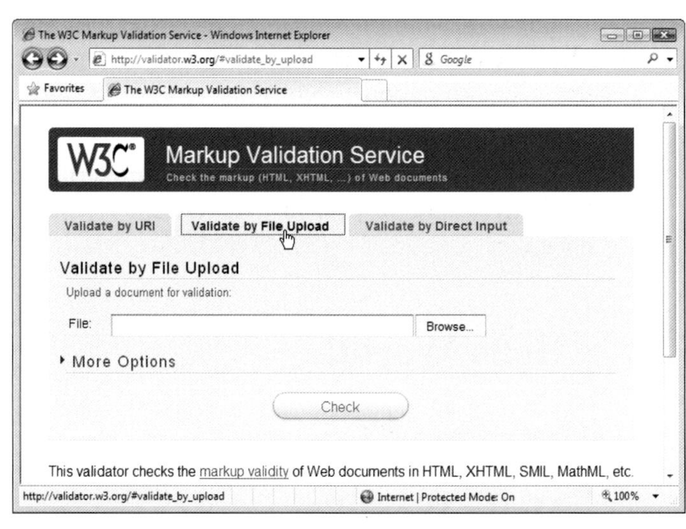

2. Click the "Browse" button to open the Windows "Choose File" dialog then select your HTML document and click the Open button – the local path now appears in the validator's File field

3. Click the validator's "Check" button to upload a copy of the HTML document and run the validation test – the result will then be displayed

[Valid] Markup Validation of hello.html

W3C® Markup Validation Service
Check the markup (HTML, XHTML, ...) of Web documents

Jump To: Congratulations Icons

This document was successfully checked as HTML 4.01 Strict!

Result: Passed

File : Browse...
Use the file selection box above if you wish to re-validate the uploaded file hello.html

iso-8859-1 (detect automatically)

Doctype : HTML 4.01 Strict (detect automatically)

Root Element: HTML

If validation fails the errors are listed so you may easily correct them. When validation succeeds you may choose to include a W3C validation icon at the end of the HTML document.

4. On the valid result page click the hyperlink to jump to the "Congratulations - Icons" section of the page

5. Copy'n'paste the HTML code of your preferred icon into the body section of your HTML document then save the document and open it in a web browser

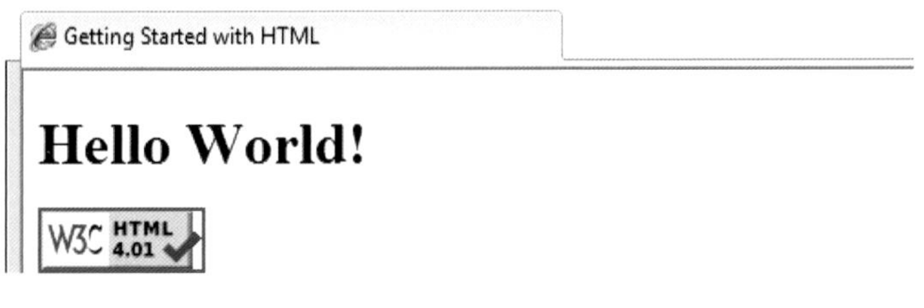

Notice that the validator automatically detects the document's character set and HTML version.

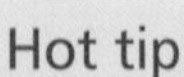

The W3C icon is also a hyperlink to the W3C validator tool – so the HTML document validation can be easily confirmed online.

Employing a HTML editor

HTML code can be created in any basic text editor and does not require any special software. In fact, many professional HTML authors use the simple Notepad application included with Microsoft Windows. As long as thc codc in the new text file is saved with a file extension of either ".htm" or ".html" a HTML document is created. This file can then be opened in any recent version of Microsoft Internet Explorer to see the browser output.

Some Netscape browsers and other older browsers may not fully recognize the HTML 4 specifications. It is best therefore to view HTML 4 web pages in a modern version of Internet Explorer or Mozilla Firefox.

Some HTML authors prefer to use specialized HTML editors that color-code the various parts of the HTML document for greater clarity. Microsoft' s Expression Web editor, shown below, provides many further features to help create great HTML code.

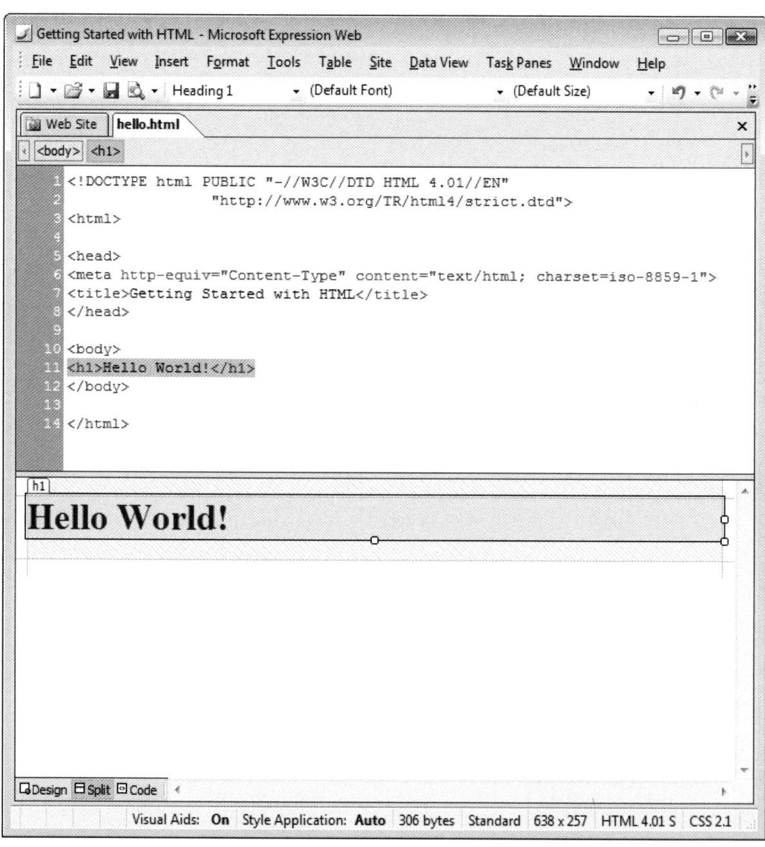

Beware

The Expression Web interface also allows web pages to be created visually by dragging components onto the Design window – but knowledge of HTML is often helpful in fine-tuning the web page.

The split view in Expression Web provides a live preview of what the HTML document will look like in a browser. Additionally a built-in menu lets you quickly view the document on any web browser installed on your computer in a variety of resolutions.

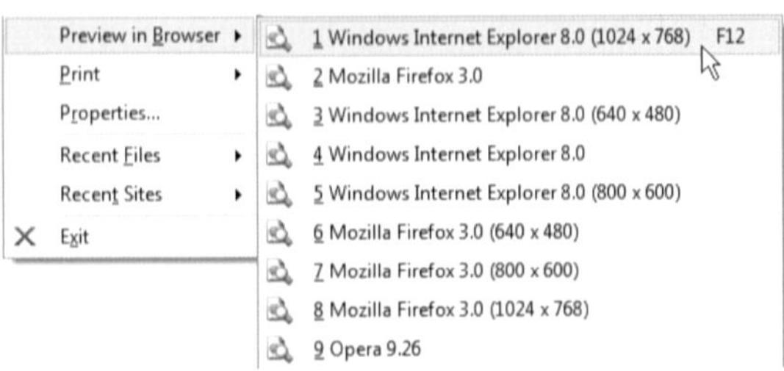

The W3C online validator tool can also be used to verify correct HTML code along with Expression Web's Compatibility Checker tool.

Expression Web's "Compatibility Checker" tool lets you easily locate code errors. For example, where a closing tag has been omitted the compatibility report provides the name of the unclosed tag and the line number where the error occurs.

Like other Microsoft development tools the Expression Web editor has "Intellisense" that provides context-sensitive menus, which can insert HTML tags compatible with the current point in the document. For example, when you type a "<" in the head section Intellisense presents a list of tags which may be inserted at that point. After selecting a tag and typing a space it then presents a list of attributes which may be inserted within that tag.

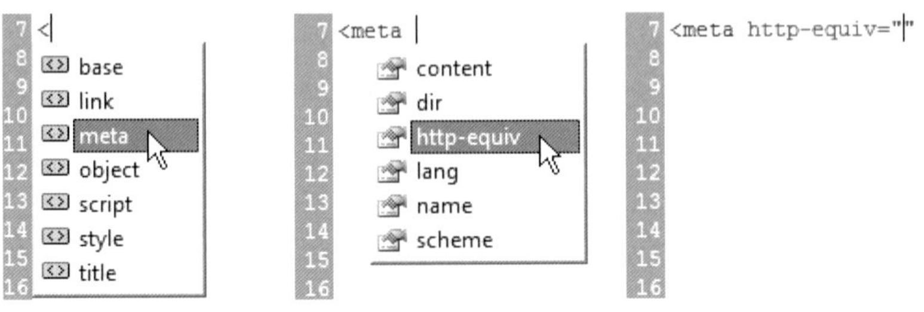

Expression Web provides Code Snippets to quickly insert frequently used chunks of code – Ctrl+Enter,dt4s inserts the entire HTML 4.01 Strict DTD.

By default Intellisense also automatically inserts a matching closing tag, if appropriate, whenever you type an opening tag. Although intended to prevent code errors some authors find this feature can be annoying but the Expression Web options allow Intellisense features to be turned on and off individually. This means that the editor can be customized to your personal taste.

Summary

- The World Wide Web Consortium (W3C) is the recognized body that oversees standards on the web
- In HTML 4 , HTML element tags define document structure but Cascading Style Sheet (CSS) rules control its presentation
- HyperText Transfer Protocol (HTTP) is the common communication standard used by web servers
- Uniform Resource Locator (URL) is an absolute web address comprising Protocol, Domain, and Path components
- A relative address can reference an adjacent file by its file name and may use the syntax "../" to reference a parent directory
- Web servers send response headers back to the requesting computer along with the files requested, or an error code
- The MIME type describing HTML documents is "text/html"
- Each HTML 4 document must have a Document Type Definition, Head section, and Body section
- There are separate specifications for Strict, Transitional, and Frameset versions of HTML 4
- The **<html> </html>** tags create a root element container
- Information about the document itself is contained in the document head section, between **<head> </head>** tags
- Document content is contained in the document body section, between **<body> </body>** tags
- A HTML 4 document should state the document title between **<title> </title>** tags and its character set in a **<meta>** tag
- The free W3C online validator tool should be used to verify the document is indeed valid against the rules of its DTD
- HTML documents can be created in any plain text editor or in a specialized HTML editor like Microsoft Expression Web

2 Providing page information

This chapter demonstrates how the head section of a HTML document can be used to describe the document and to incorporate scripts and style sheets for functionality and format.

Bestowing a title

The specifications require every HTML document to have a title, but its importance is often overlooked. The document title should be carefully considered, however, because it is used extensively:

- **Bookmarks** – save the document title to link back to its URL
- **Title Bar** – browser window displays the document title
- **Navigation tab** – browser tab displays the document title
- **History** – saves the document title to link back to its URL
- **Search engines** – read the document title and typically display the document title in search results to link back to its URL

Document titles should, ideally, be short and meaningful – the task bar typically only displays 16 characters and tabs display around 32 characters.

Document titles throughout a website should follow a consistent naming convention and capitalize all major words. One popular naming convention provides a personal or company name and brief page description separated by a colon character. For example, "Local Bookstore: HTML in easy steps". An alternative places the description first, so it remains visible when the title is truncated, and the name follows in brackets. For example, "HTML in easy steps [Local Bookstore]".

Local Bookstore: HTML in easy ste... | HTML in easy steps [Local Bookst...

You can find a list of all character entities at **www.w3.org/TR/html401/sgml/entities.html**

Document titles, and document content, may contain special characters that are defined in HTML as character "entities". Each entity reference begins with an "&" ampersand and ends with a ";" semi-colon. For example, the entity **<** (less than) produces the "<" character and the entity **>** (greater than) produces the ">" character. These are often necessary to avoid confusion with the angled brackets surrounding the HTML tags. Other commonly used entities include ** ** (non-breaking space) to produce a space, **©** (©), **®** (®), and **™** (™). These are best avoided in document titles, however, as the vocal narrator used by visually impaired viewers may read each entity character as a word.

title.html

1 Start a new HTML document with the Strict DTD

```
<!DOCTYPE HTML PUBLIC "-//W3C//DTD HTML 4.01//EN"
                    "http://www.w3.org/TR/html4/strict.dtd">
```

2 Add a root element containing head and body sections

```
<html>
  <head>
  <!-- Descriptive information to be added here. -->
  </head>
  <body>
  <!-- Actual document content to be added here. -->
  </body
</html>
```

3 Within the head section, insert an empty document title element and a meta element specifying the character set

```
<title> </title>
<meta http-equiv="Content-type"
            content="text/html;charset=ISO-8859-1" >
```

4 Within the title element, insert a title including entities

```
HTML in easy steps &lt; Local Bookstore &reg; &gt;
```

5 Save the document then open it in your web browser

HTML in easy steps <Local Bookstore ® >

6 Start a vocal narrator to hear the document title read out as "HTML-in-easy-steps-less-than-Local-Bookstore-registered-trademark-greater-than"

7 Edit the document title to make it more user-friendly

```
HTML in easy steps @ &quot; Local Bookstore &quot;
```

HTML in easy steps @ "Local Bookstore"

8 Save the document then open it in your web browser to hear the narrator now read the document title as "HTML-in-easy-steps-at-Local-Bookstore"

Don't forget 

The specifications do not define a naming scheme for HTML document titles but do encourage web page authors to consider accessibility issues in all aspects of their web page designs.

Specifying a character set

The examples in this book are each saved with ANSI encoding as described on page 15. This means that they each use the "Latin-1" character set for Western languages as defined in ISO-8859-1. Other languages may need to use a different character set to accommodate the characters of their language. The five most popular character sets are listed in the table below:

Don't forget

Character set names are not case-sensitive – therefore "BIG5", "Big5", and "big5" are equivalent.

Name	Character set
US-ASCII	US ASCII characters
ISO-8859-1	Standard ISO Latin-1 characters
UTF-8	Multi-lingual Universal Transformation Format
SHIFT_JIS	Japanese characters
BIG5	Chinese traditional characters

While US-ASCII and ISO-8859-1 exclusively support the characters used in Western languages, UTF-8, SHIFT_JIS, and BIG5 support both Western and Eastern languages. This means, for example, that a HTML document using the BIG5 character set can contain both English and Chinese characters. Similarly, both are supported in the UTF-8 character set but the characters' appearance is slightly different to that of the BIG5 character set.

big5.html

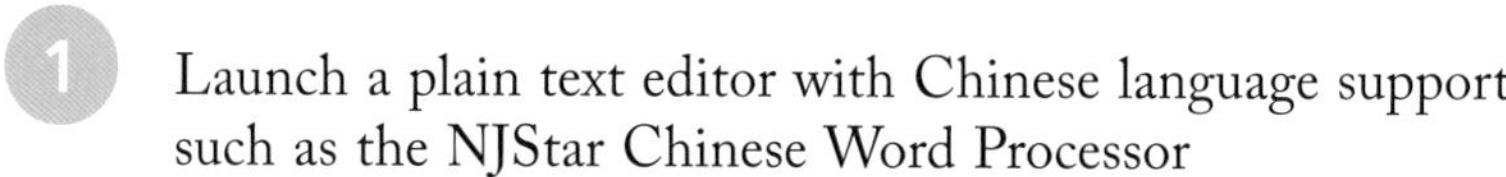

1. Launch a plain text editor with Chinese language support, such as the NJStar Chinese Word Processor

2. Start a new HTML document with the Strict DTD

```
<!DOCTYPE HTML PUBLIC "-//W3C//DTD HTML 4.01//EN"
                "http://www.w3.org/TR/html4/strict.dtd">
```

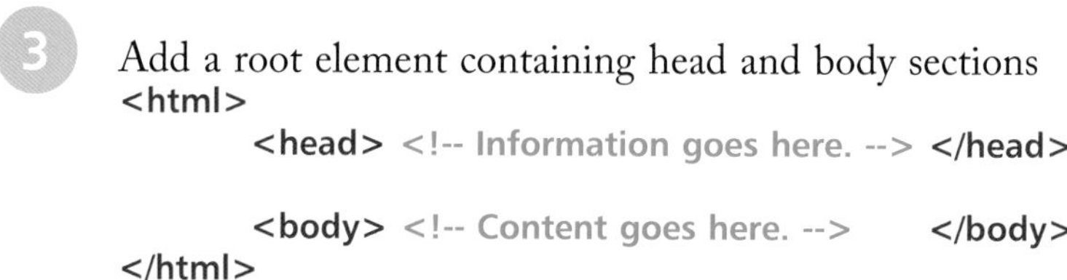

3. Add a root element containing head and body sections

```
<html>
        <head> <!-- Information goes here. --> </head>

        <body> <!-- Content goes here. -->       </body>
</html>
```

4 Within the head section, insert a document title and a meta element to specify the character set as BIG5

```
<title>Using BIG5 Encoding</title>
<meta http-equiv="Content-type"
        content="text/html;charset=BIG5" >
```

At the time of writing NJStar Chinese WP is available as a 30-day free trial at **www.njstar.com**

5 Within the body section, insert a size one heading in English and another with its Chinese equivalent

```
<h1>Fantastic Web Page</h1>
<h1>神乎其神 网页</h1>
```

6 Save the document with BIG5 encoding then open it in your web browser

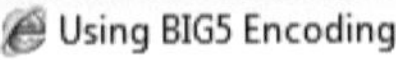

Fantastic Web Page

神乎其神 網頁

7 Make a copy of the **big5.html** document then change its character set to UTF-8

```
<meta http-equiv="Content-type"
        content="text/html;charset=UTF-8" >
```

utf-8.html

8 Save the document with UTF-8 encoding as “utf-8.html” then open it in your web browser and compare the characters of each language to those in the BIG5 version – both are correct but BIG5 encoding substitutes some traditional Chinese characters in place of their simplified equivalents used by UTF-8

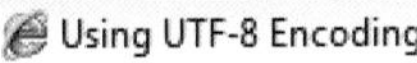

Fantastic Web Page

神乎其神 网页

Limiting page life

Meta information is simply data that describes other data. In the context of a HTML, document meta data describes the document itself – rather than the document's contents.

HTML meta data is defined in the head section of the HTML document using the **<meta>** tag. Previous examples have used this tag to specify the document's character set – as one piece of information describing that document. Further **<meta>** tags can be added to describe other aspects of the document.

The **<meta>** tag is a "single" tag that does not require a matching closing tag to create a HTML element. It is only used to specify information using its tag attributes. The **http-equiv** attribute can represent a HTTP property, such as "Content-type", and the **content** attribute can specify that property's value.

Many **<meta>** tags provide infomation for search engines such as Google and Yahoo! who typically offer cached versions of a HTML document in their search results. To ensure that readers can only view the current version of a web page **<meta>** tags can be used to limit the life span of the cached document.

The HTTP "Expires" property can be checked by search engines to determine whether they can use the cached document or must fetch a fresh copy of a web page. Where its value is a past date the web page is regarded as expired and a fresh copy is sought.

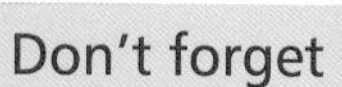

Setting a page expiry date simply indicates to search engines when the page should be removed from their database.

To set a document expiry date the **<meta>** tag's **http-equiv** attribute should specify the HTTP "Expires" property and its **content** attribute should specify the expiry date in a precise format using the GMT time zone. The date format's syntax looks like this:

Weekday, DD MMM YYYY HH:MM:SS TIMEZONE

For example, the date at midnight on the last day of 2010 would be specified as:

Sat, 01 Jan 2011 00:00:00 GMT

Users of the Mozilla Firefox browser can easily see the information contained in a HTML document's **<meta>** tags by launching the "Page Info" dialog from the Tools menu.

expires.html

1. Start a new HTML document with the Strict DTD

```
<!DOCTYPE HTML PUBLIC "-//W3C//DTD HTML 4.01//EN"
                    "http://www.w3.org/TR/html4/strict.dtd">
```

2. Add a root element containing head and body sections

```
<html>
        <head> <title>Page Expiry</title>        </head>

        <body> <h1>Good until 2011</h1>      </body>
</html>
```

3. Within the head section, insert meta elements to specify the character set and expiry date

```
<meta http-equiv="Content-type"
        content="text/html;charset=ISO-8859-1" >

<meta http-equiv="Expires"
        content="Sat, 01 Jan 2011 00:00:00 GMT" >
```

4. Save the document then open it in Firefox

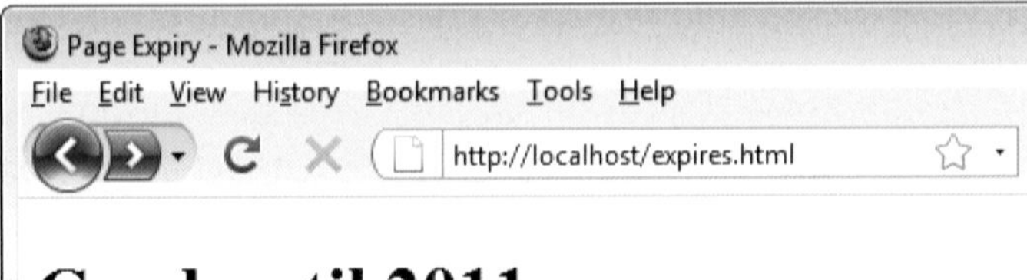

Hot tip

Notice that this example has been served to the browser by a local web server using the default "localhost" domain.

5. Click the Tools menu then choose the Page Info item to inspect the meta information for this HTML document

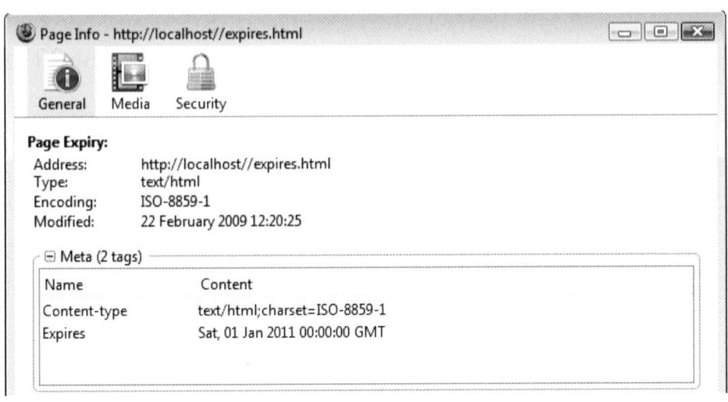

Describing the document

In addition to specifying the HTML document's character set and expiry date **<meta>** tags can be used to provide descriptive information that may be useful to search engines. This offers no guarantee of high ranking however, as search engines also use other page information for that purpose – especially the document title. Nevertheless it is helpful to provide a description and a list of keywords relevant to the contents of that page so that search engine "spiders" might usefully add the page to their index.

Don't forget

All search engine spiders find pages to add to their index – even if the page has never been submitted to them.

Descriptive **<meta>** tags always have a **name** attribute, to specify a page feature, and a **content** attribute to specify that feature's value. For example, the "description" name allows you to specify text content describing the page. This should be short succinct sentences that might appear in a search engine's results page. Any description longer than around 200 characters may get truncated.

Similarly, the "keywords" name allows you to specify text content in the format of a comma-separated list of relevant keywords. These may be used by search engines to influence their results. For example, a search for "italian ceramics" could return all web pages with "italian" and "ceramics" in their keywords list. Promotion of the page by keywords is best achieved by following some simple guidelines:

- Use only lowercase characters
- Keep all keywords on a single line
- Never repeat a keyword in the list
- Limit the keywords list to 1,000 characters or less
- Try to use the plural form for keywords – to match searches made with both the single and plural forms of that word

Hot tip

Always include the three most important keywords in the description.

To specify that a web page should not be indexed by search engines the "robots" name should have a content value of "noindex". Conversely, this may be set to "all" to explicitly allow indexing but as that is the default state it is not really necessary.

keywords.html

1. Start a new HTML document with the Strict DTD

```
<!DOCTYPE HTML PUBLIC "-//W3C//DTD HTML 4.01//EN"
                    "http://www.w3.org/TR/html4/strict.dtd">
```

2. Add a root element containing head and body sections

```
<html>
<head>
      <title>Tuscan Home Decor [Italian Ceramics]</title>
</head>
<body> <h1>Beautiful Tuscan Ceramics</h1>   </body>
</html>
```

3. Within the head section, insert meta elements to specify the character set, description, and keywords

```
<meta http-equiv="Content-type"
          content="text/html;charset=ISO-8859-1" >

<meta  name="Description"
        content="Shop for beautiful Italian Ceramics,
                 Tuscan Majolica, Home Decor, and more." >

<meta  name="Keywords"
        content="tuscan,italian,ceramics,home decor,
                 majolica,dinnerwares,vases,plates,bowls" >
```

4. Save the document then open it in Firefox and use the Page Info dialog on the Tools menu to see the meta data

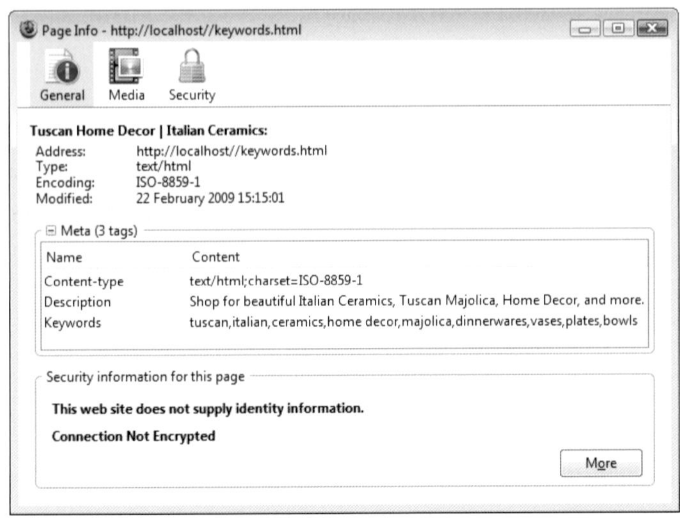

Hot tip

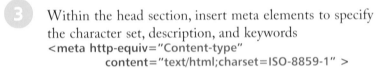

Notice that the first four meta keywords in this example also appear in the meta description.

Hot tip

There are a number of free meta tag generators available online – enter "free meta tag generator" into a search engine.

Incorporating scripts

Don't forget

As usual the content between **<noscript>** tags must be enclosed by tags defining what it is. For example as a heading using **<h1>** tags.

Scripts can be incorporated within HTML documents to interact with the user and to provide dynamic effects. This ability has become increasingly important with the development of Web 2.0 pages in which sections of the page can be dynamically updated. Previously the browser would typically request an entire new page from the web server, which was less efficient and more cumbersome, so Web 2.0 is a great improvement.

Scripts enclosed by HTML **<script> </script>** tags can be added within the head section of a document but, in line with the aim of HTML 4 to separate content from presentation, are best contained in a separate file. The **<script>** tag must specify the MIME type of the script with its **type** attribute – for JavaScript scripts the MIME type is "text/javascript". Additionally the path to the script location must be specified to its **src** attribute. When the script file is within the same directory as the HTML file the path can simply state its relative address as the script's file name. For example, to an adjacent script file named "script.js" like this:

```
<script type="text/javascript" src="script.js"></script>
```

Alternative content can be provided in the document's body section between **<noscript> </noscript>** tags, which will only be displayed when script functionality is absent or disabled.

script.html

1. Start a new HTML document with the Strict DTD and create a root element

```
<!DOCTYPE HTML PUBLIC "-//W3C//DTD HTML 4.01//EN"
                "http://www.w3.org/TR/html4/strict.dtd">
<html>
<!-- Head and body sections to go here.-->
</html>
```

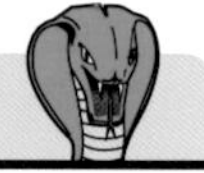

Beware

Remember that the **<script>** tag always needs to have a matching closing tag.

2. Within the root element, insert a head section specifying a document title, character set, and script location

```
<head>

  <title>Adding Scripts</title>

  <meta http-equiv="Content-type"
          content="text/html; charset=ISO-8859-1">

  <script type="text/javascript" src="script.js"></script>

</head>
```

3. Within the root element, insert a body section containing a "noscript" message heading and two regular headings

```
<body>
<noscript> <h1>JavaScript Not Enabled</h1></noscript>
<h1>Static</h1> <h1>Dynamic</h1>
</body>
```

4. Save the HTML document then open a new text editor window and precisely copy this script – exactly as listed

```
function init()
{
  var h1Tags = document.getElementsByTagName("h1");
  h1Tags[1].onclick=react;
}

function react()
{ this.innerHTML="Clicked!"; this.style.color="red"; }

window.onload=init;
```

script.js

5. Save the JavaScript file as "script.js" in the same directory as the HTML file, then open the HTML document in your web browser and click on the second **<h1>** element

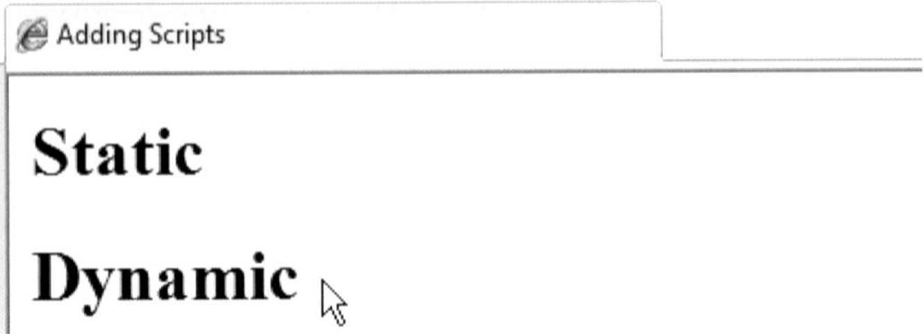

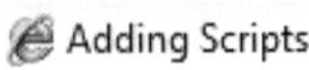

This script creates a function to respond to the click "event" that occurs when the second heading gets clicked.

Hot tip

Although JavaScript instruction is beyond the remit of this book, a few small scripts are listed to demonstrate those parts of HTML that are provided for scripting purposes. You can learn more about scripting in "JavaScript in easy steps".

Incorporating style sheets

Style sheets can be added to a HTML document by inserting **<style> </style>** tags in the head section to enclose rules governing how the content will appear. The **<style>** tag must specify the MIME type of the style sheet with its **type** attribute – for Cascading Style Sheets the MIME type is "text/css". For example, a simple style sheet containing rules that determine the appearance of all size one headings could look like this:

Hot tip

Many more style sheet examples that explain how to apply style rules can be found in chapter four of this book.

```
<style type="text/css">

h1
{
  color :  red ;
  background : yellow ;
  border : 10px dashed blue ;
  padding : 5px ;
}

</style>
```


This is acceptable and will validate but, to comply with the aim of HTML 4 to separate content from presentation, style sheets are best contained in a separate file. The great advantage of placing scripts and style sheets in their own files is that they can be applied to multiple HTML documents – so making website maintenance much easier. Editing a shared script or shared style sheet instantly affects each HTML document that shares that file.

Don't forget

MIME (Multipart Internet Mail Extension) types describe file types – **text/html** for HTML files, **text/javascript** for scripts, **text/css** for style sheets.

In order to incorporate a separate style sheet file within a HTML document a **<link>** tag can be added to the head section of the document. This must again specify the MIME type of the style sheet with its **type** attribute, and also its relationship to the HTML document with its **rel** attribute. For style sheets the correct link type value is "stylesheet". Additionally the path to the style sheet location must be specified with its **href** attribute. When the style sheet file is within the same directory as the HTML file the path can simply state its relative address as the style sheet's file name. For example, to an adjacent style sheet file named "style.css" like this:

```
<link type="text/css" rel="stylesheet" href="style.css">
```

Like the **<meta>** tag, the **<link>** tag is a single element that does not have a matching closing tag.

1. Start a new HTML document with the Strict DTD

```
<!DOCTYPE HTML PUBLIC "-//W3C//DTD HTML 4.01//EN"
                  "http://www.w3.org/TR/html4/strict.dtd">
```

style.html

2. Add a root element containing head and body sections

```
<html>
  <head> <title>Adding Style Sheets</title>   </head>

  <body> <h1>Styled Heading</h1>             </body>
</html>
```

3. Within the head section, insert a meta element to specify the character set, and a link to an adjacent style sheet

```
<meta http-equiv="Content-type"
          content="text/html;charset=ISO-8859-1" >

<link rel="stylesheet" type="text/css" href="style.css">
```

4. Save the HTML document then open a new text editor window and precisely copy this style sheet

style.css

```
h1
{
 color : red ;
 background : yellow ;
 border : 10px dashed blue ;
 padding : 5px ;
}
```

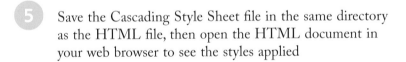

5. Save the Cascading Style Sheet file in the same directory as the HTML file, then open the HTML document in your web browser to see the styles applied

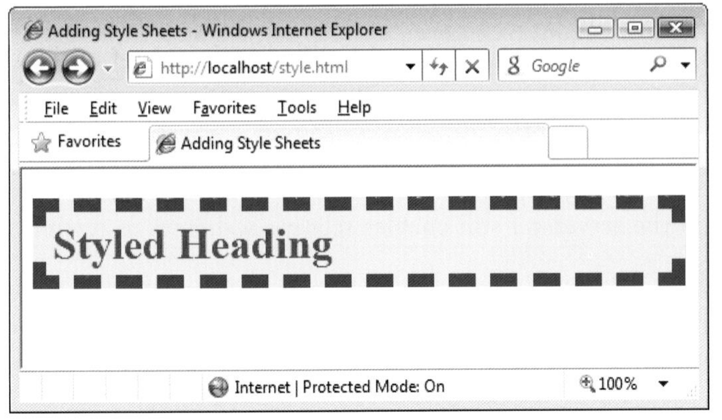

Hot tip

Coloring the **<h1>** element reveals that it occupies the entire width of the browser window – except for the default margins of the body.

Linking more resources

The <link> tag, that was used in the previous example to incorporate a style sheet in a HTML document, can also incorporate other resources into the HTML document.

This tag may only appear in the head section of the document but each head section can contain many <link> tags, and each one must contain **rel**, **type**, and **href** attributes to specify the resource's relationship, MIME type, and location respectively.

To describe a relationship the **rel** attribute may be assigned any one of the link type values in this table:

stylesheet	**alternate**	**start**	**next**	**prev**
contents	**index**	**glossary**	**copyright**	**chapter**
section	**subsection**	**appendix**	**help**	**bookmark**

Many of the link types above are intended to help search engines locate resources associated with that HTML document and may also include a **title** attribute to describe the linked resource. For example, a version of the web page in a different language:

```
<link rel="alternate" type="text/html" href="esp.html"
        title="Esta página en Español - This page in Spanish">
```

In this case the location of the resource is specified using a relative address that, by default, the browser will seek in the directory in which the HTML document is located. The browser can, however, be made to seek relative addresses in a different directory by inserting a <base> tag at the start of the document's head section. Its **href** attribute can then specify the absolute directory address. For example, to specify a separate "resources" folder like this:

```
<base href="http://localhost/resources/" >
```

This usefully separates HTML documents from other resources on the server yet still enables relative addresses to reference them.

One link type in popular use that does not appear in the HTML specifications (or the table above) is "shortcut icon". This incorporates an icon resource that appears in the web browser's address field whenever that HTML document is visited.

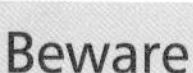

When using a **<base>** element it must be placed at the start of the head section – before any **<link>** tags.

1. Start a new HTML document with the Strict DTD

```
<!DOCTYPE HTML PUBLIC "-//W3C//DTD HTML 4.01//EN"
                  "http://www.w3.org/TR/html4/strict.dtd">
```

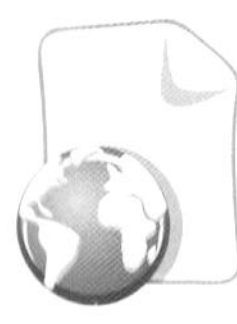

link.html

2. Add a root element containing head and body sections

```
<html>
  <head> <title>Adding Resources</title>      </head>

  <body> <h1>Linked Icon</h1>                  </body>
</html>
```

3. Within the head section, insert elements to specify a base "resources" directory, a character set, and an icon resource

```
<base href="http://localhost/resources/" >

<meta http-equiv="Content-type"
        content="text/html;charset=ISO-8859-1" >

<link   rel="shortcut icon"
        type="image/x-icon" href="favicon.ico" >
```

4. Save the HTML document then open an icon editor, such as IcoFX, and create an icon using only the 16-color palette and measuring exactly 16x16 pixels

5. Now save the icon in the "resources" directory being sure to name it exactly **favicon.ico** – no other name will work

6. Open the HTML document in your browser via a web server to see the icon resource appear in the address field

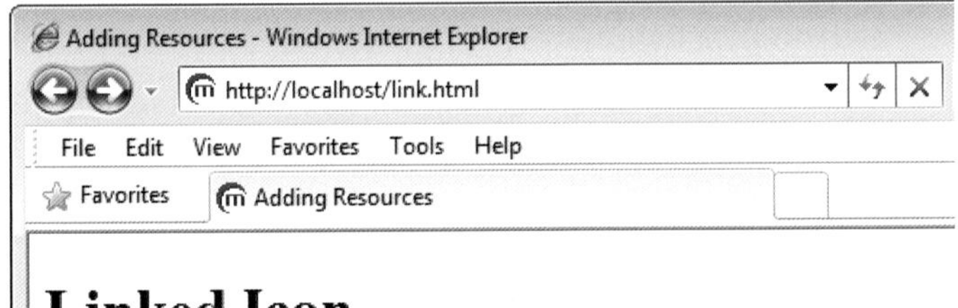

Don't forget

This page is served to the browser by a local web server using the default "localhost" domain. Simply opening a local copy of this example in a browser will not display the icon.

Hot tip

Some browsers may prefer the "icon" link type rather than "shortcut icon" – add a second <link> element to cover both link types.

Summary

- A HTML document title is used by search engines and is seen in a browser's title bar, navigation tab, bookmarks, and history
- Document content and titles can include character entity references to display special characters, such as **©** for ©
- Character sets that support Eastern language characters often also support Western language characters
- A **<meta>** tag setting the HTTP Expires property must use a precise date format to specify the expiry date – after which search engines will seek a fresh copy of the HTML document
- Search engine spiders can use the keywords and description specified in **<meta>** tags to add a web page to their index
- A keywords list should comprise only non-repeating lowercase keywords on a single line of the HTML document
- Scripts can be added to the head section of a HTML document between **<script> </script>** tags but are best created in a separate file for incorporation by the tag's **src** attribute
- Style sheets can be added to the head section of a HTML document between **<style> </style>** tags but are best created in a separate file for incorporation by a **<link>** tag
- Editing a shared script or shared style sheet instantly affects each HTML document that shares that file – making website maintenance much easier
- A **<link>** tag may only appear in the head section of a HTML document and should contain **rel**, **type**, and **href** attributes to specify a resource relationship, MIME type and location
- A **<base>** tag can be added at the start of the head section to specify a different directory in which to seek relative addresses
- A "shortcut icon" link type can incorporate an icon named **favicon.ico** that will appear in the web browser's address field

3 Creating body content

This chapter demonstrates how text and image elements can be created within the body section of a HTML document.

Working the body

Every HTML document must contain exactly one opening **<body>** tag and exactly one matching closing **</body>** tag – defining the body section to contain all document content that is intended for display in the web browser window.

The body section of a HTML document should not contain any meta data, scripts, or style sheets – **<meta>**, **<script>**, and **<link>** elements all belong in the head section.

Uniquely the opening **<body>** tag may contain attributes to reference the "load" event, which occurs when a page has completely loaded into the web browser, and the "unload" event that occurs when leaving that page or when closing the browser. These **onload** and **onunload** attributes are useful with scripting to respond to the load and unload page events.

The **onload** attribute references the same **window.load** event that was used in the script example on page 31 to create an event-handler function. Within the **<body>** tag, the **onload** attribute can specify the name of a script function to be called when the load event occurs. Similarly, the **onunload** attribute can specify a script function to be called when the unload event occurs.

Alternatively, short script "snippets" can simply be assigned to the attributes within the HTML **<body>** tag. For example, the **onload** attribute could call upon the intrinsic **window.alert()** function to launch an alert dialog whenever that page has loaded. This function can specify a message to be displayed by the dialog as a text string within quotes, between the function parentheses. As all attribute values must be enclosed within double quotes it is important to enclose the message text string within single quotes to avoid terminating the attribute value prematurely, like this:

```
<body onload = "window.alert('Greetings!')" >
```

If double quotes were used throughout the example above the attribute value would become **"window.alert("**. This principle of differentiating text strings must be applied to any attribute value that contains a "nested" quote.

The **onunload** attribute can call upon the intrinsic **window.alert()** function to display a message in an alert dialog in the same way.

Don't forget 

Scripts and style sheets are best contained in separate files and incorporated into the HTML document by **<script>** and **<link>** elements placed within its head section.

body.html

1. Start a new HTML document with the Strict DTD and create a root element

```
<!DOCTYPE HTML PUBLIC "-//W3C//DTD HTML 4.01//EN"
                  "http://www.w3.org/TR/html4/strict.dtd">
<html>
<!-- Head and body sections to go here.-->
</html>
```

2. Within the root element, insert a head section specifying a document title and character set

```
<head>
  <title>Body Attributes</title>
  <meta http-equiv="Content-type"
            content="text/html; charset=ISO-8859-1">
</head>
```

3. Within the root element, insert a body section specifying event-handlers for the load and unload events

```
<body onload="window.alert('Greetings!')"
        onunload="window.alert('...Goodbye')" >
<h1>Loaded</h1>
</body>
```

4. Save the HTML document then open it in your web browser to see the alert dialog appear when it has loaded

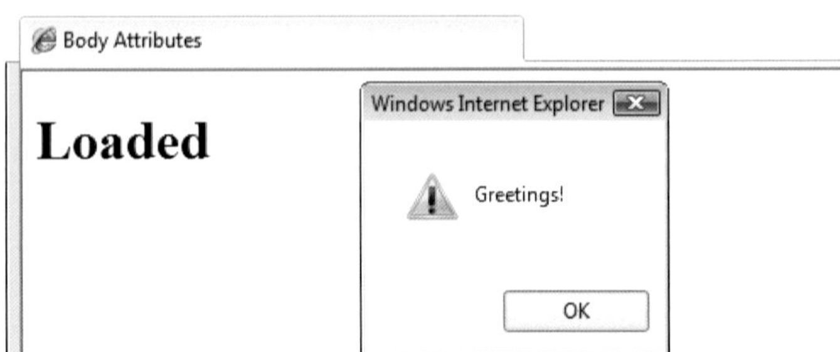

5. Click OK to close the dialog, then navigate to a different page, close the browser, or refresh the page to see the alert dialog appear when it gets unloaded

Hot tip

The **onload** and **onunload** attributes are remnants from earlier versions of HTML. It is better to specify event-handler functions in a script file rather than use these attributes – in line with the aim of HTML 4 to separate content from presentation.

Inserting paragraphs

All text content is traditionally separated into sentences and paragraphs to be more easily read and more readily understood. This is also true for text content in HTML documents and their paragraphs are contained within <p> </p> tags. Each paragraph element is visually separated from the next one by the browser – typically leaving two empty lines between them.

Text within a paragraph will normally automatically wrap to the next line when it meets the element's edge but it can be forced to wrap sooner by inserting a line break <br> tag.

For emphasis, a horizontal rule <hr> tag can be inserted between paragraphs to draw a line separating them. The <hr> tag cannot, however, be inserted inside a paragraph to separate sentences.

The <br> tag and <hr> tag are both single tags that need no closing tag.

paragraph.html

1. Start a new HTML document with the Strict DTD and create a root element

```
<!DOCTYPE HTML PUBLIC "-//W3C//DTD HTML 4.01//EN"
                    "http://www.w3.org/TR/html4/strict.dtd">
<html>
<!-- Head and body sections to go here.-->
</html>
```

2. Within the root element, insert a head section specifying a document title and character set

```
<head>
  <title>Inserting Paragraphs</title>
  <meta http-equiv="Content-type"
              content="text/html; charset=ISO-8859-1">
</head>
```

3. Within the root element, insert a body section

```
<body>

<!-- Paragraphs to go here. -->

</body>
```

4. Within the body section insert a large heading

```
<h1>The Statue of Liberty</h1>
```

5. Next within the body section, insert a paragraph containing a line break to separate two sentences
**<p>The Statue of Liberty was built over nine years by French sculptor Auguste Bartholdi.
Upon its completion in 1884 all 350 individual pieces of the statue were packed into 214 crates for the long boat ride from France to New York.</p>**

6. After the paragraph, add a horizontal ruled line
<hr>

7. After the horizontal ruled line, add a second paragraph
<p>The statue arrived in America several months later and was reconstructed on Liberty Island. Auguste Bartholdi thought that the New York harbor was the perfect setting for his masterpiece because it was where immigrants got there first view of the New World.</p>

8. Save the HTML document then open it in your web browser to see the heading, paragraphs, and a ruled line

Inserting Paragaphs

The Statue of Liberty

The Statue of Liberty was built over nine years by French sculptor Auguste Bartholdi.
Upon its completion in 1884 all 350 individual pieces of the statue were packed into 214 crates for the long boat ride from France to New York.

The statue arrived in the America several months later and was reconstructed on Liberty Island. Auguste Bartholdi thought that the New York harbor was the perfect setting for his masterpiece because it was where immigrants got their first view of the New World.

Hot tip

Use heading elements, like **<h1>**, to provide paragraph section headings and **<hr>** tags to separate sections.

Including quotations

It is important to recognize that some HTML elements produce a rectangular block area on the page in which to display content, while others merely produce a small block on a line within the outer containing block. These are generally referred to as "block-level" and "inline-level" elements. Inline-level elements must always be enclosed by a block-level element, such as **<p> </p>**.

The difference between block-level and inline-level elements can be seen by contrasting how web browsers display the two HTML elements that are used to include quotations in documents.

The **<blockquote> </blockquote>** tags are intended to surround lengthy quotations so the browser produces a rectangular block on a new line to contain the quotation – typically indented from surrounding content. So the **<blockquote>** element is block-level.

The **<q> </q>** tags on the other hand are intended to surround short quotations or snippets, so the browser produces a small block on the current line to contain the quotation – typically surrounding it with quotes. So the **<q>** element is inline-level.

Both **<blockquote>** and **<q>** tags may optionally contain a **cite** attribute to specify the location of the original source of that quotation, or information about the quotation.

Although the specifications clearly define the **<blockquote>** and **<q>** tags it does not specify exactly how these, and many other tags, should be rendered by the browser. It does, however, suggest that **<blockquote>** elements should be indented and that **<q>** elements should produce double quotes around outer quotations and single quotes around inner nested quotations. In reality, the implementation of these suggestions does vary between browsers.

quote.html

1. Start a new HTML document with the Strict DTD

```
<!DOCTYPE HTML PUBLIC "-//W3C//DTD HTML 4.01//EN"
                 "http://www.w3.org/TR/html4/strict.dtd">
```

2. Add a root element containing head and body sections

```
<html>
<head> <title>Including Quotations</title>
<meta http-equiv="Content-type"
          content="text/html; charset=ISO-8859-1">
</head>
<body> <p>A Regular Paragraph Block!</p> </body>
</html>
```

3. Within the body section, insert a blockquote element **<blockquote cite="http://www.example.com/origin.html"> </blockquote>**

4. Within the blockquote element, insert a paragraph containing two nested small quotations **<p>A Blockquote Block!
Paul said, <q>I saw Emma at lunch, she told me <q> Susan wants you to get some ice cream on your way home.</q>I think I will get some at Ben and Jerry's on Main Street.</q></p>**

5. Save the HTML document then open it in different browsers to compare the implemention of **<q>** elements

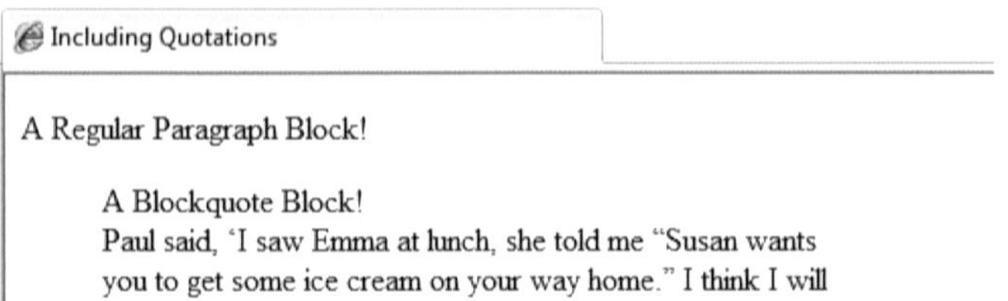
Including Quotations
A Regular Paragraph Block!
A Blockquote Block!
Paul said, 'I saw Emma at lunch, she told me "Susan wants you to get some ice cream on your way home." I think I will get some at Ben and Jerry's on Main Street.'

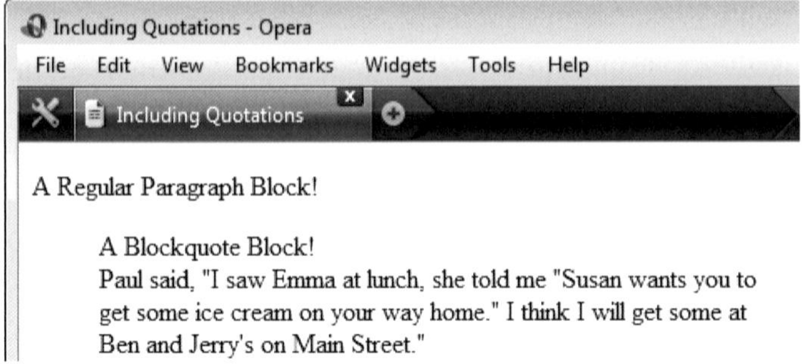
Including Quotations - Opera
File Edit View Bookmarks Widgets Tools Help
Including Quotations
A Regular Paragraph Block!
A Blockquote Block!
Paul said, "I saw Emma at lunch, she told me "Susan wants you to get some ice cream on your way home." I think I will get some at Ben and Jerry's on Main Street."

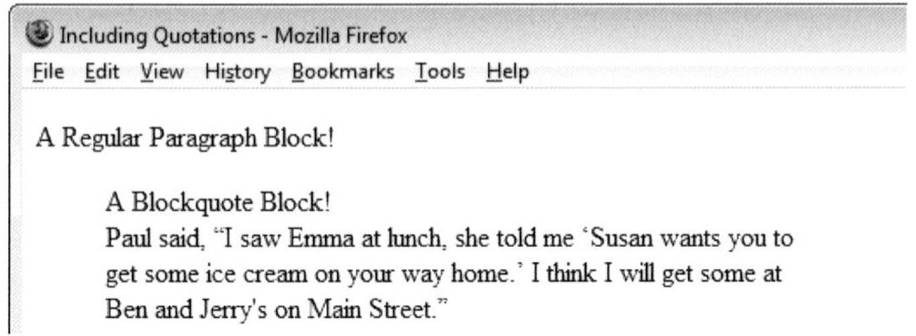
Including Quotations - Mozilla Firefox
File Edit View History Bookmarks Tools Help
A Regular Paragraph Block!
A Blockquote Block!
Paul said, "I saw Emma at lunch, she told me 'Susan wants you to get some ice cream on your way home.' I think I will get some at Ben and Jerry's on Main Street."

Hot tip

By default the paragraph element block will fill the width of its containing element – like the **<h1>** element block in the example on page 31.

Don't forget

Implementation may vary between browsers – here all three indent the **<blockquote>** element but use different quote marks.

Proclaiming headings

HTML heading elements are created using **<h1>**, **<h2>**, **<h3>**, **<h4>**, **<h5>**, and **<h6>** block-level tags – where **<h1>** has the most importance and **<h6>** has least importance. Each heading requires a matching closing tag and should contain only heading text. Typically the heading's font size and weight will reflect its importance, but headings also serve other purposes.

Heading elements should be used to convey the document structure by correctly ordering them – so **<h2>** elements follow **<h1>** elements, **<h3>** elements follow **<h2>** elements, and so on. This structure helps readers quickly skim through a document by navigating its headings.

Search engine spiders may promote documents that have correctly ordered headings as they can use the headings in their index. They assume headings are likely to describe the contents so it is especially useful to include meta keywords from the document's head section in the document's headings.

The **<h1>** element is by far the most important heading and should ideally appear just once to proclaim the document heading. Often this can be a succinct version of the document title. Below that a number of **<h2>** elements can proclaim document chapter headings for long documents. Each chapter might contain topic headings within **<h3>** elements. Similarly, each topic might in turn contain section headings in **<h4>** elements, followed by paragraph **<p>** elements containing the actual section texts.

The W3C validator tool, introduced on page 16, provides a special feature that creates a document outline from the headings it contains – so you can be sure it uses headings correctly.

heading.html

1. Start a new HTML document with the Strict DTD

```
<!DOCTYPE HTML PUBLIC "-//W3C//DTD HTML 4.01//EN"
                "http://www.w3.org/TR/html4/strict.dtd">
```

2. Add a root element containing head and body sections

```
<html>
<head> <title>Proclaiming Headings</title>
<meta http-equiv="Content-type"
        content="text/html; charset=ISO-8859-1">
</head>
<body><!-- Headings & paragraphs go here.--></body>
</html>
```

3. In the body section, insert correctly ordered headings and paragraphs defining the document's structure

```
<h1>Document Heading</h1>
  <h2>Chapter 1</h2>
    <h3>Topic 1.1</h3>
      <h4>Section 1.1.1</h4>
        <p>Section text.</p>
      <h4>Section 1.1.2</h4>
        <p>Section text.</p>
    <h3>Topic 1.2</h3>
      <h4>Section 1.2.1</h4>
        <p>Section text.</h4>      <!-- etc. -->
```

4. Save the HTML document then open it in your web browser to see the various headings

5. Now navigate to the W3C validator page at **http://validator.w3.org** and browse to select your file to "Validate by File Upload"

6. Under "More Options" select the "Show Outline" option then click the "Check" button to run the validator

Proclaiming Headings

Document Heading

Chapter 1

Topic 1.1

Section 1.1.1

Section text.

Section 1.1.2

Section text.

Topic 1.2

Section 1.2.1

Section text.

7. Upon success click the "Jump To: Outline" link to see the outline that has been generated from the document headings

Document Outline

```
[H1] Document Heading
    [H2] Chapter 1
        [H3] Topic 1.1
            [H4] Section 1.1.1
            [H4] Section 1.1.2
        [H3] Topic 1.2
            [H4] Section 1.2.1
```

Don't forget

The headings shown here demonstrate document structure, illustrated by a numbering scheme. Headings should contain descriptive text to be useful to search engines.

Beware

Never use headings for their font properties as these can be overridden by style sheet rules – always consider headings to represent structure.

Emphasizing text

HTML 4 provides four inline-level tags that can be used to emphasize text within the body of a document:

- Text can be enclosed within **<b> </b>** tags to instruct the browser to display that text with a bold font
- Text can be enclosed within **<i> </i>** tags to instruct the browser to display that text with an italic font
- Text can be enclosed within **<em> </em>** tags to suggest that the browser should emphasize that text in some way
- Text can be enclosed within **<strong> </strong>** tags to suggest that the browser should strongly emphasize that text in some way

It is somewhat surprising that the **<b>** and **<i>** tags remain in the specifications as they both suggest how content should be presented – contradicting the stated aim of HTML 4 to separate structure from presentation. These old tags may perhaps be given new purpose in future HTML specifications but, for now, it is better to use only **<em>** and **<strong>** tags for emphasis.

In any case, most browsers render text enclosed within **<em> </em>** tags with an italic font and render text enclosed within **<strong> </strong>** tags with a bold font – so the **<b>** and **<i>** tags are redundant anyway.

Don't forget

The specifications encourage web page authors to consider accessibility issues in all aspects of their web page designs.

The advantage of the **<em>** and **<strong>** tags is that they describe the importance of the text contained within those elements and let the browser choose how it should be presented. Additionally these tags are more relevant to suggest how narrators should convey the content vocally.

As with many HTML tags **<em>** and **<strong>** elements can be nested but care must be given to close nested elements in the correct order to avoid errors. For example, these nested elements:

```
<em> <strong> text </em> </strong>
```

are closed incorrectly and will not validate. The correct order is:

```
<em> <strong> text </strong> </em>
```

1. Start a new HTML document with the Strict DTD

```
<!DOCTYPE HTML PUBLIC "-//W3C//DTD HTML 4.01//EN"
                    "http://www.w3.org/TR/html4/strict.dtd">
```

emphasis.html

2. Add a root element containing head and body sections

```
<html>
<head> <title>Emphasizing Text</title>
<meta http-equiv="Content-type"
            content="text/html; charset=ISO-8859-1">
</head>
<body><!-- Document content goes here. --></body>
</html>
```

3. In the body section, insert a paragraph describing HTML

```
<p>HTML is the predominant markup language for web
pages.</p>
```

4. In the body section, insert a paragraph describing CSS

```
<p>CSS provides a richer variety of font effects using
style sheets.</p>
```

5. Edit the content to emphasize a description

```
<em>markup language</em>
```

6. Edit the content to strongly emphasize the languages

```
<strong>HTML</strong>
<strong>CSS</strong>
```

7. Edit the content to very strongly emphasize a description

```
<em><strong>style sheets</strong></em>
```

8. Save the HTML document then open it in your web browser to see how the text has been emphasized

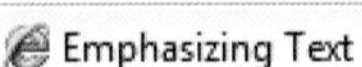

HTML is the predominant *markup language* for web pages.

CSS provides a richer variety of font effects using ***style sheets***.

Hot tip

CSS can specify fonts for emphasis and also emphasize content using background color, foreground color, and various borders – examples in the next chapter show you how.

Formatting text

HTML 4 provides three inline-level tags that can be used to format text within the body of a document:

- Text can be enclosed within **<big> </big>** tags to have a relatively larger format than that of regular text
- Text can be enclosed within **<small> </small>** tags to have a relatively smaller format than that of regular text
- Text can be enclosed within **<tt> </tt>** tags to have a monospace "teletype" format

The appearance of text content, without style sheet rules applied, is determined by the web browser's default settings or user specified preferences. For example, a browser could by default display a "medium" text of 12-point size. In this case text enclosed within HTML **<big>** elements might be displayed at 13.5-point size and text enclosed within HTML **<small>** elements might be displayed at 10-point size. The precise size adjustment is set by the browser but the size of those elements will be changed.

Further increments in size above the default size can be achieved by nesting multiple **<big>** elements. Where the default text size is 12-point the text within **<big><big> </big></big>** tags might then be displayed at 17-point size.

Don't forget

Teleprinters were made obsolete by the introduction of inkjet printers and the Internet.

Similarly, further decrements below the default size can be achieved by nesting multiple **<small>** elements. Where the default text size is 12-point text within **<small><small> </small></small>** tags might then be displayed at 7-point size.

Text within **<tt> <\tt>** tags will be displayed in a monospace as determined by the browser's default settings or user preferences. This is to emulate the teletype messages produced by the old, now largely obsolete, electro-mechanical teleprinter machines.

Although formatting text with **<big>**, **<small>**, and **<tt>** tags appears to only concern the presentation of content those tags can represent the significance of the content they contain in contrast to regular text. For example, **<big>** elements might contain content of greater significance, **<small>** elements content of lesser significance, and **<tt>** elements content of other significance.

1. Start a new HTML document with the Strict DTD

```
<!DOCTYPE HTML PUBLIC "-//W3C//DTD HTML 4.01//EN"
                   "http://www.w3.org/TR/html4/strict.dtd">
```

format.html

2. Add a root element containing head and body sections

```
<html>
<head> <title>Formatting Text</title>
<meta http-equiv="Content-type"
            content="text/html; charset=ISO-8859-1">
</head>
<body><!-- Document content goes here. --></body>
</html>
```

3. In the body section, insert a paragraph containing two lines of regular text

```
<p>A Black Hole is not a Sleeve
<br>More like a Pocket I believe.</p>
```

4. Next in the body section, insert a paragraph containing the same text as before but formatted as teletype

```
<p>     <tt>A Black Hole is not a Sleeve
        <br>More like a Pocket I believe.</tt>   </p>
```

5. Now in the body section, insert another paragraph containing the same text as before but formatting some smaller and bigger sized words

```
<p>A <small><small>Black Hole</small></small>
is not a Sleeve<br>More like a
<big><big><big>Pocket</big></big></big> I believe.
</p>
```

6. Save the document then open it in your web browser to see how text formatting affects the paragraph block sizes

Formatting Text

A Black Hole is not a Sleeve
More like a Pocket I believe.

`A Black Hole is not a Sleeve`
`More like a Pocket I believe.`

A Black Hole is not a Sleeve
More like a Pocket I believe.

Hot tip

Adjust the browser's view size preference to see that the big and small relationship to the regular text is preserved.

Retaining preformatted text

Where it is desirable to have the browser render text content that has been "preformatted" the web page author can enclose that content within **<pre> </pre>** block-level tags. These advise the browser that the following instructions may be applied:

- Preserve white space
- Render all text with a fixed-width font
- Disable automatic word wrapping
- Do not disable bidirectional processing

Preserving the white space retains all spaces, tabs, and line breaks. This is great to display lengthy poems in which every second line is indented. For example, with this verse:

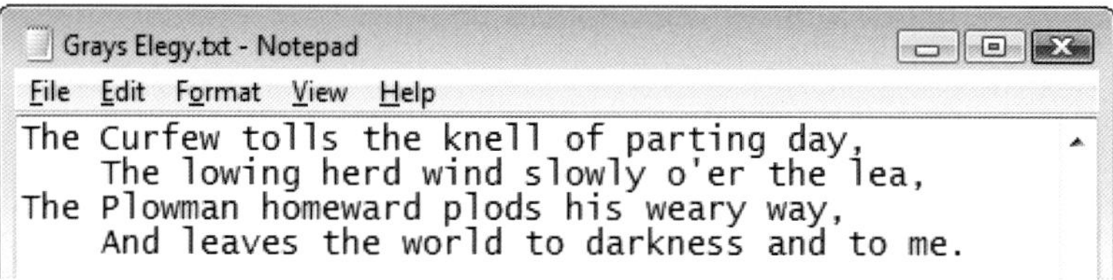

Grays Elegy.txt - Notepad
File Edit Format View Help
The Curfew tolls the knell of parting day,
    The lowing herd wind slowly o'er the lea,
The Plowman homeward plods his weary way,
    And leaves the world to darkness and to me.

In this case each second line is indented from the previous line by four character widths – created by hitting the space bar four times to insert four invisible space characters. These indents will be exactly preserved by the **<pre>** element to reproduce indents that are four characters wide.

Use spaces rather than tabs when preparing preformatted text.

Tab characters, on the other hand, can present some surprises as they are usually interpreted by a web browser to be eight characters wide. This agrees with the tab size in Notepad but other text editors may have their tab width set differently. This means that preformatted content may appear to have been misaligned by the **<pre>** tag. For example, preformatted text produced with four-character wide tabs in an editor will appear with eight-character wide tabs in the browser. It is for this reason that the HTML specifications strongly discourage the use of tabs when creating preformatted characters.

The **<pre> </pre>** tags can also be useful to ensure "Text-Art", sometimes used in web forum signatures, will appear as intended.

1. Start a new HTML document with the Strict DTD

```
<!DOCTYPE HTML PUBLIC "-//W3C//DTD HTML 4.01//EN"
                    "http://www.w3.org/TR/html4/strict.dtd">
```

2. Add a root element containing head and body sections

```
<html>
<head> <title>Retaining Preformatted Text</title>
<meta http-equiv="Content-type"
          content="text/html; charset=ISO-8859-1">
</head>
<body><!-- Document content goes here. --></body>
</html>
```

3. In the body section, insert a document heading

```
<h1>Preformatted Text-Art Signature</h1>
```

4. Ensure that the font in your text editor is set to a fixed width font, such as Lucida Console for Notepad

5. Next in the body section, insert a **<pre>** element containing preformatted content in a fixed width font – and produced without any tab characters

```
<pre>
     ---- __@
   ---- _`\<,_
  ---- (*)/ (*)      MIKE'S PUSHBIKES
~~~~~~~~~~~~~~~~~~~~~~~~~~~~~~~~~~~~~~~~
</pre>
```

6. Save the HTML document then open it in your web browser to ensure the content retains preformatting

preformat.html

Hot tip

You can use any character within a fixed width font to create your text art – Windows users can use the Character Map program in System Tools to select special characters from the Lucida Console font.

Don't forget

Notice that the **<pre>** element is block-level so it does not need to be enclosed within a paragraph – it creates its own block.

Modifying text

Regular text in a paragraph area of a web page is displayed on invisible baselines that automatically wrap content to the next line. The vertical line spacing is determined by the font height to allow space between characters that extend below the line above such as “p”, and tall characters on the current line, such as “l”.

You can find a list of all character entities at **www.w3.org/TR/html401/sgml/entities.html**

Text on a line in a paragraph content box.
See how the lines are nicely spaced so characters do not collide. ™

The standard vertical line spacing will accommodate “superscript” such as the trade mark symbol ™ produced by the **™** character entity. Superscript is any text, number, or symbol that appears smaller than the regular text and is set above the baseline. Mathematical formulae can use superscript to indicate numeric powers using the character entities **²** for ^{2} and **³** for ^{3}. The standard line spacing will also accommodate “subscript” – that appears smaller than the regular text and is set below the baseline.

The height available for superscript and subscript in the standard vertical line spacing is limited so their character size is restricted. Rather than use character entities for this purpose it is usually better to use the HTML **** tags for superscript and **** for subscript. These elements increase the vertical line spacing to allow more prominent subscript and superscript characters. For example, **²** is larger than **²** . Additionally, any content can be included within these elements so you are not restricted to available character entity references.

Don't forget

The specifications allow the browser to choose how to render **<del>** and **<ins>** element content – adding a strikethrough for **<del>** and an underline for **<ins>** is typical.

Text on a line in a paragraph content box with ^{superscript} and $_{\text{subscript}}$
See how the lines are spaced so characters do not collide with subscript.

Text can be modified to indicate that a newer version of text replaces a previous version using **<del> </del>** tags, to strike through the old version, and **<ins> </ins>** tags to underline its replacement. These elements can be used to advise a new version number and the version number it replaces.

Unusually both **<del>** and **<ins>** elements may be either block-level or inline-level. This means they can create a block area for lengthy content or appear within a paragraph for short content.

1. Start a new HTML document with the Strict DTD

```
<!DOCTYPE HTML PUBLIC "-//W3C//DTD HTML 4.01//EN"
                    "http://www.w3.org/TR/html4/strict.dtd">
```

2. Add a root element containing head and body sections

```
<html>
<head> <title>Modifying Text</title>
<meta http-equiv="Content-type"
          content="text/html; charset=ISO-8859-1">
</head>
<body><!-- Document content goes here. --></body>
</html>
```

3. In the body section, insert a paragraph containing superscript and subscript produced by character entities

```
<p>     Square of four: 4&sup2; = 16.
        Cube of four: 4&sup3; = 64.
</p>
```

4. In the body section, insert a paragraph containing superscript and subscript produced by HTML elements

```
<p>     Square of four: 4<sup>2</sup> = 16.
        Cube of four: 4<sup>3</sup> = 64.
</p>
```

5. Next in the body section, insert block-level replacements

```
<del>HTML 4.0</del> <ins>HTML 4.01</ins>
```

6. Now in the body section, insert inline-level replacements

```
<p>SALE! <del>50%</del> <ins>75%</ins> OFF!</p>
```

7. Save the HTML document then open it in your browser to compare superscript, subscript, and replacement text

Modifying Text

Square of four: 4^2 = 16. Cube of four: 4^3 = 64.

Square of four: 4^2 = 16. Cube of four: 4^3 = 64.

~~HTML 4.0~~ HTML 4.01

SALE! ~~50%~~ 75% OFF!

Hot tip

When using superscript ^{2} in paragraphs to denote area, such as 10 feet^2, you may prefer to use the entity **²** rather than **²** to keep line spacings equal.

Displaying code in text

HTML 4 provides three inline-level tags specifically to display computer program code within the body of a document:

- Complete program code, or program snippets, can be enclosed within **<code> </code>** tags to be displayed in a suitable font
- Program variable instances can be enclosed within **<var> </var>** tags to differentiate them from regular text
- Sample program input and output can be enclosed within **<samp> </samp>** tags to differentiate that from regular text

The source of the program code can be provided by block-level **<address> </address>** tags inserted at the end of the body. This element is generally useful to supply contact information and may alternatively appear at the start of the body.

code.html

1. Start a new HTML document with the Strict DTD

```
<!DOCTYPE HTML PUBLIC "-//W3C//DTD HTML 4.01//EN"
        "http://www.w3.org/TR/html4/strict.dtd">
```

2. Add a root element containing head and body sections

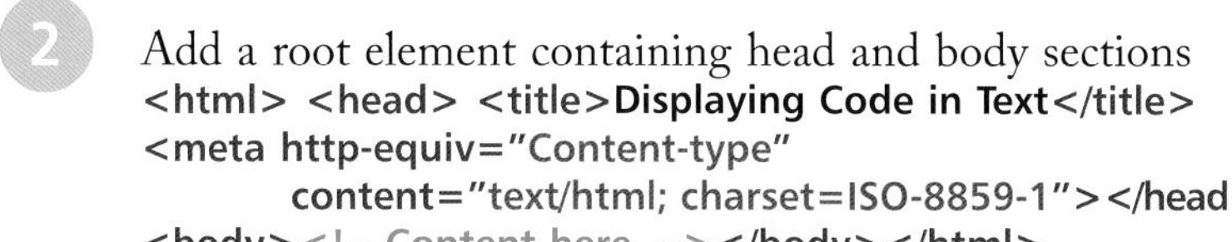

```
<html> <head> <title>Displaying Code in Text</title>
<meta http-equiv="Content-type"
      content="text/html; charset=ISO-8859-1"></head>
```

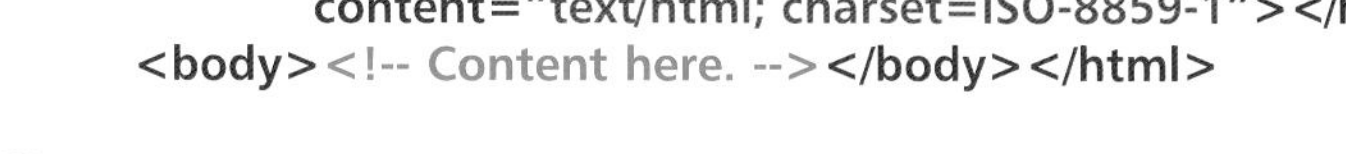

```
<body><!-- Content here. --></body></html>
```

Hot tip

Insert the inline-level **<code>** element within a block-level **<pre>** element to preserve program code layout in a HTML document.

3. In the body section, insert this program code

```
<pre><code>
#include &lt;iostream&gt;
using namespace std;
int main()
{
  float degF, degC;
  cout << "Enter Fahrenheit Temperature: ";
  cin >> degF;
  degC = ((degF - 32.0 ) * (5.0 / 9.0));
  cout << degF << "F is " << degC << "C";
  cout << endl;
  return 0;
}
</code></pre>
```

4 Now in the body section, insert a program description **<p>This program assigns an input value to <var>degF</var> then performs a conversion on that value, assigning the result to <var>degC</var> for output. For example, input of <samp>98.6</samp> will output <samp>37C</samp>.</p>**

5 In the body section, state the program source **<address>Adapted from "C++ Programming in easy steps"
Available at www.ineasysteps.com</address>**

6 Save the HTML document then open it in your browser to see how the program code and address appear

Displaying Code in Text

```
#include <iostream>
using namespace std;

int main()
{
  float degF, degC;
  cout << "Enter Fahrenheit Temperature: ";
  cin >> degF;
  degC = ((degF - 32.0 ) * (5.0 / 9.0));
  cout << degF << "F is " << degC << "C";
  cout << endl;
  return 0;
}
```

This program assigns an input value to *degF* then performs a conversion on that value, assigning the result to *degC* for output. For example, input of `98.6` will output `37C`.

Adapted from "C++ Programming in easy steps"
Available at www.ineasysteps.com

Notice that the angled brackets on the first line of program code have been replaced by character entities in the HTML document to prevent confusion with HTML elements. Double angled brackets elsewhere in the program code do display correctly.

Don't forget

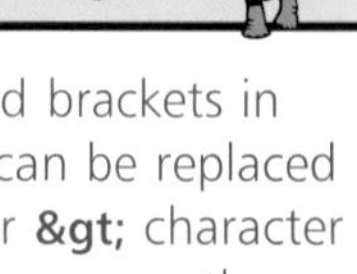

All angled brackets in content can be replaced by **<** or **>** character entities to ensure they are not confused with the angled brackets around HTML elements.

Giving tooltip advice

HTML 4 provides four further inline-level tags that can be used to designate advisory phrases within the body of a document:

- Text can be enclosed within **<abbr> </abbr>** tags to indicate it is an abbreviation
- Text can be enclosed within **<dfn> </dfn>** tags to indicate it is the definitive instance of that term
- Text can be enclosed within **<cite> </cite>** tags to provide a citation or reference to other sources
- Text can be enclosed within **<kbd> </kbd>** tags to indicate text to be entered by the user from a keyboard

Every HTML element that may legally appear within the body section of a HTML document, except the **<param>** element that is used to supply parameters for embedded objects, may optionally include a **title** attribute. Values assigned to the **title** attribute are typically displayed as tooltips by the web browser – that pop up when the user places the cursor over that element.

Each of the phrase elements listed above can usefully include a **title** attribute to expand on the meaning of its content.

advice.html

1. Start a new HTML document with the Strict DTD

```
<!DOCTYPE HTML PUBLIC "-//W3C//DTD HTML 4.01//EN"
                "http://www.w3.org/TR/html4/strict.dtd">
```

2. Add a root element containing head and body sections

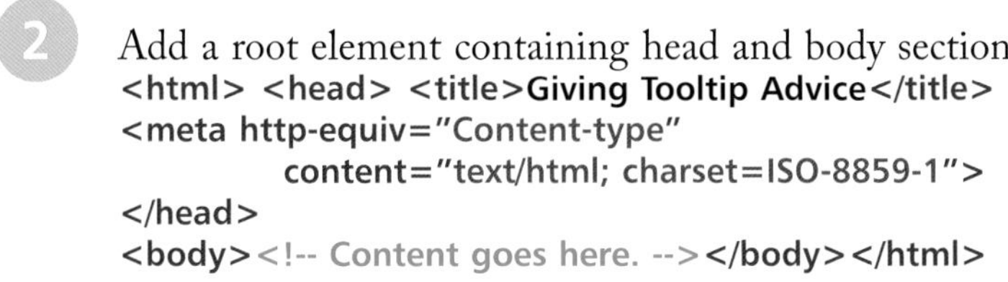

```
<html> <head> <title>Giving Tooltip Advice</title>
<meta http-equiv="Content-type"
          content="text/html; charset=ISO-8859-1">
</head>
<body><!-- Content goes here. --></body></html>
```

3. In the body section, insert a paragraph containing an abbreviation with tooltip advice

```
<p>
<abbr title="HyperText Markup Language">HTML</abbr>
in easy steps</p>
```

4. Next in the body section, insert a paragraph containing a definitive term with tooltip advice
```
<p><dfn title="The popular language of the
WorldWideWeb. Commonly abbreviated to 'HTML'">
HyperText Markup Language</dfn> </p>
```

Remember to use single quotes for quotes nested within other quotes – as with 'HTML' in step 4.

5. Now in the body section, insert a paragraph containing a citation with tooltip advice
```
<p><cite title="Inventor of the HyperText Markup
Language">Sir Tim Berners-Lee</cite></p>
```

6. Finally in the body section, insert a paragraph containing a keyboard instruction with tooltip advice
```
<p> <kbd title="Press the Y key on your keyboard to
execute a script. This requires JavaScript to be enabled in
your browser">Hit Y to Continue</kbd> </p>
```

7. Save the HTML document then open it in your web browser and place your cursor over each element in turn

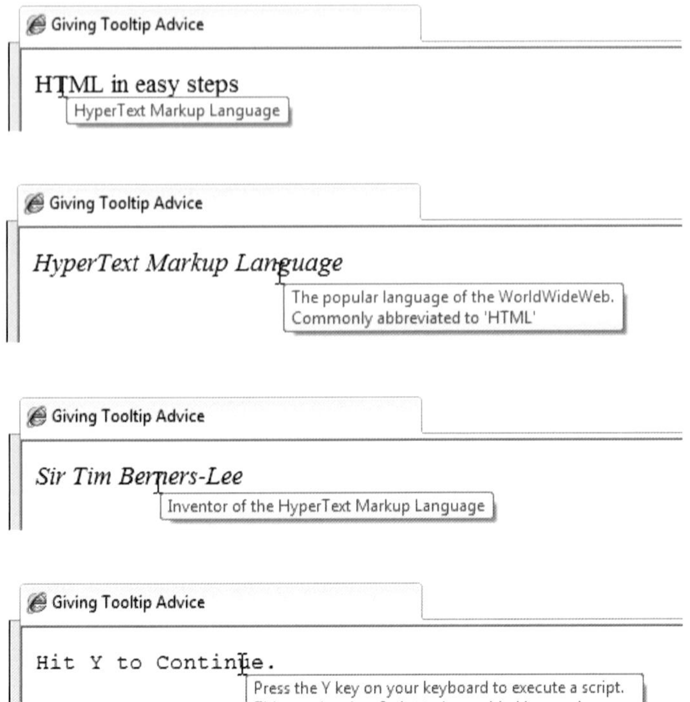

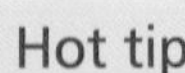

Add a **<script>** element in the head section of this example to incorporate a script to react to the Y key press. This is complete in the download archive – available from the Resource Center at **www.ineasysteps.com**.

Adding images

The ability to add images to HTML document content introduces lots of exciting possibilities. An image is easily added to the document using the inline-level **<img>** tag, which should always include these four attributes:

- A **src** attribute must specify the image location by its absolute or relative path
- A **width** attribute must specify the pixel width of the area it will occupy on the page
- A **height** attribute must specify the pixel height of the area it will occupy on the page
- An **alt** attribute must specify text briefly describing the image for circumstances where the image cannot be seen

The values assigned to the **width** and **height** attributes instruct the web browser to create a content area on the web page of that size. This need not be the actual dimensions of the image as the web browser can resize the image to suit the specified size. This is not recommended, however, as this can easily distort the appearance. Always adjust the image size to the dimensions it will occupy on the web page using a graphics editor, such as Windows Paint. Importantly this can also reduce the file size so your image will download faster and allow the web page to load quicker.

Beware

Avoid the Bitmap (BMP) file format for web images – saving the original image shown here as **fish.bmp** creates a file of 1.31Mb!

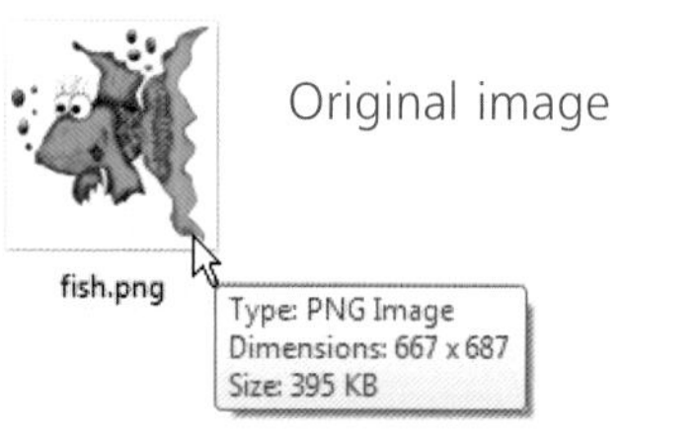

Original image

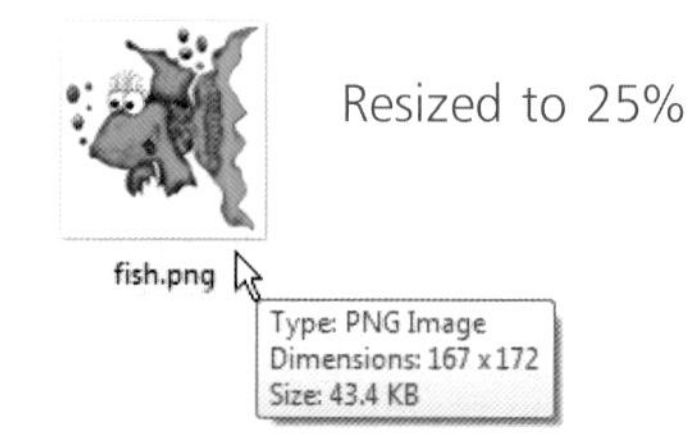

Resized to 25%

The optimum file type for web graphics is the non-proprietary Portable Network Graphics (PNG) file format, which produces compact files and supports transparency. Graphics without anti-aliasing, not blending to a background color, have sharp edges and can be created with transparent backgrounds. On the web page their transparent area will adopt the page's background color so the image will appear to be more an intrinsic part of the page.

image.html

1. Start a new HTML document with the Strict DTD

```
<!DOCTYPE HTML PUBLIC "-//W3C//DTD HTML 4.01//EN"
                "http://www.w3.org/TR/html4/strict.dtd">
```

2. Add a root element containing head and body sections

```
<html> <head> <title>Adding Images</title>
<meta http-equiv="Content-type"
        content="text/html; charset=ISO-8859-1">
</head>
<body><!-- Content goes here. --></body> </html>
```

3. In the body section, insert a paragraph containing an image, stating its actual dimensions

```
<p> <img src="fish.png" alt="Goofy Fish Picture"
      width="167" height="172">            </p>
```

4. Save the HTML document then open it in your browser and place the cursor over the image to see its alternative text description

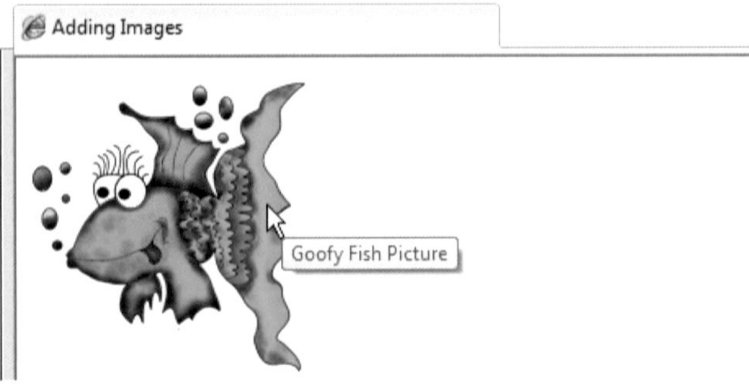

5. Change the browser's default background color from white to see the color shine through transparent areas

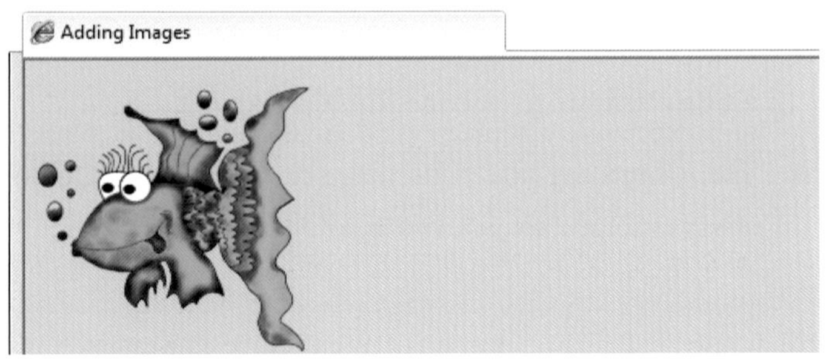

Don't forget

Attributes in HTML tags can appear in any order.

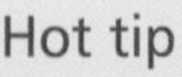
Hot tip

To change Internet Explorer's default background color select Tools, Internet Options, General, Colors, uncheck Use Windows Colors, click Background then choose a new color.

Summary

- The HTML **<body>** element encloses the document content and may include **onload** and **onunload** attributes
- A paragraph is enclosed within a **<p>** element and may use the **
** tag to force breaks between lines of text
- Block-level elements create a rectangular block area on the page in which to display content, inline-level elements create a small block on a line within the outer containing block
- Quotations may be enclosed within a **<blockquote>** element for block display or within a **<q>** element for inline display
- Headings of varying importance can be created as **<h1>**, **<h2>**, **<h3>**, **<h4>**, **<h5>** or **<h6>** elements
- The **<em>** and **<strong>** elements are preferred over the **<b>** and **<i>** elements to emphasize text
- Text can be formatted with **<big>**, **<small>** and **<tt>** elements
- To avoid misalignment tab spacing should be avoided when creating preformatted text for inclusion within a **<pre>** element
- Superscript and subscript can be included using character entities or using the **<sup>** and **<sub>** elements
- The **<del>** and **<ins>** elements indicate replaced text and **<abbr>**, **<dfn>**, **<cite>**, and **<kbd>** elements provide advice
- Program code can be included within a HTML document using the **<code>**, **<var>** and **<samp>** elements
- Contact information can be stated with the **<address>** element
- Most elements that appear in the document body may include a **title** attribute to provide Tooltip text
- The **<img>** tag places an image on the web page and should always include **src**, **alt**, **width**, and **height** attributes

4 Adding style to content

This chapter demonstrates how style sheet rules control the presentation of content within the body section of a HTML document.

Understanding style rules

Every CSS style rule consists of these three components:

- **Selector** – selecting one or more HTML elements to style
- **Property** – naming the property to be styled
- **Value** – specifying how the property should be affected

The W3C's online CSS validator can be found at **http://jigsaw.w3.org/css-validator**.

Each rule starts with the selector followed by the property and value enclosed within **{ }** curly brackets. The property is followed by a : colon character and the value is followed by a ; semicolon. For example, a style rule to set the **<body>** element's background color to yellow looks like this:

```
body { background : yellow ; }
```

A single style rule can include multiple property/value pairs within its brackets to set many properties of the selected element.

In order to use style sheets effectively it is essential to understand the properties of the rectangular blocks the web browser creates to accommodate content. In CSS these are called "content boxes" and have separate properties that can be styled by rules:

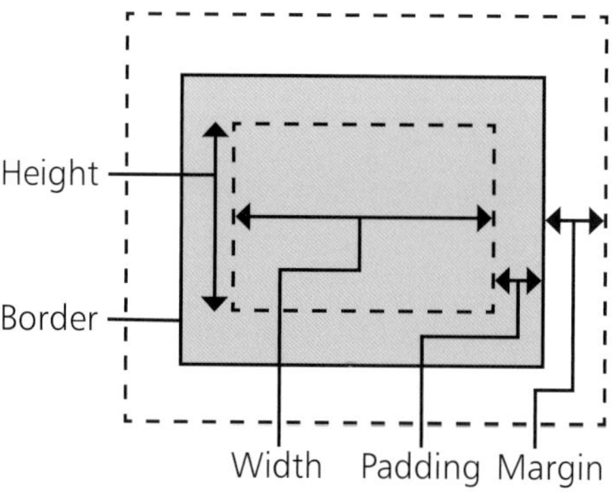

By default the padding and border properties are zero, so they occupy no space, but the browser does supply default sizes for the invisible margin property that separates the content boxes. Typically, Internet Explorer will set the body element's left and right margins to ten pixels and its top margin to 15 pixels. That is why the first content box appears with space above and to each side – as seen with the **<h1>** element on page 33.

Hot tip

The body's top margin sets the distance of the first content box from the top of the window but subsequent content-boxes typically have a default top-margin value of 19px to space them apart vertically.

Many of the properties found in CSS style sheets are listed in the table below. Size values can be specified as pixels with a "px" suffix and colors can be specified as hexadecimal values in the range **#000000** to **#FFFFFF**, or by one of the predefined listed names.

Property	Example Values	Specifies
margin	**5px | 10% | auto**	margin size
padding	**5px | 10%**	padding size
border	**3px solid black**	border size, type, and color
display	**block | inline**	level type
width	**5px | 10%**	width
height	**5px | 10%**	height
position	**absolute | relative**	positioning scheme
top	**5px | 10%**	distance from top
left	**5px | 10%**	distance from left
visibility	**visible | hidden**	show/hide element
overflow	**visible | hidden**	show/hide overflow
color	**red | #FF0000**	foreground color
background	**white | url(tile.png)**	background color or background image
font	**large "Arial", sans-serif**	font size and name
cursor	**pointer | default**	cursor type
text-align	**center | left**	inner text alignment

Black	**#000000**	Green	**#008000**
Silver	**#C0C0C0**	Lime	**#00FF00**
Gray	**#808080**	Olive	**#808000**
White	**#FFFFFF**	Yellow	**#FFFF00**
Maroon	**#800000**	Navy	**#000080**
Red	**#FF0000**	Blue	**#0000FF**
Purple	**#800080**	Teal	**#008080**
Fuchsia	**#FF00FF**	Aqua	**#00FFFF**

Don't forget

CSS provides many more properties than those listed here. More comprehensive information is available in "CSS in easy steps".

Hot tip

Three-figure hexadecimal shorthand values can also be used for color values. For example **#0F8** for **#00FF88**.

Styling individual tags

Any HTML tag that can contain displayable content may include a **style** attribute to determine how its content should be presented. This attribute acts as the style rule selector and allows property/value pairs to be specified, just as they are in a style sheet.

tags.html

1. Start a new HTML document with the Strict DTD

```
<!DOCTYPE HTML PUBLIC "-//W3C//DTD HTML 4.01//EN"
          "http://www.w3.org/TR/html4/strict.dtd">
```

2. Add a root element containing head and body sections

```
<html> <head> <title>Styling Individual Tags</title>
<meta http-equiv="Content-type"
        content="text/html; charset=ISO-8859-1">
</head>
<body><!-- Content goes here. --></body> </html>
```

3. In the body section, insert a heading and a paragraph

```
<h1>Heading</h1>
<p>Paragraph</p>
```

4. In the **<h1>** tag, insert a **style** attribute specifying property/value pairs for this element

```
style="color: red; background: yellow;
        border: 1px solid black;"
```

5. In the **<p>** tag, insert a **style** attribute specifying property/value pairs for that element

```
style="font: large 'Lucida Handwriting',cursive ;
color: blue; background: yellow; border: 1px solid black;"
```

6. Save the HTML document then open it in your browser to see the styles applied to each element

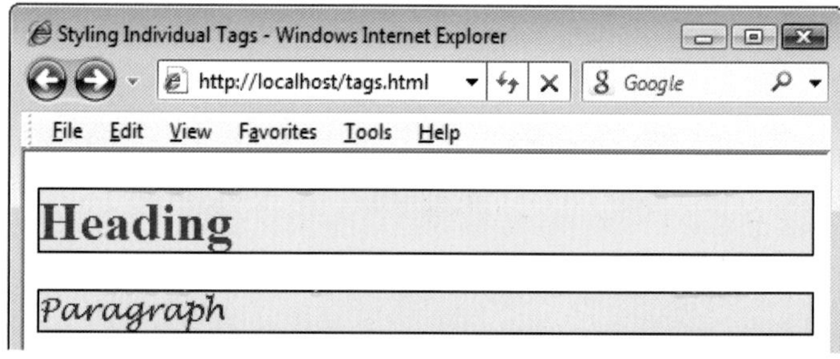

Beware

Notice that this font name must be enclosed within quotes because it contains a space. Single quotes are used to avoid conflict with the outer double quotes.

The heading content box is separated from the paragraph content box by a default margin set by the browser. This separation can be removed by setting the margin property of both content boxes to zero – overriding the default margin between them.

7 In the **<h1>** tag, edit the **style** attribute to add another property/value pair
margin:0px ;

8 Likewise edit the **style** attribute in the **<p>** tag to add another property/value pair
margin:0px ;

9 Save the document then open it in your web browser to see that the heading and paragraph margin has now gone

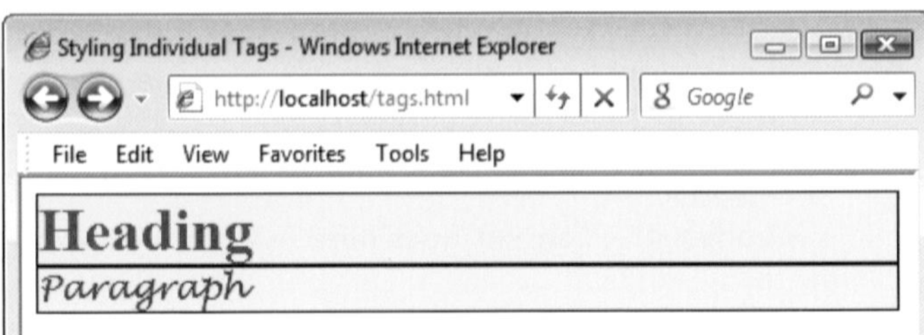

The default margins of the **<body>** element can also be overridden:

10 In the **<body>** tag, insert a **style** attribute specifying a property/value pair for that element then save the document and open it in your web browser once more
<body style="margin: 0px;">

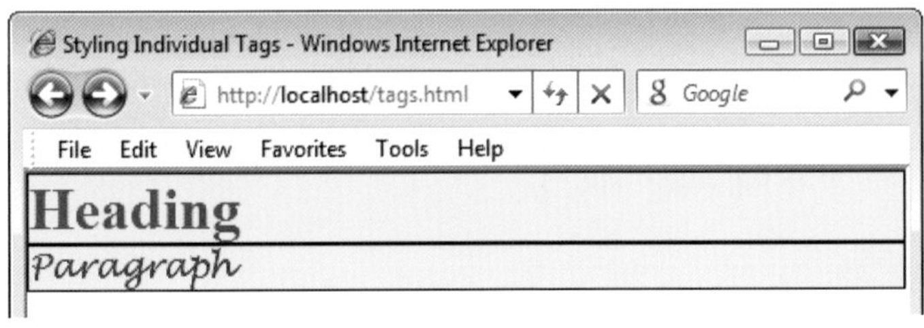

Hot tip

Many border styles are available – increase the border size to 5px and try the dashed, dotted, double, and groove styles. For example, **border: 5px groove red;**

Hot tip

Where the Lucida Handwriting font is not available the paragraph content will appear in a font chosen by your system from the "cursive" font family. Other font families are fantasy, serif, sans-serif, and monospace.

Styling with style sheets

The HTML **style** attribute, that was introduced in the previous example, is perfectly valid but is not the preferred method of applying styles to HTML documents as it can be cumbersome. For instance, where a document contains multiple identically styled paragraphs each **<p>** tag would require an identical **style** attribute. Changing the style of those paragraphs would tediously require each individual **style** attribute to be edited.

A much better solution is to style all those paragraphs with a single rule within a linked style sheet. If any paragraph needs to be styled differently a **style** attribute could then be added to its **<p>** tag to override the rule in the style sheet.

sheet.html

1. Start a new HTML document with the Strict DTD
```
<!DOCTYPE HTML PUBLIC "-//W3C//DTD HTML 4.01//EN"
            "http://www.w3.org/TR/html4/strict.dtd">
```

2. Add a root element containing head and body sections
```
<html> <head> <title>Styling with Style Sheets</title>
<meta http-equiv="Content-type"
        content="text/html; charset=ISO-8859-1">
</head>
<body><!-- Content goes here. --></body> </html>
```

3. In the body section, insert a heading and three paragraphs
```
<h1>Heading</h1>
<p>Paragraph</p>
<p>Paragraph</p>
<p>Paragraph</p>
```

4. In the head section, insert an element to incorporate a linked style sheet into this HTML document
```
<link rel="stylesheet" type="text/css" href="sheet.css">
```

sheet.css

5. Save the HTML document then open a text editor and add a rule to select the heading and style its foreground
```
h1 { color: red; }
```

6. Add a second rule to select all three paragraph elements and to style their background color and font
```
p { background: yellow;
        font: large "Lucida Handwriting",cursive ; }
```

7 Save the Cascading Style Sheet, in the same directory as the HTML document, then open the HTML document in your web browser to see the styles applied

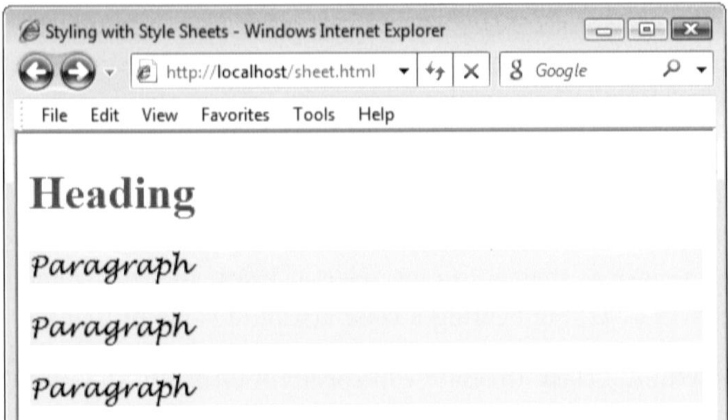

Don't forget

Block-level elements, like the paragraphs shown here, have content boxes that extend to the right edge of their containing box. Change the paragraphs to inline content boxes by adding a **display:inline;** rule to see the difference.

8 In the HTML document, edit the second paragraph element to change its background color and add padding

```
<p style="background:aqua; padding:50px;">
```

9 Save the HTML document then open it in your browser once more to see the overriding styles applied

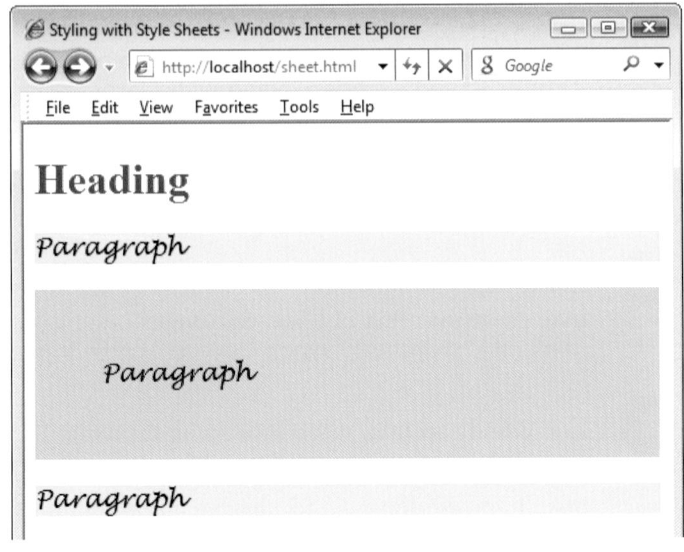

Hot tip

You can find more on incorporating style sheets into a HTML document back on page 32.

Styling with class

Hot tip

A **class** attribute can appear in any HTML displayable element.

The HTML **style** attribute, introduced in the previous examples, contradicts the stated aim of HTML 4 to separate structure from presentation by including CSS style rules within HTML tags. A cleaner solution is to insert a **class** attribute in a HTML tag to nominate the name of a CSS "class". This is simply a name of your choice stated as the selector within a style rule. Class selectors must always be prefixed by a "." period in the style sheet. For example, a selector for a class named "blue-text" must appear as **.blue-text** in the style sheet.

Property/value pairs are specified to a class rule in exactly the same way as they are to tag selector rules. The rule is applied to any HTML tag bearing a **class** attribute value of that class name.

Usefully, a **class** attribute can specify multiple CSS class selector names as a space-separated list. This allows class rules to style different properties of a HTML tag. In the event that more than one class rule attempts to style the same property of a HTML tag the rule nearest to the end of the style sheet will be applied. This principle applies to all CSS style sheets as the browser reads them from start (top) to finish (bottom).

class.html

1. Start a new HTML document with the Strict DTD

```
<!DOCTYPE HTML PUBLIC "-//W3C//DTD HTML 4.01//EN"
                "http://www.w3.org/TR/html4/strict.dtd">
```

2. Add a root element containing head and body sections

```
<html> <head> <title>Styling with Class</title>
<meta http-equiv="Content-type"
        content="text/html; charset=ISO-8859-1">
</head>
<body><!-- Content goes here. --></body> </html>
```

3. In the head section, insert an element to incorporate a style sheet into this HTML document

```
<link rel="stylesheet" type="text/css" href="class.css">
```

4. In the body section, insert a heading element

```
<h1>This heading has no class</h1>
```

5. Next in the body section, insert a paragraph styled with a class attribute

```
<p class="blue-text">This paragraph does have class</p>
```

6. Now in the body section, insert a paragraph styled with a class attribute

```
<p class="on-yellow">This paragraph has other class</p>
```

7. Finally in the body section, insert a paragraph styled with a class attribute specifying two selectors

```
<p class="red-text on-yellow">
        This paragraph has lots of class!</p>
```

8. Save the HTML document, then open a text editor and add three rules to apply the class styles

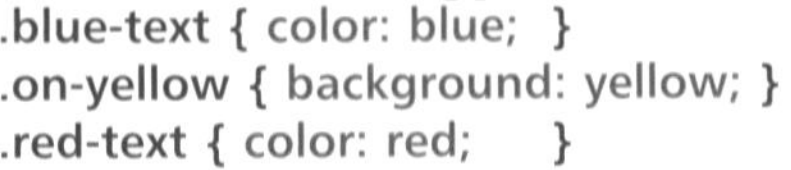

```
.blue-text { color: blue;  }
.on-yellow { background: yellow; }
.red-text { color: red;     }
```

class.css

9. Save the Cascading Style Sheet, in the same directoy as the HTML document, then open the web page in your browser to see the class styles applied

Styling with Class

This heading has no class

This paragraph does have class

This paragraph has other class

This paragraph has lots of class!

10. Edit the class attribute value in the final paragraph to introduce conflicting foreground color rules

```
<p class="red-text on-yellow blue-text">
        This paragraph has lots of class!</p>
```

11. Save the HTML document then reopen it in your web browser to see the blue foreground color is not applied to the final paragraph – because the rule setting the red foreground appears last in the style sheet

Don't forget

For conflicting rules, the rule order in the style sheet determines which value to apply – not the order of the class selector list supplied to the HTML **class** attribute.

Styling by identity

HTML provides an **id** attribute that can be used to uniquely identify each single element within an entire HTML document. Different styles can then be applied to each element using their **id** attribute value as the style sheet selector. Identity selectors must always be prefixed by a "#" hash character in the style sheet. For example, a selector for an identity named "chapter1" must appear as **#chapter1** in the style sheet. Property/value pairs are specified to an identity rule in the same way as they are for all other rules.

Style sheets can often employ a combination of tag, **class**, and **id** selectors, for optimum performance and ease of maintenance. The ability to uniquely identify any HTML element within the document is especially useful for scripting dynamic web pages.

Hot tip 

An **id** attribute can appear in any HTML displayable element.

id.html

1. Start a new HTML document with the Strict DTD

```
<!DOCTYPE HTML PUBLIC "-//W3C//DTD HTML 4.01//EN"
          "http://www.w3.org/TR/html4/strict.dtd">
```

2. Add a root element containing head and body sections

```
<html> <head> <title>Styling by Identity</title>
<meta http-equiv="Content-type"
        content="text/html; charset=ISO-8859-1">
</head>
<body><!-- Content goes here. --></body> </html>
```

Hot tip 

You can find more on incorporating scripts into a HTML document back on page 30.

3. In the head section, insert an element to incorporate a style sheet into this HTML document

```
<link rel="stylesheet" type="text/css" href="id.css">
```

4. In the body section, insert a large heading element

```
<h1>Contents</h1>
```

5. In the body section, insert a smaller heading and a paragraph styled with identity attributes

```
<h3 id="chapter1">Chapter One Title</h3>
<p id="chapter1contents">
Topic 1.1<br>Topic 1.2<br>Topic 1.3</p>
```

6. Next in the body section, insert another heading and a paragraph styled with identity attributes

```
<h3 id="chapter2">Chapter Two Title</h3>
<p id="chapter2contents">
Topic 2.1<br>Topic 2.2<br>Topic 2.3</p>
```

7 Now in the body section, insert yet another heading and a paragraph styled with identity attributes

```
<h3 id="chapter3">Chapter Three Title</h3>
<p id="chapter3contents">
Topic 3.1<br>Topic 3.2<br>Topic 3.3</p>
```

8 Save the HTML document then open a text editor and add rules to apply identity styles

id.css

```
#chapter1 { color: red; }
#chapter2 { color: green; }
#chapter3 { color: blue; }

#chapter1contents { background: fuchsia; }
#chapter2contents { background: lime; }
#chapter3contents { background: aqua; }
```

9 Save the Cascading Style Sheet, in the same directory as the HTML document, then open the web page in your browser to see the identity styles applied

Styling by Identity

Contents

Chapter One Title

Topic 1.1
Topic 1.2
Topic 1.3

Chapter Two Title

Topic 2.1
Topic 2.2
Topic 2.3

Chapter Three Title

Topic 3.1
Topic 3.2
Topic 3.3

Dividing content

In addition to the body content tags, introduced in the previous chapter, HTML provides a generic block-level **<div> </div>** element to contain any type of content. This tag is favored by web page authors who wish to present content with absolute precision.

The position of an element on the page is, by default, relative to other elements but can be precisely specified by setting the element's CSS **position** property to an **absolute** value. In so doing the element's **top**, **left**, and **width** properties should also be given a size value to determine its position and width.

Absolute control over HTML elements allows the web page author to micro-manage multiple elements within a single "wrapper" element to produce some exciting Web 2.0 designs.

Beware

If you absolutely control the position of one element you must absolutely control the position of all other elements on that page.

div.html

1. Start a new HTML document with the Strict DTD

```
<!DOCTYPE HTML PUBLIC "-//W3C//DTD HTML 4.01//EN"
                    "http://www.w3.org/TR/html4/strict.dtd">
```

2. Add a root element containing a head section incorporating a style sheet, and a body section

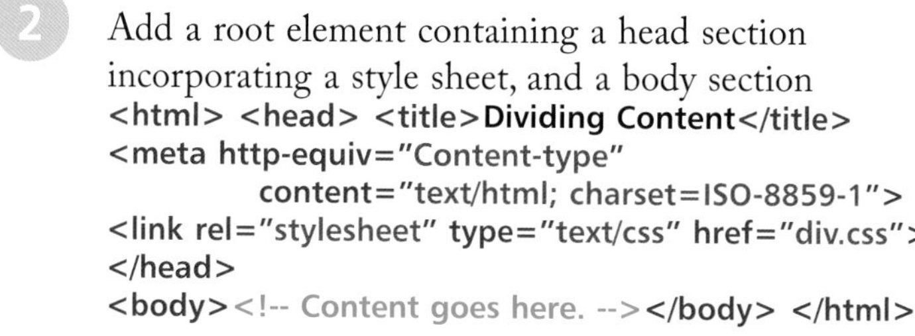

```
<html> <head> <title>Dividing Content</title>
<meta http-equiv="Content-type"
          content="text/html; charset=ISO-8859-1">
<link rel="stylesheet" type="text/css" href="div.css">
</head>
<body><!-- Content goes here. --></body> </html>
```

3. In the body section, insert all these container elements

```
<div id="wrapper-1">
  <div class="d1"></div> <div class="d2"></div>
  <div class="d3"></div> <div class="d4"></div>
  <div class="d8">Web 2.0 Panel</div>
  <div class="d9" id="content-1" >
  Content appears here.<br>
  This area expands to accommodate content size.</div>
  <div class="d7"></div> <div class="d6"></div>
  <div class="d5"></div> <div class="d1"></div>
</div>
```

4. Save the HTML document then open a text editor and carefully copy the advanced style sheet listed opposite to precisely style each of the **<div>** elements above

Don't forget

Notice that the inner content panel has an **id** attribute so it can easily be referenced by scripts.

```
#wrapper-1
{ position: absolute; top: 20px; left: 20px; width: 450px; }

.d1, .d2, .d3, .d4, .d5, .d6, .d7
{ font: 1px cursive; overflow:hidden;      }

.d1, .d2, .d3, .d4, .d8     { background: #FF6600; }
.d5, .d6, .d7, .d9          { background: #FEEDB7; }

.d1, .d2, .d3, .d5, .d6     { height: 1px;   }
.d4, .d7                    { height: 2px;   }

.d1             { margin: 0px 5px;        }
.d2, .d5        { margin: 0px 3px;        }
.d3, .d6        { margin: 0px 2px;        }
.d4, .d7        { margin: 0px 1px;        }

.d2, .d5
{ border-right:2px solid #FF6600; border-left:2px solid #FF6600; }

 .d3, .d4, .d6, .d7, .d8, .d9
{ border-right:1px solid #FF6600; border-left:1px solid #FF6600; }

.d8     { color:#FEEDB7; padding-left: 10px;
                font: medium "Lucida Handwriting", cursive ; }

.d9     { padding: 10px; font: medium cursive;   }
```

Hot tip

The margin, border, and padding properties also have individual properties to control each side, such as **border-left**.

5. Save the Cascading Style Sheet then open the HTML document in your web browser to see a "rounded" rectangular panel appear – without the use of graphics

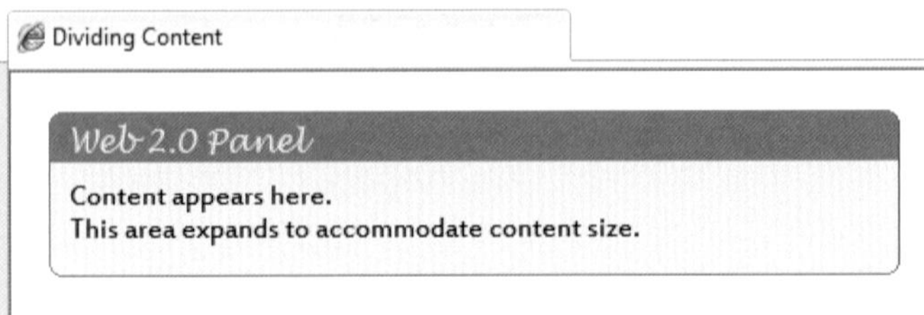

The Web 2.0 rounded rectangle is a welcome relief after many years of square-cornered rectangles in web page design but there is some debate over the best method of their production. Images with anti-aliasing can be used to display smooth rounded corners that blend with a known background color. The CSS technique employed in this example creates a number of one-pixel high **<div>** elements that produce steps to simulate rounded corners and can be used on any color background.

Centering with style

Although CSS style rules allow the web page author to absolutely specify the position and size of a HTML element consideration must be given to how the web page might be viewed. For instance, a web page designed for the popular resolution of 1024x768 pixels will overflow at a resolution of 640x480 pixels.

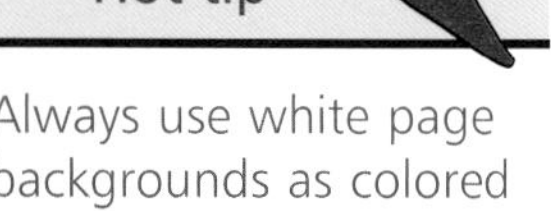

Always use white page backgrounds as colored backgrounds can make content difficult to read.

A compromise adopted by many web page authors is to design for a resolution of 800x600 pixels which displays reasonably well in both larger and smaller resolutions. Some prefer to leave the page's content box fixed horizontally at the default left position while others prefer to center the page content. Centering the page is achieved using a **<div>** element as a "wrapper" for the content and applying a style rule to set its **margin** property to **auto.**

Additionally, many web page authors use the special * universal CSS selector to set the initial **padding**, **border**, and **margin** property of all elements to zero. This removes the default **margin** areas of the body element so a **<div>** wrapper element gets positioned at the very top of the browser window.

The margins at each side of a centered wrapper element reveal the background of the <body> element. This can be styled to match the wrapper's background color, set to a different color for contrast, or styled with a background image tile.

Note that the **margin** property determines the position of the content box itself. Alignment of content inside the content box is determined by its **text-align** property.

center.html

1. Start a new HTML document with the Strict DTD

```
<!DOCTYPE HTML PUBLIC "-//W3C//DTD HTML 4.01//EN"
                "http://www.w3.org/TR/html4/strict.dtd">
```

2. Add a root element containing a head section incorporating a style sheet, and a body section

```
<html> <head> <title>Centering with Style</title>
<meta http-equiv="Content-type"
        content="text/html; charset=ISO-8859-1">
<link rel="stylesheet" type="text/css" href="center.css">
</head>
<body><!-- Content goes here. --></body> </html>
```

3. In the body section, insert a wrapper element

```
<div id="content-wrapper">    </div>
```

4. In the wrapper element, insert a heading and a paragraph

```
<h1>Centered Heading</h1>
<p>Centered Paragraph</p>
```

5. Save the HTML document then open a text editor and add a style rule to remove all default content box values

```
* { padding: 0px; border: 0px; margin:0px; }
```

center.css

6. Next add a style rule to center the wrapper element and set its size and background color

```
#content-wrapper
{
        margin: auto; background: white;
        width: 800px; height: 1000px;
}
```

Hot tip

Notice how two selectors are used in a single rule to style both the **<h1>** and **<p>** elements.

7. Now add a style rule to set the body background

```
body { background: url( stripes.png ); }
```

8. Finally add a style rule to center the content inside the heading and paragraph elements and to set their border

```
h1, p { text-align: center; border: 5px dashed red; }
```


9. Save the Cascading Style Sheet alongside the HTML document and image then view the web page in your browser to see the wrapper and text content centered

Don't forget

The browser repeats the image across the page to fill the margins.

stripes.png

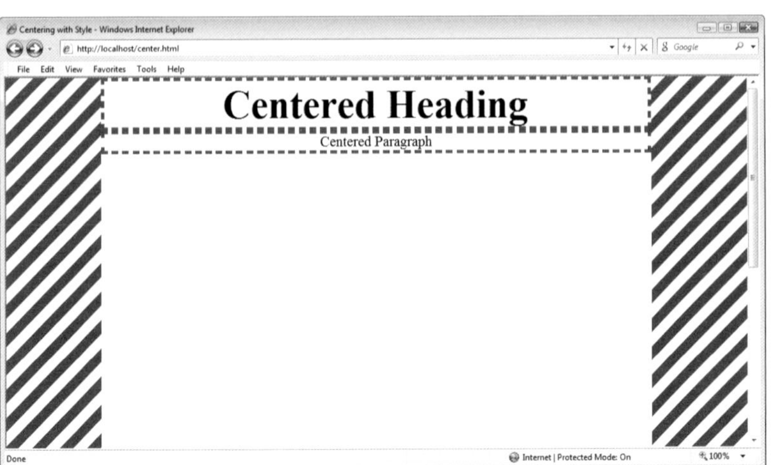

Styling inline content

Just as HTML provides the generic block-level **<div>** element it also provides a generic inline-level **<span> </span>** element to contain text content. Unlike the **<div>** tag, the **<span>** tag is not used for positioning but specifies display characteristics for pieces of text, such as syntax highlighting for programming code.

span.html

1. Start a new HTML document with the Strict DTD

```
<!DOCTYPE HTML PUBLIC "-//W3C//DTD HTML 4.01//EN"
                "http://www.w3.org/TR/html4/strict.dtd">
```

2. Add a root element containing a head section incorporating a style sheet, and a body section

```
<html> <head> <title>Styling Inline Content</title>
<meta http-equiv="Content-type"
        content="text/html; charset=ISO-8859-1">
<link rel="stylesheet" type="text/css" href="span.css">
</head>
<body><!-- Content goes here. --></body> </html>
```

3. In the body section, insert a heading and a preformatted programming code sample

```
<h1>A First C++ Program</h1>
<pre id="sample">
#include &lt;iostream&gt;
using namespace std;

int main()
{
  // The traditional beginning.
  cout << "Hello World!" << endl;
  return 0;
}
</pre>
```

4. Insert elements around the keywords in the programming code sample

```
<span class="keyword">#include</span>
<span class="keyword">using namespace</span>
<span class="keyword">int</span>
<span class="keyword">return</span>
```

5. Next insert an element around the code comment

```
<span class="comment">
        // The traditional beginning.</span>
```

Don't forget

Remember to use **<** and **>** character entities in place of angled brackets where they may be confused with those surrounding HTML tags.

6. Now insert elements around the library name and namespace name

```
<span class="name">&lt;iostream&gt;</span>
<span class="name">std</span>
```

7. Finally insert elements around the literal values

```
<span class="literal">Hello World!</span>
<span class="literal">0</span>
```

8. Save the HTML document then open a plain text editor and add these rules to style the elements

```
#sample     { color: black; padding:10px; width:450px;
              font-weight:bold; border:1px solid black;}
.keyword    { color: blue;      }
.comment    { color: green;     }
.name       { background: #FFA500; }
.literal    { color: red;       }
```

span.css

9. Save the Cascading Style Sheet alongside the HTML document then view the web page in your browser to see the syntax color highlighting applied

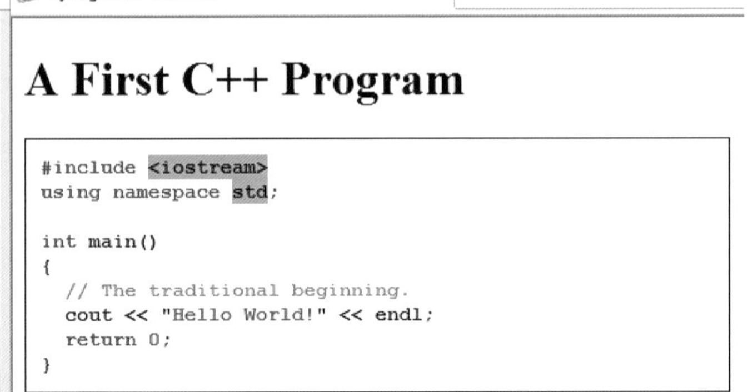
Styling Inline Content
A First C++ Program
#include <iostream>
using namespace std;
int main()
{
// The traditional beginning.
cout << "Hello World!" << endl;
return 0;
}

Hot tip

The hexadecimal value **#FFA500** represents the color orange.

10. Add a **title** attribute to any **<span>** tag to describe that piece of code when the cursor is placed over it

```
<span class="keyword"
        title="Integer Data Type">int</span>
```

```
int main()
{  Integer Data Type
  // The traditional beginning.
```

Summary

- Every CSS style rule has a selector and property/value pairs
- Content boxes have **width**, **height**, **padding**, **border**, and **margin** properties, which can be styled by CSS rules
- Size values expressed in pixels have the suffix **px** and color values can be specified by name or hexadecimal value
- Any HTML element that can contain displayable content can include a **style** attribute to specify rules – but it is preferable to list rules in style sheets for ease of maintenance
- Style rule tag selectors simply select an element by its tag name
- The **class** attribute nominates one or more CSS class rules to be applied to that HTML element
- Style rule **class** selectors prefix the class name with a . period
- Rules can be overridden by other rules selecting the same element that appears later in the style sheet
- All HTML elements in a document can include an **id** attribute to uniquely identify each element
- Style rule **id** selectors prefix the identity name with a **#** hash
- The generic block-level **<div>** element can contain any type of content and can be precisely positioned on the page
- Style rules that set an **absolute** value for a **position** property should also specify values for **top**, **left**, and **width** properties
- A **<div>** element can be used as a wrapper to contain other elements for graphical effect and page centering
- The **margin** property specifies the position of a content box and the **text-align** property specifies the alignment of its content
- The generic inline-level **<span>** element is used to specify display characteristics for pieces of text

5 Writing lists

This chapter demonstrates how to create and present lists of items within a HTML document.

Creating unordered lists

Unordered lists, where the sequence of list items is not important, typically place a bullet-point before each item to differentiate list items from regular text.

In HTML unordered lists are created with **<ul> </ul>** tags. These produce a block-level **<ul>** container element for list items. A list item can be created using **<li> </li>** tags, to enclose the item, or optionally just using **<li>** to precede the item – either form of **<li>** element validates as correct HTML. An unordered list **<ul>** element can contain numerous list item **<li>** elements.

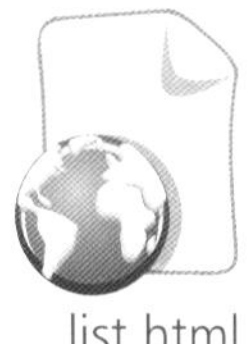
list.html

1. Start a new HTML document with the Strict DTD

```
<!DOCTYPE HTML PUBLIC "-//W3C//DTD HTML 4.01//EN"
                "http://www.w3.org/TR/html4/strict.dtd">
```

2. Add a root element containing a head section incorporating a style sheet, and a body section

```
<html> <head> <title>Creating Unordered Lists</title>
<meta http-equiv="Content-type"
        content="text/html; charset=ISO-8859-1">
<link rel="stylesheet" type="text/css" href="list.css">
</head>
<body><!-- Content goes here. --></body> </html>
```

3. In the body section, insert a wrapper element

```
<div id="recipe">        </div>
```

4. Within the wrapper element, insert a small heading and an unordered list containing three list items

```
<h3>Ingredients:</h3>
<ul>
<li>2 Large Eggs</li>
<li>Salt and Pepper</li>
<li>1 Tablespoon Oil or Butter</li>
</ul>
```

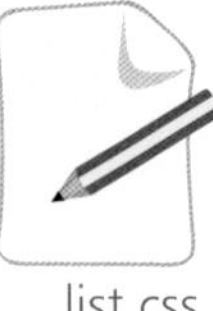
list.css

5. Save the HTML document then open a text editor and add style rules for the wrapper and list elements

```
#recipe { background: #FEEDB7 ; width: 300px; }
ul      { background: #FF6600 ; margin-bottom: 0px; }
```

6. Save the Cascading Style Sheet alongside the HTML document then open the web page in your web browser

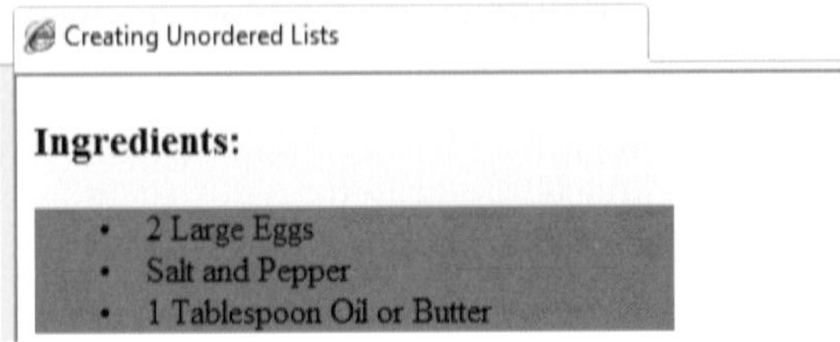

Viewed with Internet Explorer 8 (or Firefox 3) the list appears as shown above – the wrapper element's background color shines through the heading element and the list element's background color fills its content box. The bullet-point list item markers are actually positioned within the left padding area of the list element. Viewed with Internet Explorer 7 the list appears as shown below:

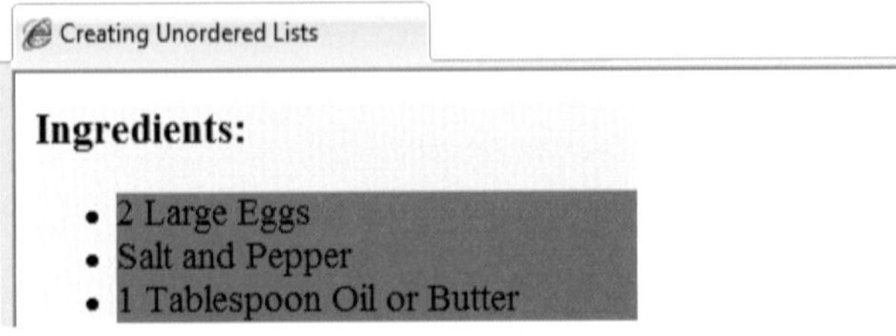

Here the bullet-point list item markers are actually positioned within the left margin area of the list element. The list element's background color fills its content box and the wrapper element's background color shines through the heading element – and the list element's left margin!

7. Add a further style rule to the Cascading Style Sheet to adjust the list's left padding and position

```
ul {     list-style-position: inside;
         padding-left: 30px; margin-left:0px ; }
```

8. Save the modified Cascading Style Sheet then open the HTML document in Internet Explorer 7 to see that the list now appears like it does in Internet Explorer 8 – as illustrated in the screenshot at the top of this page.

Hot tip

Do always use the optional **</li>** closing tag – it clearly marks the end of list item content.

Specifying bullet-point styles

The bullet-point that differentiates list items from regular text may be any one of these three marker types:

- **Disc** – a filled circular bullet-point (the default style)
- **Circle** – an unfilled circular bullet-point
- **Square** – a filled square bullet-point

A style rule can specify any one of these values to the list's **list-style-type** property to determine which bullet-point to use. Alternatively a **none** value can be used to suppress bullet-points.

Each HTML list also has a **list-style-image** property that can specify the path to an image file to be used for the bullet-points. This will appear in place of any of the marker type bullet-points. Where the web browser cannot use the specified image the marker specified to its **list-style-type** property will be used. When there is no other marker specified the default marker will be used.

bullet.html

1. Start a new HTML document with the Strict DTD

```
<!DOCTYPE HTML PUBLIC "-//W3C//DTD HTML 4.01//EN"
                "http://www.w3.org/TR/html4/strict.dtd">
```

2. Add a root element containing a head section incorporating a style sheet, and a body section

```
<html> <head> <title>Bullet-point Styles</title>
<meta http-equiv="Content-type"
          content="text/html; charset=ISO-8859-1">
<link rel="stylesheet" type="text/css" href="bullet.css">
</head>
<body><!-- Content goes here. --></body> </html>
```

3. In the body section, insert a small heading and an unordered list containing three list items

```
<h3>Disc Bullets:</h3>
<ul class="bullet">
<li>Item 1</li>
<li>Item 2</li>
<li>Item 3</li>
</ul>
```

4. Copy'n'paste four lists below the first then change their heading and class to "circle", "square", "none" and "image"

5. Save the HTML document then open a text editor and add class style rules for each list marker type

```
.disc   { list-style-type: disc ; }
.circle { list-style-type: circle ; }
.square { list-style-type: square ; }
.none   { list-style-type: none ; }
```

bullet.css

6. Now add a class style rule specifying an image in the same directory to be used for bullet-points

```
.image { list-style-image: url(bullet.png) ; }
```

bullet.png

7. Save the Cascading Style Sheet alongside the HTML document and bullet image then open the web page in your web browser to see the various bullet-points

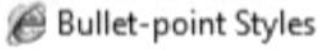

Disc Bullets:

- Item 1
- Item 2
- Item 3

Circle Bullets:

- Item 1
- Item 2
- Item 3

Square Bullets:

- Item 1
- Item 2
- Item 3

None Bullets:

Item 1
Item 2
Item 3

Image Bullets:

- Item 1
- Item 2
- Item 3

Beware

Notice that the items in the list without markers are aligned with all other items as the bullet-points are drawn in the left padding area.

Creating ordered lists

Ordered lists, where the sequence of list items is important, number each item to differentiate list items from regular text.

In HTML ordered lists are created with **<ol> </ol>** tags. These produce a block-level **<ol>** container element for list items. A list item can be created using **<li> </li>** tags, to enclose the item, or optionally just using **<li>** to precede the item – either form of **<li>** element validates as correct HTML. An ordered list **<ol>** element can contain numerous list item **<li>** elements.

order.html

1. Start a new HTML document with the Strict DTD

```
<!DOCTYPE HTML PUBLIC "-//W3C//DTD HTML 4.01//EN"
                 "http://www.w3.org/TR/html4/strict.dtd">
```

2. Add a root element containing a head section incorporating a style sheet, and a body section

```
<html> <head> <title>Creating Ordered Lists</title>
<meta http-equiv="Content-type"
        content="text/html; charset=ISO-8859-1">
<link rel="stylesheet" type="text/css" href="order.css">
</head>
<body><!-- Content goes here. --></body> </html>
```

3. In the body section, insert a wrapper element

```
<div id="prepare">      </div>
```

4. Within the wrapper element, insert a small heading and an ordered list containing four list items

```
<h3>Directions:</h3>
<ol>
<li>Whisk the Eggs</li>
<li>Add Salt and Pepper to taste</li>
<li>Heat the Oil then add the Eggs</li>
<li>Serve when set</li>
</ol>
```

order.css

5. Save the HTML document then open a text editor and add style rules for the wrapper and list elements

```
#prepare { background: #FEEDB7 ; width: 300px; }
ol       { background: #FF6600 ; margin-bottom: 0px; }
```

6. Save the Cascading Style Sheet alongside the HTML document then open the web page in your web browser

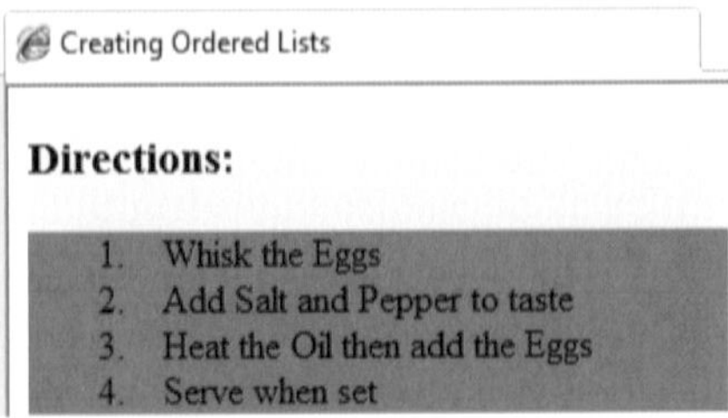

Viewed with Internet Explorer 8 (or Firefox 3) the list appears as shown above – the wrapper element's background color shines through the heading element and the list element's background color fills its content box. The list item numbers are actually positioned within the left padding area of the list element. Viewed with Internet Explorer 7 the list appears as shown below:

Creating Ordered Lists

Directions:

1. Whisk the Eggs
2. Add Salt and Pepper to taste
3. Heat the Oil then add the Eggs
4. Serve when set

Here the list item numbers are actually positioned within the left margin area of the list element. The list element's background color fills its content box and the wrapper element's background color shines through the heading element – and the list element's left margin!

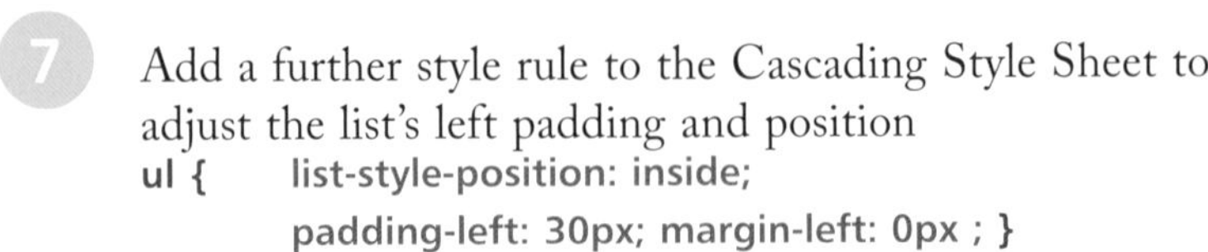

7. Add a further style rule to the Cascading Style Sheet to adjust the list's left padding and position

```
ul {    list-style-position: inside;
        padding-left: 30px; margin-left: 0px ; }
```

8. Save the modified Cascading Style Sheet then open the HTML document in Internet Explorer 7 to see that the list now appears just like it does in Internet Explorer 8 – as seen in the screenshot at the top of this page.

Hot tip

List item numbers are positioned by default in the same way as markers in unordered lists.

Specifying numbering styles

The automatic numbering that differentiates ordered list items from regular text may be any one of these four numbering types:

- **Decimal** – traditional numerals (the default style)
- **Roman** – classical numerals
- **Latin** – traditional alphabetical lettering
- **Greek** – classical alphabetical lettering

A style rule can specify any one of these to the list's **list-style-type** property to determine which numbering style to use. Optionally decimal numbering can include a leading zero. All other numbering types must specify whether to display in uppercase or lowercase. Alternatively a **none** value can be used to suppress numbering. When no numbering type is specified the default bullet-point style will be used.

number.html

1. Start a new HTML document with the Strict DTD

```
<!DOCTYPE HTML PUBLIC "-//W3C//DTD HTML 4.01//EN"
                "http://www.w3.org/TR/html4/strict.dtd">
```

2. Add a root element containing a head section incorporating a style sheet, and a body section

```
<html> <head> <title>List-number Styles</title>
<meta http-equiv="Content-type"
        content="text/html; charset=ISO-8859-1">
<link rel="stylesheet" type="text/css" href="number.css">
</head>
<body><!-- Content goes here. --></body> </html>
```

3. In the body section, insert a small heading and an ordered list containing three list items

```
<h3>Decimal Numbers:</h3>
<ol class="decimal">
<li>Item 1</li>
<li>Item 2</li>
<li>Item 3</li>
</ol>
```

4. Copy'n'paste four lists below the first then change their heading and class to "roman", "latin", "none" and "greek"

5. Save the HTML document then open a text editor and add class style rules for each numbering type

```
.decimal { list-style-type: decimal ; }
.roman  { list-style-type: upper-roman ; }
.latin   { list-style-type: upper-latin ; }
.none   { list-style-type: none ; }
.greek  { list-style-type: lower-greek ; }
```

number.css

6. Save the Cascading Style Sheet alongside the HTML document then open the web page in your web browser to see the various numbering styles

List-number Styles

Decimal Numbers:

1. Item 1
2. Item 2
3. Item 3

Roman Numbers:

I. Item 1
II. Item 2
III. Item 3

Latin Letters:

A. Item 1
B. Item 2
C. Item 3

None Numbers:

Item 1
Item 2
Item 3

Greek Letters:

α. Item 1
β. Item 2
γ. Item 3

Other possible numbering style values are **decimal-leading-zero, lower-roman, lower-latin** and **upper-greek**. Support for alphabetical numbering was introduced in Internet Explorer 8 – previous versions only support decimal and roman numbering.

Beware

Notice that the items in the list without numbers are aligned with all other items as the numbers are drawn in the left padding area.

Creating definition lists

A definition list is a unique type of list where each list item typically consists of a term and a description of that term.

In HTML definition lists are created with **<dl> </dl>** tags. These produce a block-level **<dl>** container element for list items. A list item can be created using **<dt> </dt>** tags, to enclose the definition term, and **<dd> </dd>** tags, to enclose the definition description. Optionally the **</dt>** and **</dd>** closing tags can be omitted – either form validates as correct HTML.

A definition list **<dl>** element can contain numerous list item **<dt>** and **<dd>** elements but these need not be in pairs. For example, two terms might have the same single description.

define.html

1. Start a new HTML document with the Strict DTD

```
<!DOCTYPE HTML PUBLIC "-//W3C//DTD HTML 4.01//EN"
                    "http://www.w3.org/TR/html4/strict.dtd">
```

2. Add a root element containing a head section incorporating a style sheet, and a body section

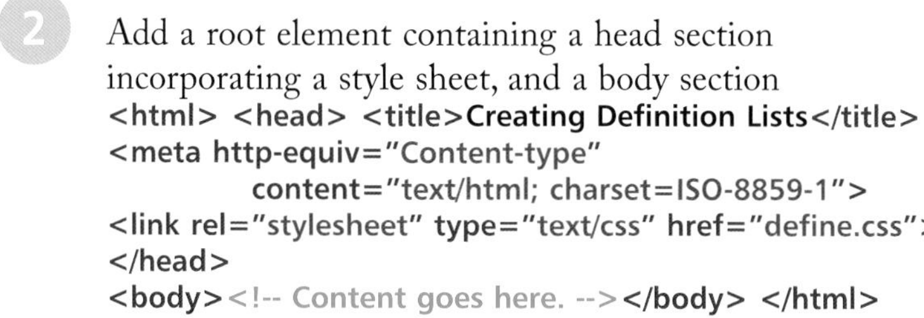

```
<html> <head> <title>Creating Definition Lists</title>
<meta http-equiv="Content-type"
          content="text/html; charset=ISO-8859-1">
<link rel="stylesheet" type="text/css" href="define.css">
</head>
<body><!-- Content goes here. --></body> </html>
```

3. In the body section, insert a definition list element

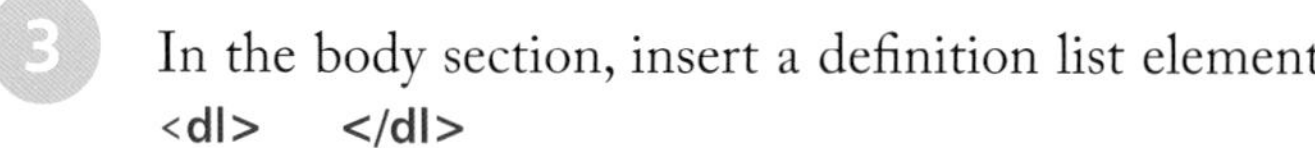

```
<dl>    </dl>
```

4. Within the definition list element, insert a definition term and description for the HyperText Markup Language

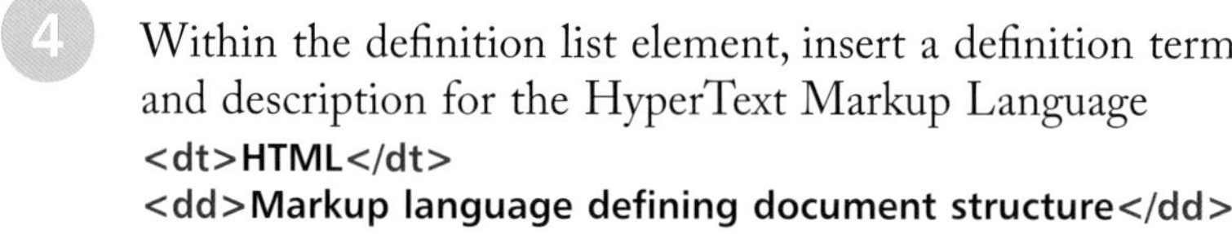

```
<dt>HTML</dt>
<dd>Markup language defining document structure</dd>
```

5. Next within the definition list element, insert a definition term and description for Cascading Style Sheets

```
<dt>CSS</dt>
<dd>Style language defining content presentation</dd>
```

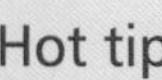

Hot tip

Always use the optional **</dt>** and **</dd>** closing tags – they clearly mark the end of each term and description.

6 Now within the definition list element, insert a definition term and description for JavaScript

```
<dt>JavaScript</dt>
<dd>Client-side scripting language for functionality</dd>
```

7 Finally within the definition list element, insert a definition term and description for both Perl and PHP

```
<dt>Perl</dt>
<dt>PHP</dt>
<dd>Server-side scripting language for functionality</dd>
```

8 Save the HTML document then open a text editor and add style rules for each definition list element

```
dl { background: lime ; width: 350px ; }
dt { background: yellow ; }
dd { background: #FFA500 ; }
```

define.css

9 Save the Cascading Style Sheet alongside the HTML document then open the web page in your web browser to see the definition list

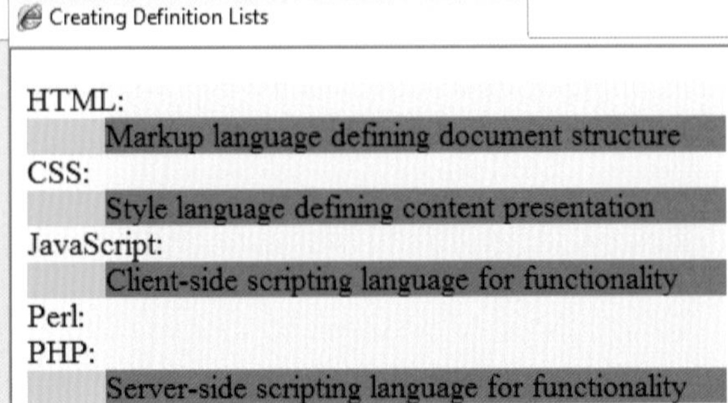

The definition term's background color fills its content box across the entire width of the definition list content box. The definition description background color fills its content box revealing an automatic left margin, which the definition list element's background color shines through.

Don't forget

Definition lists are useful to display movie dialog – using **<dt>** elements for the speaker's name and the **<dd>** element for their lines.

Styling definitions

Although the benefits of definition lists may not be immediately obvious they can, with a little imagination, be extremely useful. Multiple **<dd>** description elements can be applied to a single **<dt>** definition term and can include images to illustrate the term. This is often used to create a definition box "floating" around text and positioned to the right of a web page:

box.html

1. Start a new HTML document with the Strict DTD

```
<!DOCTYPE HTML PUBLIC "-//W3C//DTD HTML 4.01//EN"
                 "http://www.w3.org/TR/html4/strict.dtd">
```

2. Add a root element containing a head section incorporating a style sheet, and a body section

```
<html> <head> <title>Creating Definition Boxes</title>
<meta http-equiv="Content-type"
        content="text/html; charset=ISO-8859-1">
<link rel="stylesheet" type="text/css" href="box.css">
</head>
<body><!-- Content goes here. --></body> </html>
```

3. In the body section, insert a wrapper element

```
<div id="wrapper-1">  </div>
```

4. Within the wrapper, insert a definition list element

```
<dl>    </dl>
```

5. Within the definition list, insert a definition term

```
<dt>Scarlet Cob</dt>
```

6. Next within the definition list insert, insert multiple definition descriptions for the definition term

```
<dd> <img src="cactus.jpg" alt="Scarlet Cob Image"
       width="192" height="180" ></dd>
<dd><em>Echinopsis hertrichiana</em> </dd>
<dd>Native Habitat: Peru</dd>
```

7. After the definition list, insert a descriptive paragraph

```
<p><em>Subfamily:</em> Cactoideae<br>
<em>Tribe:</em> Trichocereeae<br>
<em>Habit:</em> Globose<br>
<em>Flower:</em> Red<br>
<em>Synonyms:</em> Lobivia <!-- Etcetera. --> </p>
```

Don't forget

Always include **width**, **height**, and **alt** attributes in every image element.

8 Save the HTML document then open a text editor and add a style rule for the definition list element

```
dl {      border: 1px solid #FF6600; background: #FEEDB7;
          width: 212px; text-align: center;
          margin-top: 0px; float: right;      }
```

box.css

9 Next add a style rule for the definition term element

```
dt {      background: #FF6600; color: #FEEDB7;
          font-weight: bold; padding: 5px;
          margin-bottom: 10px;                }
```

10 Add a style rule for the definition description elements

```
dd {      margin: 0px; padding: 0px 10px 5px 10px;
          font-size: 85%;                     }
```

11 Finally add rules to to put a border around the image and set the wrapper width

```
img {    border: 1px solid #FF6600 ;          }
#wrapper-1 { width: 450px;                    }
```

12 Save the Cascading Style Sheet alongside the HTML document then open the web page in your web browser to see the definition box float to the right of the text

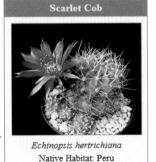

Creating Definition Boxes

Scarlet Cob

Echinopsis hertrichiana
Native Habitat: Peru

Subfamily: Cactoideae
Tribe: Trichocereeae
Habit: Globose
Flower: Red
Synonyms: Lobivia hertrichiana, Neolobivia hertrichiana, Echinopsis backebergii, Lobivia allegraiana, Lobivia binghamiana, Lobivia incaica, Neolobivia incaica, Lobivia planiceps, Lobivia huilcanota, Lobivia minuta, Neolobivia minuta, Lobivia vilcabambae, Neolobivia vilcabambae, Lobivia simplex, Lobiva echinata, Neolobivia echinata, Lobivia laui. Lobivia hertrichiana, Neolobivia hertrichiana, Echinopsis backebergii, Lobivia allegraiana, Lobivia binghamiana, Lobivia incaica, Neolobivia incaica, Lobivia planiceps, Lobivia huilcanota, Lobivia minuta, Neolobivia minuta, Lobivia vilcabambae, Neolobivia vilcabambae, Lobivia simplex,

Hot tip

The multiple values specified to the **padding** property in this example are applied in order to its to top, right, bottom, and left areas.

Beware

Photographic images are often better compressed by the JPG format, rather than the PNG format used for web graphics.

Summary

- The sequence of list items is unimportant in unordered lists
- Unordered lists typically place a bullet-point before each list item to differentiate the list item from regular text
- The HTML **<ul>** element creates an unordered list, which contains list items within **<li>** elements
- A **list-style-type** property can specify that unordered list items should have a **disc**, **circle**, or **square** bullet-point
- A **list-style-image** property can specify the path to an image that should appear in place of bullet-points
- The sequence of list items is important in ordered lists
- The HTML **<ol>** element creates an ordered list, which contains list items within **<li>** elements
- A **list-style-type** property can specify that ordered list items should be automatically numbered with **decimal** numbers or **roman**, **latin**, or **greek** letters in uppercase or lowercase
- Bullet-points and numbering can be suppressed by specifying a **none** value to a **list-style-type** property
- Each list item in a definition list has both a definition term and a definition description
- The HTML **<dl>** element creates a definition list, which contains list items within **<dt>** and **<dd>** elements
- A **<dt>** element contains the definition term and a **<dd>** element contains the definition description
- Any definition term may have multiple descriptions and any description can be applied to multiple terms
- A **<dl>** element can be styled to create a definition box and positioned relative to other content by its **float** property

6 Making tables

This chapter demonstrates how to create and present tables for tabular data within a HTML document.

Producing a simple table

Data is often best presented in tabular form, arranged in rows and columns, to logically group related items so it is easily understood.

In HTML tables are created with **<table> </table>** tags, which produce a block-level **<table>** container element for table rows. Each table row is created with **<tr> </tr>** tags, which produce an inline-level **<tr>** container element for items of table data. Items of table data are contained within **<td> </td>** tags, which produce a **<td>** element – an individual table data "cell".

Hot tip

The closing tags **</tr>**, **</td>**, and **</th>** are optional but it is best to always use them – to clearly mark the end of rows, headers, and data.

The number of cells in a row determine the number of columns that table will have. The top row may, optionally, contain only table header cells between **<th> </th>** tags in place of table data. Similarly the first column may, optionally, contain only table header cells between **<th> </th>** tags in place of table data.

The **<table>** tag provides a **width** attribute to specify the table width and a **border** attribute to specify its border width. When the **border** attribute is included each cell also gets a border, and gets spaced apart from its adjacent cells. This is usually desirable.

A brief description of the table can be assigned to the **<table>** tag's **summary** attribute and between **<caption> </caption>** tags. The specifications do not stipulate a caption position, so it varies between browsers, but if a caption is provided the **<caption>** element must immediately follow the opening **<table>** tag.

table.html

1. Start a new HTML document with the Strict DTD

```
<!DOCTYPE HTML PUBLIC "-//W3C//DTD HTML 4.01//EN"
                    "http://www.w3.org/TR/html4/strict.dtd">
```

2. Add a root element containing a head section incorporating a style sheet, and a body section

```
<html> <head> <title>Producing a Simple Table</title>
<meta http-equiv="Content-type"
          content="text/html; charset=ISO-8859-1">
<link rel="stylesheet" type="text/css" href="table.css">
</head>
<body><!-- Content goes here. --></body> </html>
```

3. In the body section, insert a table element

```
<table border="5" width="450"
                    summary="A Table Demonstration">
</table>
```

4 Within the table, insert a table caption

```
<caption>A Simple Table</caption>
```

5 After the table caption, insert a table row element

```
<tr>    </tr>
```

6 Within the table row, insert four table header cells

```
<th></th> <th>Column 1</th>
<th>Column 2</th> <th>Column 3</th>
```

7 Next within the table, insert three rows – each containing one table header cell and three table data cells, numbered by row and column

```
<tr> <th>Row 1</th>
<td>Cell 1.1</td> <td>Cell 1.2</td> <td>Cell 1.3</td>
</tr>
<tr> <th>Row 2</th>
<td>Cell 2.1</td> <td>Cell 2.2</td> <td>Cell 2.3</td>
</tr>
<tr> <th>Row 3</th>
<td>Cell 3.1</td> <td>Cell 3.2</td> <td>Cell 3.3</td>
</tr>
```

8 Save the HTML document then open a text editor and add a style rule for all table data elements

```
td { background: #FFBF23; }
```

9 Save the Cascading Style Sheet alongside the HTML document then open the web page in your web browser

Producing a Simple Table

A Simple Table

	Column 1	Column 2	Column 3
Row 1	Cell 1.1	Cell 1.2	Cell 1.3
Row 2	Cell 2.1	Cell 2.2	Cell 2.3
Row 3	Cell 3.1	Cell 3.2	Cell 3.3

Subsequent examples in this chapter will build on this simple table as more table features are introduced.

Beware

Do not confuse the table's HTML **border** attribute with its CSS **border** property.

table.css

Don't forget

The table border width increases as the **border** attribute value increases but the cell border appearance is fixed.

Spanning cells over rows

An individual table cell can be combined with others to span down over multiple rows of a table. The number of rows to span is specified to the **rowspan** attribute of a **<td>** tag. Cells in the rows being spanned must be removed to maintain the table symmetry.

rowspan.html

1. Make a copy of the **table.html** document, created in the previous example, and rename it "rowspan.html"

2. Change the document title, style sheet and table caption

```
<title>Spanning Table Rows</title>
<link rel="stylesheet" type="text/css" href="rowspan.css">
<caption>A Table Spanning Rows</caption>
```

3. In the table data element containing the text "Cell 1.1", insert an attribute in its opening tag and edit its contents

```
<td rowspan="2">Cell 1.1+2.1</td>
```

4. Now delete the table data element containing the text "Cell 2.1" – as this cell is now spanned

rowspan.css

5. Save the HTML document then open a text editor and add style rules for table data elements spanning rows

```
td[rowspan|="2"] { background: #FF9A66; }
td[rowspan|="3"] { background: #84C984; }
```

6. Save the Cascading Style Sheet alongside the HTML document then open the web page in your web browser to see the modified cell span over two rows

Hot tip

Insert tab spaces between all table data elements in the HTML code to align them so it's easier to configure the table row layout.

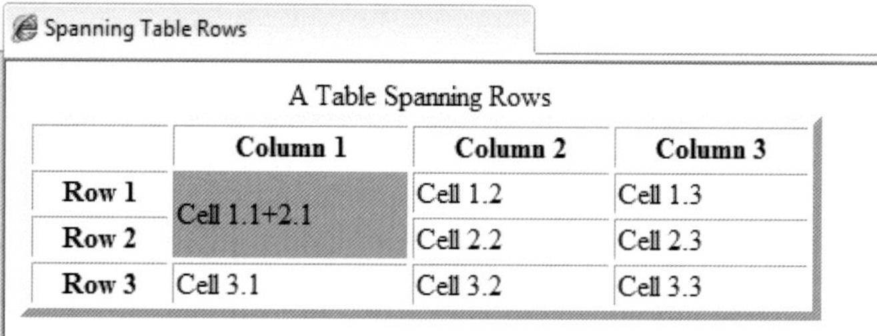

A Table Spanning Rows

	Column 1	Column 2	Column 3
Row 1	Cell 1.1+2.1	Cell 1.2	Cell 1.3
Row 2		Cell 2.2	Cell 2.3
Row 3	Cell 3.1	Cell 3.2	Cell 3.3

7. Reopen the HTML document in a plain text editor then insert an attribute into the table data element containing the text "Cell 2.2" and edit its contents

```
<td rowspan="2">Cell 2.2+3.2</td>
```

8. Now delete the table data element containing the text "Cell 3.2" – as this cell is now spanned

9. Save the amended HTML document then open it in your web browser again to see the modified cell span two rows

Spanning Table Rows

A Table Spanning Rows

	Column 1	Column 2	Column 3
Row 1	Cell 1.1+2.1	Cell 1.2	Cell 1.3
Row 2		Cell 2.2+3.2	Cell 2.3
Row 3	Cell 3.1		Cell 3.3

10. Reopen the HTML document in a plain text editor then insert an attribute into the table data element containing the text "Cell 1.3" and edit its contents

```
<td rowspan="3">Cell 1.3+2.3+3.3</td>
```

11. Now delete the table data elements containing the text "Cell 2.3" and "Cell 3.3" – as these cells are now spanned

12. Save the amended HTML document again then open it in your web browser once more to see the modified cell span over all three rows in the third table column

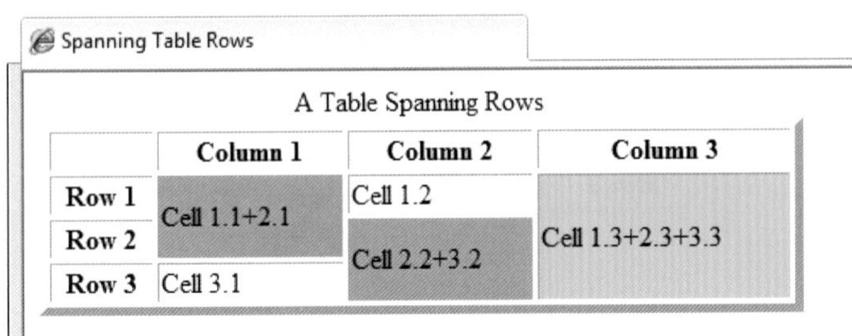
Spanning Table Rows

A Table Spanning Rows

	Column 1	Column 2	Column 3
Row 1	Cell 1.1+2.1	Cell 1.2	Cell 1.3+2.3+3.3
Row 2		Cell 2.2+3.2	
Row 3	Cell 3.1		

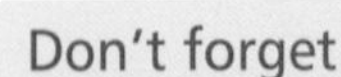

Don't forget

Notice that, by default, text in each cell is left-aligned and horizontally centered in merged cells.

Spanning cells across columns

An individual table cell can be combined with others to span to the right, across multiple columns of a table. The number of columns to span is specified to the **colspan** attribute of a **<td>** tag. Cells in the columns being spanned must be removed to maintain the table symmetry.

colspan.html

1. Make a copy of the **table.html** document, created on page 94, and rename it "colspan.html"

2. Change the document title, style sheet and table caption

```
<title>Spanning Table Columns</title>
<link rel="stylesheet" type="text/css" href="colspan.css">
<caption>A Table Spanning Columns</caption>
```

3. In the table data element containing the text "Cell 1.1", insert an attribute in its opening tag and edit its contents

```
<td colspan="2">Cell 1.1+1.2</td>
```

4. Now delete the table data element containing the text "Cell 1.2" – as this cell is now spanned

colspan.css

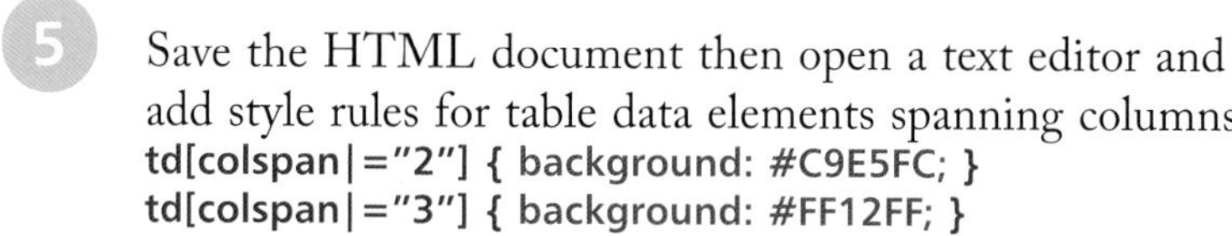

5. Save the HTML document then open a text editor and add style rules for table data elements spanning columns

```
td[colspan|="2"] { background: #C9E5FC; }
td[colspan|="3"] { background: #FF12FF; }
```

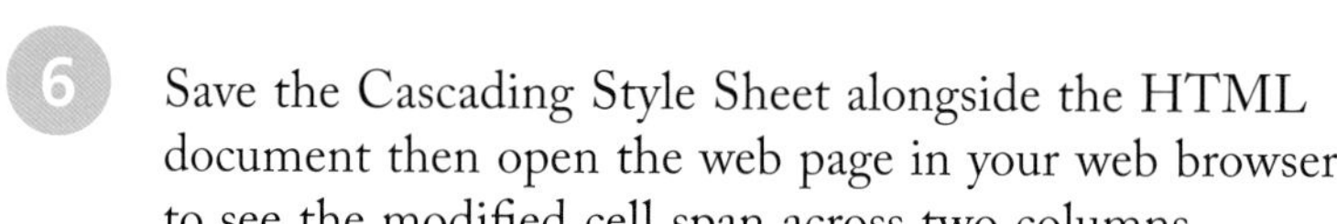

6. Save the Cascading Style Sheet alongside the HTML document then open the web page in your web browser to see the modified cell span across two columns

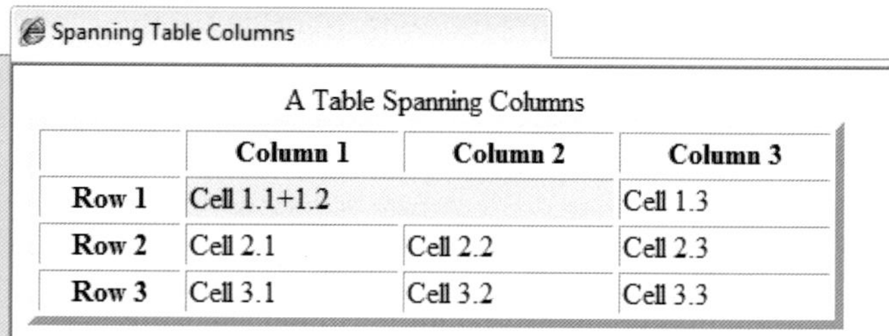

A Table Spanning Columns

	Column 1	Column 2	Column 3
Row 1	Cell 1.1+1.2		Cell 1.3
Row 2	Cell 2.1	Cell 2.2	Cell 2.3
Row 3	Cell 3.1	Cell 3.2	Cell 3.3

Hot tip

Insert line breaks between all table row elements in the HTML code to align them so it's easier to configure the table column layout.

7. Reopen the HTML document in a plain text editor then insert an attribute into the table data element containing the text "Cell 2.1" and edit its contents
   <td colspan="3">Cell 2.1+2.2+2.3</td>

8. Now delete the table data elements containing the text "Cell 2.2" and "Cell 2.3" – as these cells are now spanned

9. Save the amended HTML document then open it in your web browser to see the modified cell span three columns

Spanning Table Columns

A Table Spanning Columns

	Column 1	Column 2	Column 3
Row 1	Cell 1.1+1.2		Cell 1.3
Row 2	Cell 2.1+2.2+2.3		
Row 3	Cell 3.1	Cell 3.2	Cell 3.3

10. Reopen the HTML document in a text editor then insert another attribute into the table data element containing the text "Cell 2.1+2.2+2.3" and edit its contents
    <td colspan="3" rowspan="2">
    Cell 2.1+2.2+2.3 and 3.1+3.2+3.3</td>

11. Now delete the table data elements containing the text "Cell 3.1", "Cell 3.2" and "Cell 3.3"

12. Save the amended HTML document again then open it in your web browser once more to see the modified cell span across all three columns over two rows

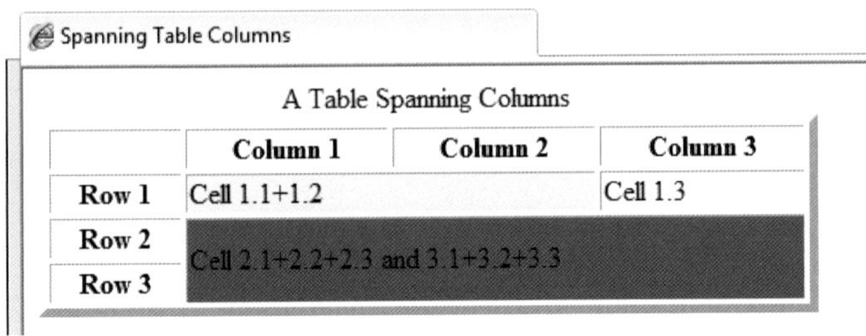
Spanning Table Columns

A Table Spanning Columns

	Column 1	Column 2	Column 3
Row 1	Cell 1.1+1.2		Cell 1.3
Row 2	Cell 2.1+2.2+2.3 and 3.1+3.2+3.3		
Row 3			

Hot tip 

Column spanning and row spanning can be combined to create large rectangular cell blocks, which can extend over multiple rows and multiple columns.

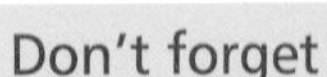 

Don't forget

Combined spans are rectangular – they cannot span an L-shape.

Adding a header & footer

Additional special rows can be added above a table to contain header information using **<thead> </thead>** tags.

Similarly, additional special rows can be added below a table to contain footer information using **<tfoot> </tfoot>** tags.

When a table has **<thead>** or **<tfoot>** elements all regular table row elements must be enclosed in **<tbody> </tbody>** tags. Also note that the **<thead>** and **<tfoot>** elements must appear before the **<tbody>** element between the **<table> </table>** tags.

In long tables, rows can be grouped into separate table body sections using multiple **<tbody>** elements. When these are printed each page can repeat the header and footer information.

info.html

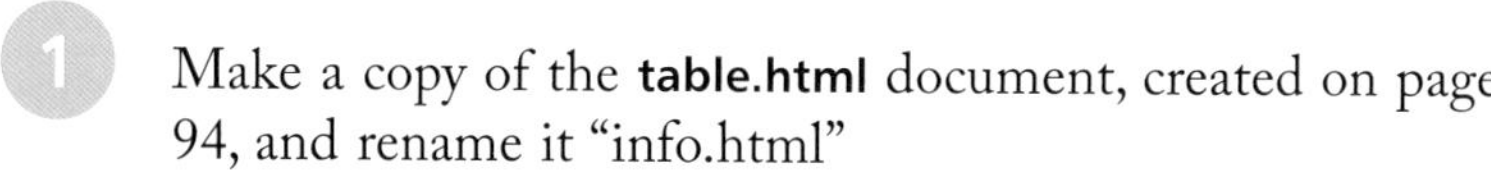

1. Make a copy of the **table.html** document, created on page 94, and rename it "info.html"

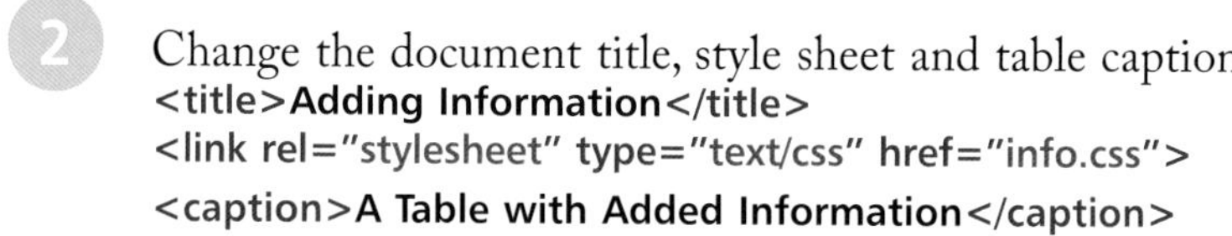

2. Change the document title, style sheet and table caption

```
<title>Adding Information</title>
<link rel="stylesheet" type="text/css" href="info.css">
<caption>A Table with Added Information</caption>
```

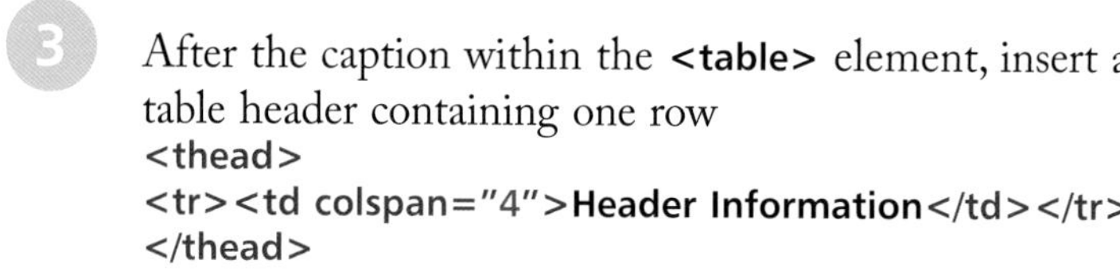

3. After the caption within the **<table>** element, insert a table header containing one row

```
<thead>
<tr><td colspan="4">Header Information</td></tr>
</thead>
```

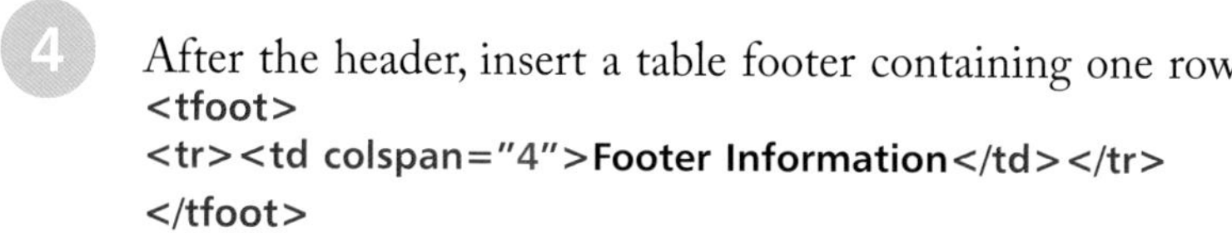

4. After the header, insert a table footer containing one row

```
<tfoot>
<tr><td colspan="4">Footer Information</td></tr>
</tfoot>
```

5. After the footer, insert a table body element to enclose all regular existing table row elements

```
<tbody id="tb-1">
        <!-- Existing row elements go here. -->
</tbody>
```

Don't forget

Table headers and footers should only contain information – data should appear in the table body.

6 After the table body element, insert a second table body element containing four more rows

```
<tbody id="tb-2" >
<tr><th colspan="4">Next Section</th></tr>
<tr> <th>Row 4</th>
<td>Cell 4.1</td> <td>Cell 4.2</td> <td>Cell 4.3</td>
</tr>
<tr> <th>Row 5</th>
<td>Cell 5.1</td> <td>Cell 5.2</td> <td>Cell 5.3</td>
</tr>
<tr> <th>Row 6</th>
<td>Cell 6.1</td> <td>Cell 6.2</td> <td>Cell 6.3</td>
</tr>
</tbody>
```

7 Save the HTML document then open a text editor and add style rules for the table header, table footer, and each table body element

```
thead    { background: #FFBF23;          }
tfoot    { background: #84C984;          }
th       { background: #FF6600;          }
#tb-1 td { background: #C9E5FC;          }
#tb-2 td { background: #FEEDB7;          }
```

info.css

8 Save the Cascading Style Sheet alongside the HTML document then open the web page in your web browser to see the table header, footer, and table body sections

Adding Information

A Table with Added Information

Header Information			
	Column 1	**Column 2**	**Column 3**
Row 1	Cell 1.1	Cell 1.2	Cell 1.3
Row 2	Cell 2.1	Cell 2.2	Cell 2.3
Row 3	Cell 3.1	Cell 3.2	Cell 3.3
Next Section			
Row 4	Cell 4.1	Cell 4.2	Cell 4.3
Row 5	Cell 5.1	Cell 5.2	Cell 5.3
Row 6	Cell 6.1	Cell 6.2	Cell 6.3
Footer Information			

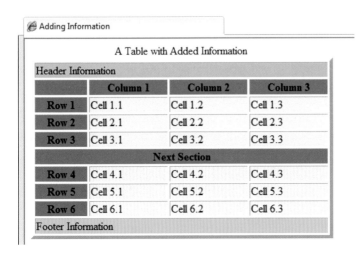

Hot tip

Notice the syntax used here by the style rule selectors to select all **<td>** elements of each **<tbody>** element.

Aligning cell content

Typically, the default position of content in a table data cell is horizontally left-aligned and vertically centered, while table header cells generally center their content both horizontally and vertically. These may be overridden using HTML **align** and **valign** attributes.

An **align** attribute can specify the horizontal alignment of cell content – with possible values of **left**, **center**, or **right**. Similarly, the **valign** attribute can specify the vertical alignment of cell content – with possible values of **top**, **middle**, or **bottom**.

The **align** and **valign** attributes can be included in **<td>** and **<th>** tags, to control the horizontal and vertical content position in individual cells. Additionally these attributes can be included in the **<tr>**, **<tbody>**, **<thead>**, and **<tfoot>** tags to control the horizontal and vertical content position in groups of cells. This means they can automatically specify a new "default" position for content within all the **<td>** and **<th>** elements they contain.

align.html

1. Make a copy of the **table.html** document, created on page 94, and rename it "align.html"

2. Change the document title, style sheet and table caption

```
<title>Aligning Cell Content</title>
<link rel="stylesheet" type="text/css" href="align.css">
<caption>A Table with Realigned Content</caption>
```

align.css

3. Save the HTML document then open a text editor and add style rules to standardize cell appearance

```
td,th    { height: 50px ; background: #FEEDB7 ;
              font-weight:bold ; color: red ;          }
```

4. Save the Cascading Style Sheet alongside the HTML document then open the web page in your web browser to see the default positioning in table header and data cells

	Column 1	Column 2	Column 3
Row 1	Cell 1.1	Cell 1.2	Cell 1.3

5 Edit the HTML document by inserting a table body element to enclose all regular existing table row elements – and specifying their new "default" cell content position

```
<tbody align="center" valign="middle" >
        <!-- Existing row elements go here. -->
</tbody>
```

6 Insert an attribute to right-align content in the final column header cell

```
<th align="right" >Column 3</th>
```

7 Next insert an attribute to top-align content in the central table data cell

```
<td valign="top" >Cell 2.2</td>
```

8 Now insert attributes to bottom-align and right-align all content in the final table row, but left-align its header

```
<tr align="right" valign="bottom" >
<th align="left">Row 3</th>
<td>Cell 3.1</td> <td>Cell 3.2</td> <td>Cell 3.3</td>
</tr>
```

9 Save the HTML document once more, then open it in your web browser again to see that the cell content has been horizontally and vertically realigned

Aligning Cell Content

A Table with Realigned Content

	Column 1	Column 2	Column 3
Row 1	Cell 1.1	Cell 1.2	Cell 1.3
Row 2	Cell 2.1	Cell 2.2	Cell 2.3
Row 3	Cell 3.1	Cell 3.2	Cell 3.3

Hot tip

Notice the syntax used here by the single style rule selector to select all <td> elements and all <th> elements.

Styling cell content

Before the introduction of Cascading Style Sheets tables were extensively used for web page layout – creating grids to contain text and images. Today table cells should only contain data as CSS style rules provide much more flexibility and far greater precision.

Don't forget

The presence of a HTML **border** attribute with any positive value ensures cells will be spaced apart and each have a border.

The HTML **<table>** tag provides two attributes that may be used to specify the layout of cells and their content. The space between table cells can be modified using the **cellspacing** attribute, and padding can be added around cell content using the **cellpadding** attribute. By default the padding area size is zero so adding padding increases the overall size of every cell.

Padding can also be added to cells using the CSS **padding** property, as usual, but cell spacing cannot be modified using the **margin** property. Cell borders, and spacing around cells, use a different border model to that of other content boxes but spacing can be eliminated using a special **border-collapse** property. Assigning this property a **collapse** value removes spacing and unites common borders. The border can normally be removed from an individual cell by setting its **border** property to **none** but when borders are collapsed those from adjacent cells remain.

The CSS **text-align** and **vertical-align** properties can be used to position cell content – instead of the HTML **align** and **valign** attributes. Where both types are specified for the same element the CSS values are applied.

Cell size can be specified using CSS **height** and **width** properties. Fonts and colors are specified in the normal way. Class style rules can usefully be employed for those tables with alternate row color.

cell.html

1. Make a copy of the **table.html** document, created on page 94, and rename it "cell.html"

2. Change the document title, style sheet and table caption

```
<title>Styling Cell Content</title>
<link rel="stylesheet" type="text/css" href="cell.css">
<caption>A Table with Stylish Cells</caption>
```

3. Insert a class attribute to remove the outer table border

```
<table class="no-border" border="5" width="450"
                    summary="A Table Demonstration">
```

4. Next insert a class attribute to remove the border from around the first (empty) table header cell
```
<th class="no-border"></th>
```

5. Next insert class attributes to alternate row colors
```
<tr class="positive"> <!-- Existing cell elements. --> </tr>
<tr class="negative"> <!-- Existing cell elements. --></tr>
<tr class="positive"> <!-- Existing cell elements. --> </tr>
```

6. Save the HTML document then open a text editor and add a class style rule to remove borders
```
.no-border       { border: none ;          }
```

cell.css

7. Next add a style rule to unite all common table borders
```
table    { border-collapse: collapse ; }
```

8. Now add a style rule to specify the font and height, and to center the content in each cell
```
td { font: medium "Lucida Handwriting", cursive ;
height: 50px ; text-align: center ; vertical-align: middle ;  }
```

9. Finally insert style rules to apply alternate row colors
```
.positive td { background: #C9E5FC ; color: #327EBE ; }
.negative td { background: #327EBE ; color: #C9E5FC ; }
```

10. Save the Cascading Style Sheet alongside the HTML document then open the web page in your web browser to see the cell styles applied

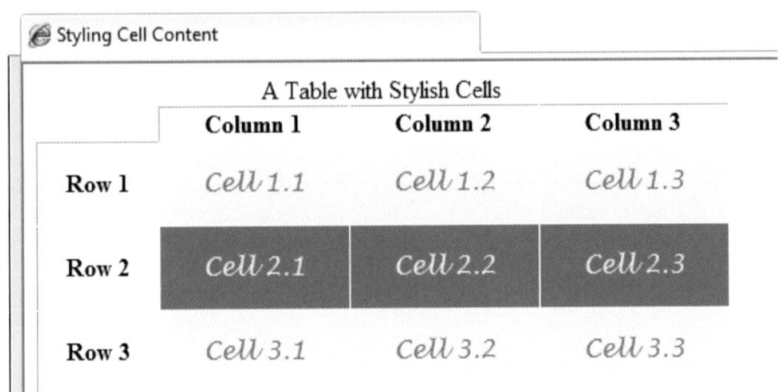

Hot tip

The **border-collapse** property can alternatively be set to **separate** – the normal state showing individual cell borders.

Asserting table frame rules

The HTML **<table>** tag provides a **frame** attribute, which may be used to specify which sides of the outer table border are visible, and a **rules** attribute, which may be used to specify which sides of the inner table border are visible. Their possible values are listed in the table below together with a description of their display effect:

Frame	Display	Rules	Display
above	top side only	**groups**	ruled lines between table header, table body, and table footer
below	bottom side only		
hsides	horizontal sides	**cols**	lines between columns
vsides	vertical sides	**rows**	lines between rows
lhs	left-hand side		
rhs	right-hand side	**all**	ruled lines between all rows and columns
box	all four sides		

rules.html

1. Make a copy of the **table.html** document, created on page 94, and rename it "rules.html"

2. Change the document title, style sheet and table caption

```
<title>Asserting Table Frame Rules</title>
<link rel="stylesheet" type="text/css" href="rules.css">
<caption>A Table with Frame Rules</caption>
```

3. After the caption within the **<table>** element, insert a table header containing one row

```
<thead>
<tr><td colspan="4">Header Information</td></tr>
</thead>
```

4. After the header, insert a table footer containing one row

```
<tfoot>
<tr><td colspan="4">Footer Information</td></tr>
</tfoot>
```

5. After the footer, insert a table body element to enclose all regular existing table row elements

```
<tbody>
        <!-- Existing row elements go here. -->
</tbody>
```

6. Insert an attribute to display vertical frame borders only

```
<table border="5" width="450" frame="vsides"
                summary="A Table Demonstration">
</table>
```

7. Next in the **<table>** tag, insert an attribute to display ruled lines between table groups only

```
rules="groups"
```

8. Save the HTML document then open a text editor and add a style rule to color the table frame borders

```
table    { border-color: #FFBF23 ;          }
```

9. Now add style rules to color and style each table group

```
thead { background: #C9E5FC ;
        font: medium "Lucida Handwriting", cursive ; }
tbody { background: #FEEDB7 ; }
tfoot { background: #84C984 ; font-size: small ; }
```

10. Save the Cascading Style Sheet alongside the HTML document then open the web page in your web browser to see the frame and rules applied

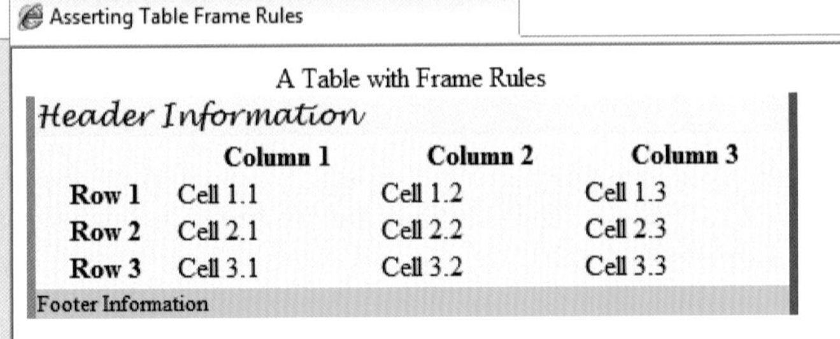

The width of the vertical sides is determined by the **border** attribute. When this is zero or absent vertical sides are not displayed.

rules.css

Grouping columns

Table columns can be grouped together using the HTML **<colgroup> </colgroup>** tags to create a **<colgroup>** element. The number of columns to include in the group is specified to a **span** attribute in the **<colgroup>** tag. This tag may also usefully include a **width** attribute to specify the width of each column.

A table may contain one or many column groups and each group may be styled individually to differentiate it from other columns. Additionally the **rules** attribute of the **<table>** tag can be used to rule a line between column groups and other table groups:

group.html

1. Start a new HTML document with the Strict DTD

```
<!DOCTYPE HTML PUBLIC "-//W3C//DTD HTML 4.01//EN"
                "http://www.w3.org/TR/html4/strict.dtd">
```

2. Add a root element containing a head section incorporating a style sheet, and a body section

```
<html> <head> <title>Grouping Table Columns</title>
<meta http-equiv="Content-type"
          content="text/html; charset=ISO-8859-1">
<link rel="stylesheet" type="text/css" href="group.css">
</head>
<body><!-- Content goes here. --></body> </html>
```

3. In the body section, insert a table element including an attribute to rule lines between groups

```
<table rules="groups" width="450" cellpadding="3"
                              summary="Calendar Table">
</table>
```

4. Within the table element, insert a table caption

```
<caption>Monthly Calendar</caption>
```

5. After the table caption, insert an element creating a group of five columns with a specified class name for styling

```
<colgroup class="weekday" span="5" width="14%">
</colgroup>
```

6. Now insert an element creating a group of two columns with a specified class name for styling

```
<colgroup class="weekend" span="2" width="15%">
</colgroup>
```

Beware

When specifying sizes by percentage ensure they total 100% – here the groups are 70% + 30%.

7 Next within the table, insert a table header group and a table footer group – each spanning seven columns

```
<thead>
<tr><th colspan="7">February 2010</th></tr></thead>
<tfoot>
<tr><td colspan="7">Birthday</td></tr></tfoot>
```

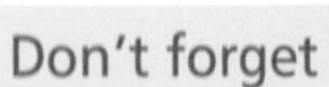

Don't forget

The table body in this example omits the optional </td> and </tr> closing tags to save page space.

8 Now insert a table body group, containing seven columns – with one cell given an identity for unique styling

```
<tbody>
<tr><td>1<td>2<td>3<td>4<td>5<td>6<td>7
<tr><td>8<td>9<td>10<td>11<td>12<td>13<td>14
<tr><td>15<td>16<td>17<td>18<td>19<td>20
                                    <td id="birthday">21<tr>
<td>22<td>23<td>24<td>25<td>26<td>27<td>28
</tbody>
```

9 Save the HTML document then open a text editor and add rules to style each column group and table group

```
.weekday { background: #FFBF23 ; }
.weekend { background: #FEEDB7 ; }

thead { background: #FFF ; color: #ED2024 ;
        font: medium "Lucida Handwriting", cursive ; }
tbody { text-align: center ; }
tfoot { background: #FFF ; font-size: small ; }

#birthday { border: 3px solid #ED2024 ; }
```

group.css

10 Save the Cascading Style Sheet alongside the HTML document then open the web page in your web browser to see the table group styles applied

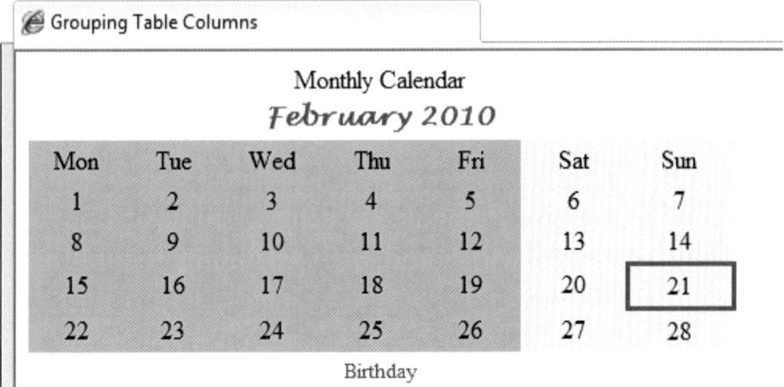

Grouping Table Columns
Monthly Calendar
February 2010
Mon Tue Wed Thu Fri Sat Sun
1 2 3 4 5 6 7
8 9 10 11 12 13 14
15 16 17 18 19 20 21
22 23 24 25 26 27 28
Birthday

Specifying column widths

Where a table has a width specified by the **width** attribute of the **<table>** tag the web browser will, by default, calculate the width of each table column according to its content – columns with wide content will be wider than columns with slender content. Greater control over column width is possible by specifying each column's width to the **width** attribute of HTML **<col>** tags as a fixed pixel value or as a percentage of the containing element.

A single **<col>** tag can specify the same width for multiple columns using its **span** attribute to specify the number of columns. The **<col>** tag simply contains attributes to specify width or for styling, so it has no closing tag. It may be used alone or within a **<colgroup>** element that structurally groups columns:

column.html

1. Start a new HTML document with the Strict DTD

```
<!DOCTYPE HTML PUBLIC "-//W3C//DTD HTML 4.01//EN"
                  "http://www.w3.org/TR/html4/strict.dtd">
```

2. Add a root element containing a head section incorporating a style sheet, and a body section

```
<html> <head> <title>Specifying Column Widths</title>
<meta http-equiv="Content-type"
        content="text/html; charset=ISO-8859-1">
<link rel="stylesheet" type="text/css" href="column.css">
</head>
<body><!-- Content goes here. --></body> </html>
```

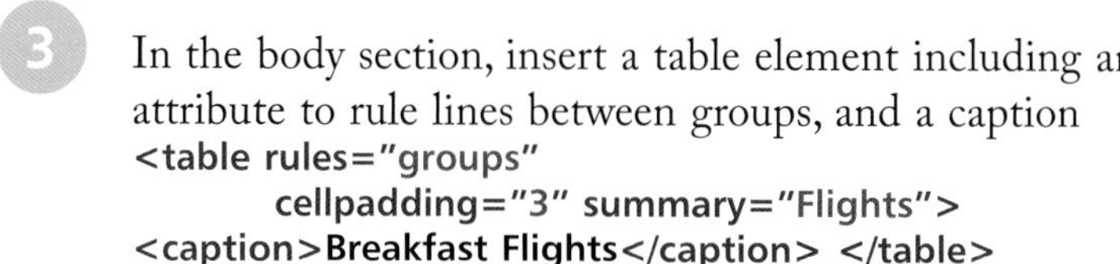

3. In the body section, insert a table element including an attribute to rule lines between groups, and a caption

```
<table rules="groups"
       cellpadding="3" summary="Flights">
<caption>Breakfast Flights</caption> </table>
```

Don't forget

In this example the table width of 470 pixels (5x80+70) is determined by the column widths – so the **<table>** element needs no **width** attribute.

4. After the table caption, insert elements creating a group of one column with a specified width

```
<colgroup> <col width="70"> </colgroup>
```

5. Next insert elements creating a group of three columns of a specified width and with attributes for styling

```
<colgroup>
<col width="80" class="stripe">
<col width="80">
<col width="80" class="stripe">
</colgroup>
```

6. Now insert elements creating a group of two columns of a specified width and with an attribute for styling

```
<colgroup>
<col width="80"> <col width="80" class="stripe">
</colgroup>
```

7. Insert the table header and table footer – each spanning six columns

```
<thead>
<tr><th colspan="6"><!-- Header --></th></tr></thead>
<tfoot>
<tr><td colspan="6"><!-- Footer --></th></tr></tfoot>
```

Hot tip

The **•** character entity is used in this table footer to create bullet points.

8. Insert the table body – containing six columns

```
<tbody>
<tr><th></th> <th>American<br>Airlines</th>
<th>Delta<br>Air Lines</th>
<th>Alaska<br>Airlines</th><th>United</th>
<th>Continental<br>Airlines</th></tr>
<!-- Body rows with six cells each. -->
</tbody>
```

9. Save the HTML document then open a text editor and add rules to style the columns and table groups

```
.stripe  { background: #C9F2BA ; }
table    { font-family: sans-serif ; }
tbody th { background: #84C984; color: #FFF ; }
tfoot    { font-size: small ; }
```

column.css

10. Save the Cascading Style Sheet alongside the HTML document then open the web page in your web browser to see the table group styles applied

Breakfast Flights

New York (JFK) - Los Angeles

	American Airlines	Delta Air Lines	Alaska Airlines	United	Continental Airlines
Departure	8:30am	7:00am	7:30am	7:54am	8:35am
Arrival	12:05pm	10:30am	10:45am	11:30am	12:02pm
Duration	6h35min	6h30min	6h15min	6h26min	6h27min
Price	$155	$155	$195	$466	$526

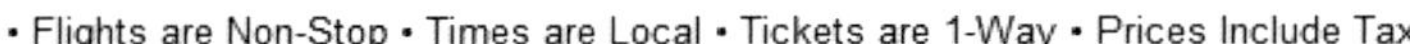

• Flights are Non-Stop • Times are Local • Tickets are 1-Way • Prices Include Tax

Summary

- A **<table>** element is a block-level container for table data within table row **<tr>** elements
- Each **<table>** element can include a **summary** attribute and a **<caption>** element describing that table
- Each table row **<tr>** element can contain table headings within **<th>** elements and table data within **<td>** elements
- Any table heading **<th>** element and any table data **<td>** element may include a **rowspan** attribute, to span multiple rows, and a **colspan** attribute to span multiple columns
- Header information can be added to a table using a **<thead>** element and footer information added with a **<tfoot>** element
- Table rows can be grouped into sections by **<tbody>** elements
- Most HTML table elements can include an **align** attribute, to align content horizontally, and a **valign** attribute to align content vertically
- Including a **border** attribute with a positive value within a **<table>** element causes the table to have an outer border of the specified width and its cells to have individual borders
- Cell borders can be united using a CSS style rule to assign the table's **border-collapse** property a **collapse** value
- The **<table>** tag may include a **frame** attribute, to determine which sides of its outer border is visible, and a **rules** attribute to determine which sides of its cell borders are visible
- Table columns can be structurally grouped together by the **span** attribute of the **<colgroup>** element
- The width of a table can be specified by a **width** attribute, within the **<table>** tag, or by **width** attributes in **<col>** tags
- HTML tables should not be used for page layout because CSS style rules provide more flexibility and greater precision

7 Embedding objects

This chapter demonstrates how to create content-rich web pages by embedding various media objects within a HTML document.

Embedding image objects

External resources can be embedded into a HTML document using the **<object> </object>** tags to create an **<object>** element. The **<object>** tag can include a **width** and **height** attribute to specify dimensions on the page where the resource will appear. Its **data** attribute can specify the path to the resource and its **type** attribute can describe the resource type as one of the universally recognized MIME types, such as those below:

For details of all MIME types please refer to the W3C website online at **http://www.w3.org**.

MIME type	Object
image/png	PNG image resource
image/jpeg	JPG, JPEG, JPE image resource
image/gif	GIF image resource
text/plain	TXT regular text document resource
text/html	HTM, HTML markup text resource
audio/x-wav	WAV sound resource
audio/x-mpeg	MP3 music resource
video/mpeg	MPEG, MPG, MPE video resource
video/x-msvideo	AVI video resource
video/x-ms-wmv	WMV video resource
application/java	CLASS java resource
application/pdf	PDF portable document resource
application/msword	DOC word document resource

An **<object>** element can contain a text description of the resource that will be displayed when, for some reason, it cannot be embedded in the HTML document. For example, the location of an image will appear when that image cannot be embedded:

embed.html

1. Start a new HTML document with the Strict DTD

```
<!DOCTYPE HTML PUBLIC "-//W3C//DTD HTML 4.01//EN"
                "http://www.w3.org/TR/html4/strict.dtd">
```

2. Add a root element containing a head and body section

```
<html> <head> <title>Embedding an Image</title>
<meta http-equiv="Content-type"
  content="text/html; charset=ISO-8859-1"></head>
<body><!-- Content goes here. --></body> </html>
```

3. Within the body section, insert a paragraph

```
<p>This is text in the main document that<br>

<br>continues around an embedded resource.</p>
```

4. Between the line breaks in the paragraph, insert an image object with alternative descriptive location text

```
<object type="image/png" data="embed.png"
        height="227" width="218">
[Image @ http://localhost/embed.png] </object>
```

5. Save the HTML document alongside the image resource then open the web page in your web browser to see the embedded image

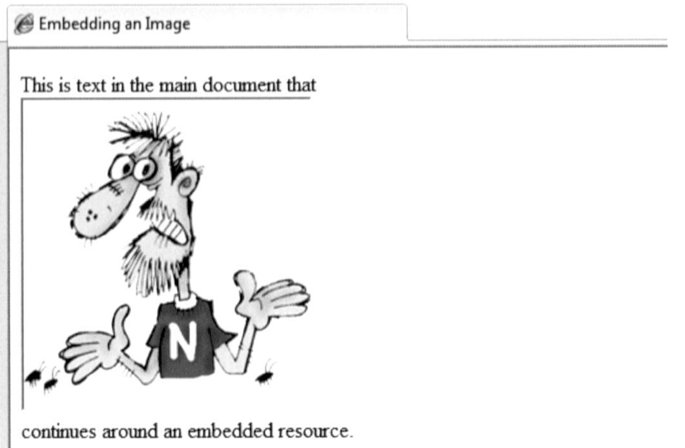

6. Open the web page in a browser that has disabled embedding to see the alternative descriptive text

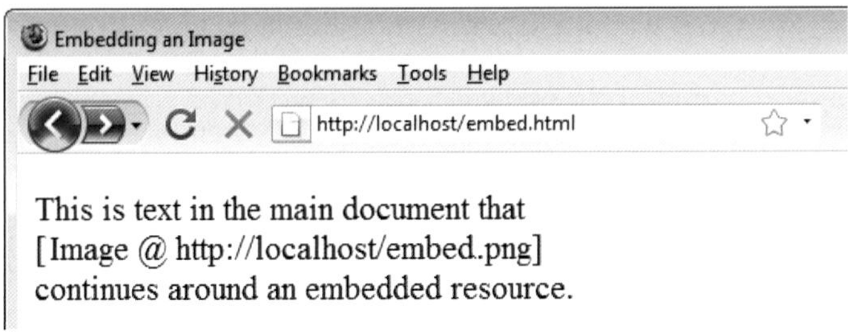

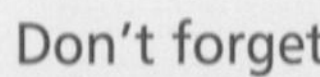

Don't forget

The description in an **<object>** element is ignored unless the resource cannot be embedded.

Hot tip

The browser calls upon the application on your system that is associated with the specified MIME type to display an embedded resource.

Embedding documents

Documents that contain rich content, such as charts and graphs, can be embedded into a HTML document as **<object>** elements. This is particularly useful to embed documents in the versatile Portable Document Format (PDF) that have a compact file size:

1. Open an application that can create documents in PDF file format, such as Word or OpenOffice Writer, then create a pie chart document and name it "chart.pdf"

Hot tip

When creating a web PDF document with Word be sure to check the box for minimum size in the "Publish as PDF" dialog.

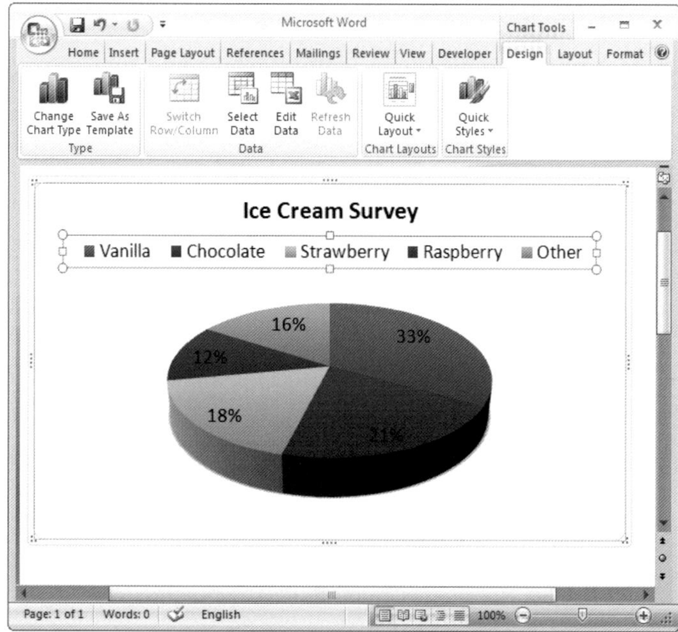

chart.html

2. Start a new HTML document with the Strict DTD

```
<!DOCTYPE HTML PUBLIC "-//W3C//DTD HTML 4.01//EN"
                "http://www.w3.org/TR/html4/strict.dtd">
```

3. Add a root element containing a head and body section

```
<html> <head> <title>Embedding a Document</title>
<meta http-equiv="Content-type"
  content="text/html; charset=ISO-8859-1"></head>
<body><!-- Content goes here. --></body> </html>
```

4. Within the body section, insert a paragraph

```
<p>This is text in the main document that<br>

<br>continues around an embedded resource.</p>
```

5. Between the line breaks in the paragraph, insert a PDF document object with alternative descriptive location text

```
<object type="application/pdf" data="chart.pdf"
        height="450" width="325">
[Survey Chart @ http://localhost/chart.pdf] </object>
```

6. Save the HTML document alongside the PDF document resource then open the web page in your web browser to see the embedded document displayed by the browser's Adobe Reader plugin

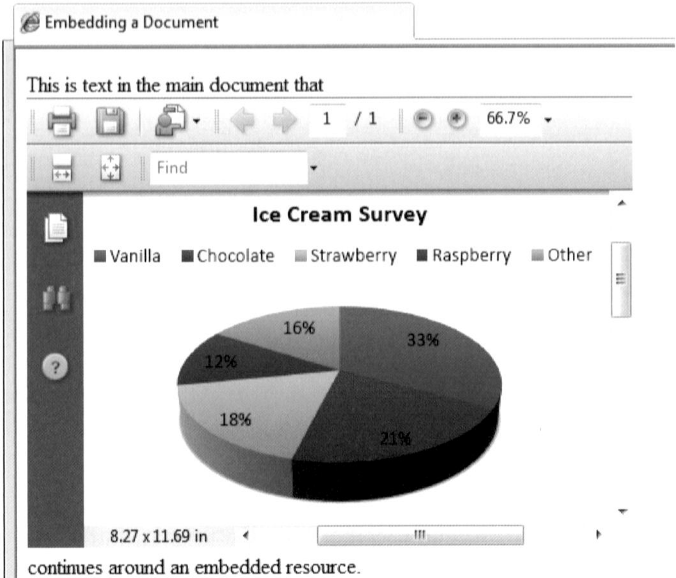

7. Open the web page in a browser that has disabled the Adobe Reader plugin to see the alternative text

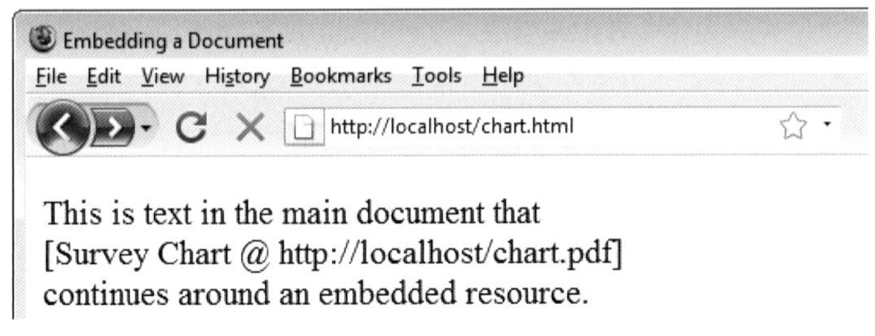

Don't forget

The Adobe Reader plugin that displays embedded PDF documents also displays controls to scroll, zoom, and print that document.

Hot tip

The free Adobe Reader plugin can be found at **www.adobe.com /products/reader**.

Embedding Flash media

Interactive and animated content in the Shockwave Flash format can be embedded into a HTML document as **<object>** elements. The **<object>** tag must include a **type** attribute, describing the MIME type as "application/x-shockwave-flash", and a **data** attribute to specify the media's path for Firefox. It should also contain **width** and **height** attributes to specify the display size.

The **<object>** element can enclose **<param>** elements that specify parameters for the Flash media with **name** and **value** attributes. The media may allow multiple parameters but there must always be one **<param>** element to specify its path for Internet Explorer.

Additionally the **<object>** element can include a text description of the Flash media that will be displayed when, for some reason, it cannot be embedded in the HTML document.

flash.html

1. Start a new HTML document with the Strict DTD

```
<!DOCTYPE HTML PUBLIC "-//W3C//DTD HTML 4.01//EN"
                "http://www.w3.org/TR/html4/strict.dtd">
```

2. Add a root element containing a head and body section

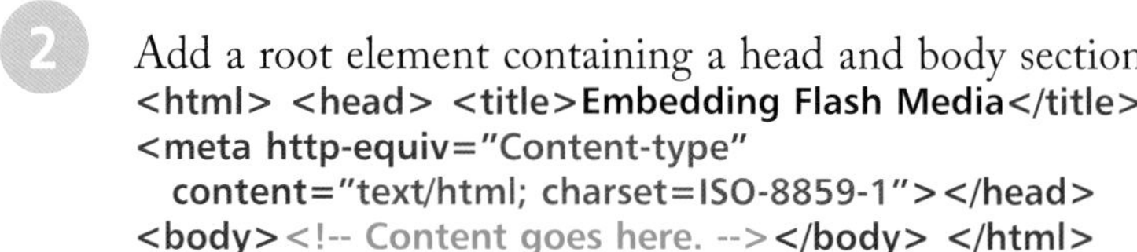

```
<html> <head> <title>Embedding Flash Media</title>
<meta http-equiv="Content-type"
  content="text/html; charset=ISO-8859-1"></head>
<body><!-- Content goes here. --></body> </html>
```

3. Within the body section, insert a paragraph

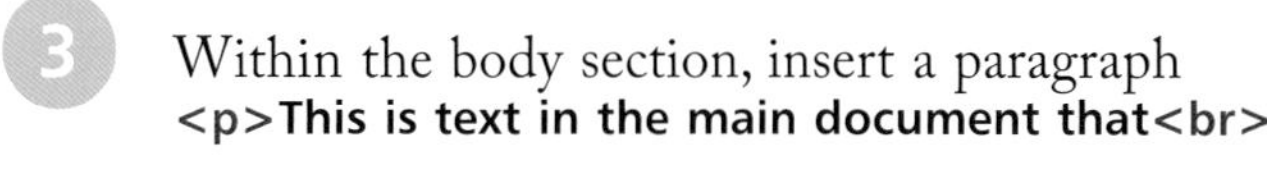

```
<p>This is text in the main document that<br>

<br>continues around embedded objects.</p>
```

4. Between the line breaks in the paragraph, insert a Flash movie object with alternative descriptive location text

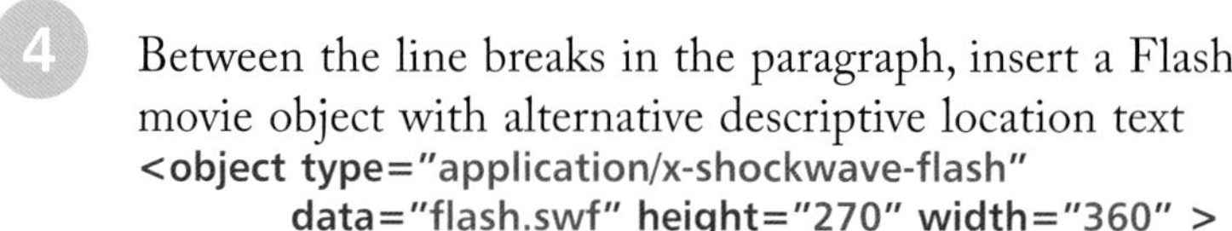

```
<object type="application/x-shockwave-flash"
        data="flash.swf" height="270" width="360" >

<param name="movie" value="flash.swf" >
[Flash Media @ http://localhost/flash.swf] </object>
```

5. Save the HTML document alongside the Flash media resource then open the web page in your web browser to see the embedded media displayed by the browser's Flash Player plugin

Beware

This modern method of embeddding Flash media is not supported by older web browsers.

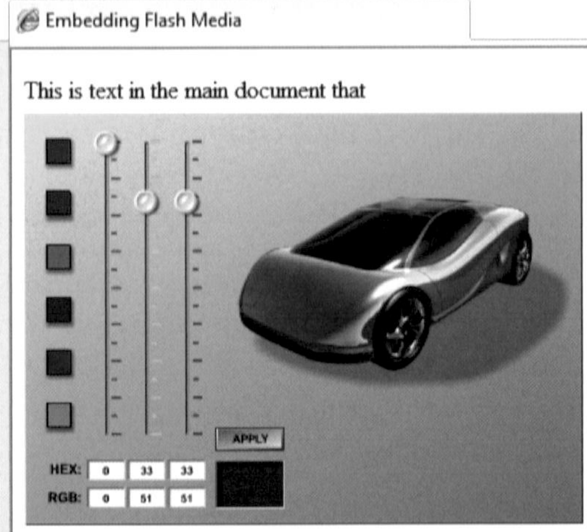

6 This Flash media example is an interactive color selector demonstration – drag the slider controls then click the Apply button to apply that color to the car

7 Open the web page in a browser that has disabled the Flash Player plugin to see the alternative text

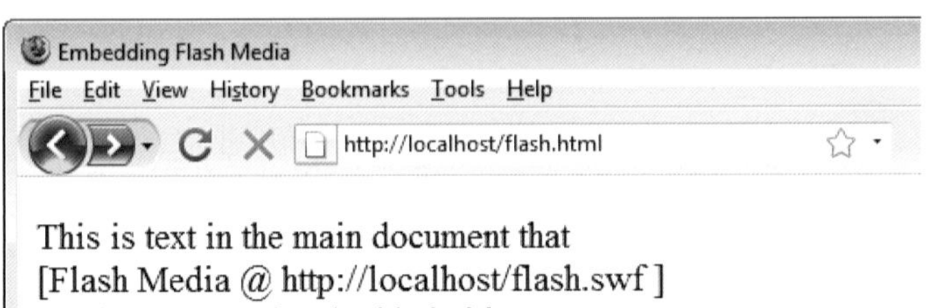

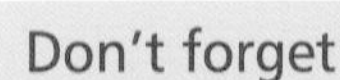

The free Flash Player plugin that displays Flash media can be found at **www.adobe.com/go/getflashplayer**.

Embedding audio media

Windows Media Player can be embedded into a HTML document as an **<object>** element to play audio media, with **width** and **height** attributes to specify its size on the web page. Sadly the technique to embed the Windows Media Player plugin is not consistent among browsers. Internet Explorer requires the **<object>** tag to include a **classid** attribute specifying a lengthy ActiveX component identifier with the precise value of "CLSID:6BF52A52-394A-11D3-B153-00C04F79FAA6". Other browsers, such as Firefox, require the tag to include a **type** attribute specifying a MIME type of "application/x-ms-wmp" instead of the **classid** attribute. This means that cross-browser support requires two **<object>** elements – nesting one **<object>** element within another allows the browser to apply the appropriate technique while ignoring that which is inappropriate.

Beware

When an **<object>** tag includes a **classid** attribute the resource path is specified by a parameter – not by its **data** attribute.

The **<object>** element can enclose **<param>** elements to specify parameters for the plugin with **name** and **value** attributes. The path to the media must be specified to a parameter named "URL" and the parameter named "autostart" must be given a "false" value to prevent automatic playback – unless that is desirable.

audio.html

1. Start a new HTML document with the Strict DTD

```
<!DOCTYPE HTML PUBLIC "-//W3C//DTD HTML 4.01//EN"
        "http://www.w3.org/TR/html4/strict.dtd">
```

2. Add a root element containing a head and body section

```
<html> <head>
<title>Embedding Audio Media</title>
<meta http-equiv="Content-type"
  content="text/html; charset=ISO-8859-1"></head>
<body><!-- Content goes here. --></body> </html>
```

3. Within the body section, insert a paragraph

```
<p>This is text in the main document that<br>
   <br>continues around an embedded resource.</p>
```

4. Between the line breaks in the paragraph, insert a Windows Media Player object for Internet Explorer

```
<object height="65" width="250"
classid="CLSID:6BF52A52-394A-11D3-B153-00C04F79FAA6">
<param name="URL" value="audio.mp3">
<param name="autostart" value="false">
<!-- Nested object to go here. -->
</object>
```

5 Now insert a nested Windows Media Player object for Firefox and other browsers

```
<object type="application/x-ms-wmp" data="audio.mp3"
        height="65" width="250" >
<param name="autostart" value="false">
[Audio Media @ http://localhost/audio.mp3]
</object>
```

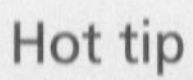

Hot tip

Set the **width** and **height** to zero, so no controls are displayed, then set **autostart** to **true** to automatically play an audio file once whenever that web page loads.

6 Save the HTML document alongside the audio media then open the web page in Internet Explorer to see the embedded Windows Media Player from the outer object

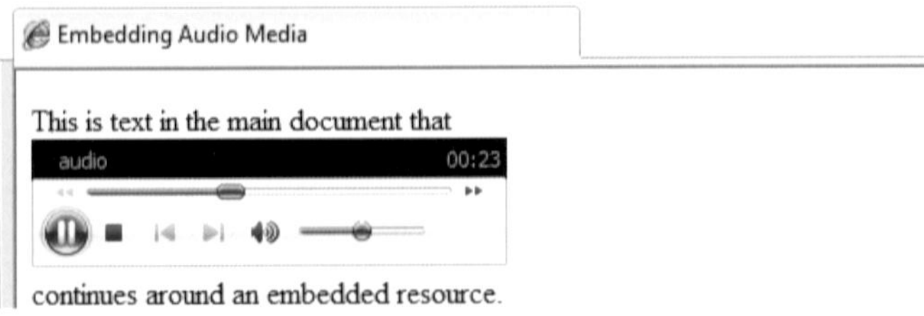

7 Open the web page in a different web browser to see the embedded Windows Media Player from the nested object

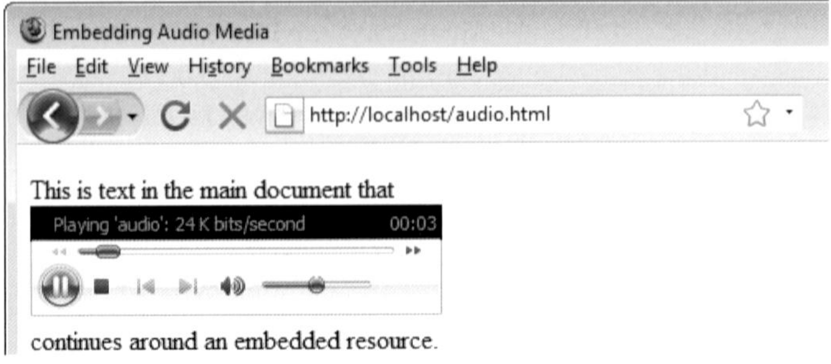

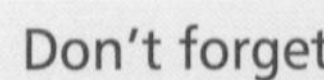

Don't forget

No alternative text has been specified for the outer object here – so none will be displayed if the Windows Media Player plugin is disabled in Internet Explorer.

8 Disable the Windows Media Player plugin to see the alternative text from the nested object

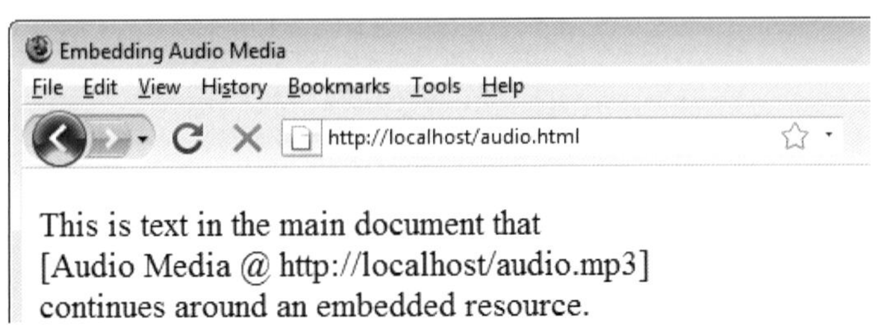

Embedding video media

Windows Media Player can be embedded into a HTML document as an **<object>** element to play video using the same technique described in the previous example – but the **width** and **height** attributes must specify a suitable display size. Additional parameters may be added to specify how the video appears:

Hot tip

Additional parameters are available for scripting purposes – they can be found online at **msdn2.microsoft.com**.

Parameter	Default	Description
autoStart	**true**	automatically begin playing
balance	**0**	stereo balance (-100 to 100)
fullScreen	**false**	play in full screen mode
PlayCount	**1**	number of times to play
stretchToFit	**false**	fit to width and height
uiMode	**full**	which controls to display (full, mini, invisible, none)
URL (required)	**-**	path to media file
Volume	**last setting**	Volume level (0 to 100)

video.html

1. Start a new HTML document with the Strict DTD
```
<!DOCTYPE HTML PUBLIC "-//W3C//DTD HTML 4.01//EN"
                "http://www.w3.org/TR/html4/strict.dtd">
```

2. Add a root element containing a head and body section
```
<html> <head>
<title>Embedding Video Media</title>
<meta http-equiv="Content-type"
  content="text/html; charset=ISO-8859-1"></head>
<body><!-- Content goes here. --></body> </html>
```

3. Within the body section, insert a paragraph
```
<p>This is text in the main document that<br>
   <br>continues around embedded objects.</p>
```

4. Between the line breaks in the paragraph, insert a default Windows Media Player object for Internet Explorer
```
<object height="250" width="250"
classid="CLSID:6BF52A52-394A-11D3-B153-00C04F79FAA6">
<param name="URL" value="video.mpg">
<param name="uiMode" value="full">
<!-- Nested object to go here. --> </object>
```

5 Now insert a nested Windows Media Player default object for Firefox and other browsers

```
<object type="application/x-ms-wmp" data="video.mpg"
        height="250" width="250" >
<param name="uiMode" value="full">
[Video Media @ http://localhost/video.mpg]
</object>
```

6 Save the HTML document alongside the video media then open the web page in your browser to see the video automatically play once – with visible player controls

7 Edit the object's **height** attribute, reducing its value to "200", and change the parameter's **uiMode** attribute value to "none"

8 Save the amended HTML document alongside the video media then open it in your browser to see the video automatically play once – without visible player controls

9 Right-click anywhere on the video area and use the context menu that appears to control the video

Don't forget

Setting the **uiMode** to "none" removes the controls but setting it to "invisible" hides the entire video – but it still plays so you can hear its audio track.

Embedding QuickTime

The Apple QuickTime Player can be embedded into a HTML document as an **<object>** element to play multi-media, with **width** and **height** attributes to specify its size on the web page. Sadly the technique to embed the QuickTime Player plugin is not consistent among browsers. Internet Explorer requires the **<object>** tag to include a **classid** attribute specifying a lengthy ActiveX component identifier with the precise value of "CLSID:02BF25D5-8C17-4B23-BC80-D3488ABDDC6B". Other browsers, such as Firefox, require the tag to include a **type** attribute specifying a MIME type of "video/quicktime" and a **data** attribute specifying the media path. This means that cross-browser support requires two **<object>** elements – nesting one **<object>** element within another allows the browser to apply the appropriate technique while ignoring that which is inappropriate.

You can discover more about the QuickTime player online at **www.apple.com/quicktime**

The **<object>** element can enclose **<param>** elements to specify parameters for the plugin with **name** and **value** attributes. The path to the media is specified to a parameter named "src" and the parameter named "autoplay" must be given a "false" value to prevent automatic playback – unless that is desirable.

quicktime.html

1. Start a new HTML document with the Strict DTD

```
<!DOCTYPE HTML PUBLIC "-//W3C//DTD HTML 4.01//EN"
                  "http://www.w3.org/TR/html4/strict.dtd">
```

2. Add a root element containing a head and body section

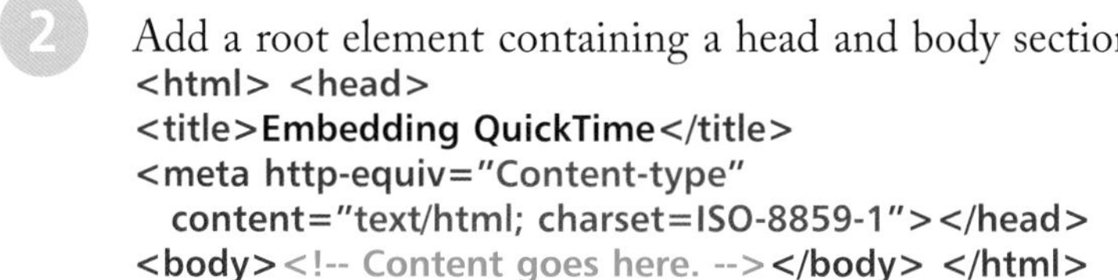

```
<html> <head>
<title>Embedding QuickTime</title>
<meta http-equiv="Content-type"
  content="text/html; charset=ISO-8859-1"></head>
<body><!-- Content goes here. --></body> </html>
```

3. Within the body section, insert a paragraph

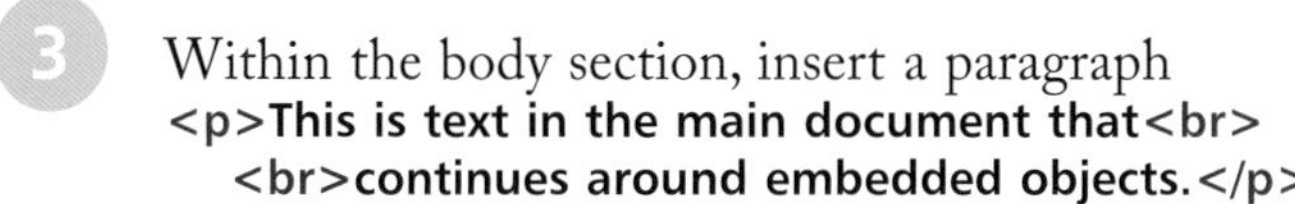

```
<p>This is text in the main document that<br>
   <br>continues around embedded objects.</p>
```

4. Between the line breaks in the paragraph, insert a QuickTime Player object for Internet Explorer

```
<object height="255" width="195"
classid="CLSID:02BF25D5-8C17-4B23-BC80-D3488ABDDC6B">
<param name="src" value="quicktime.mov">
<param name="autoplay" value="false">
<!-- Nested object to go here. -->
</object>
```

5. Now insert a nested QuickTime Player object for Firefox and other browsers

```
<object type="video/quicktime" data="quicktime.mov"
        height="255" width="195" >
<param name="autoplay" value="false">
[QuickTime Media @ http://localhost/quicktime.mov]
</object>
```

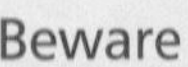

Beware

This example embeds QuickTime version 7. Earlier versions were embedded using the, now deprecated, HTML **<embed>** tag.

6. Save the HTML document alongside the QuickTime media then open the web page in Internet Explorer to see the embedded QuickTime Player from the outer object

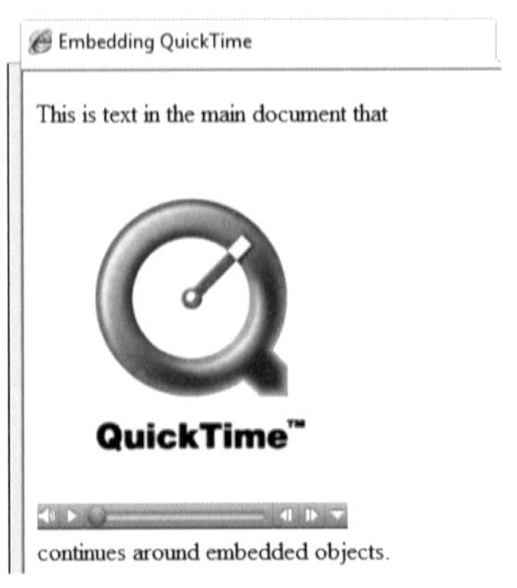

7. Open the web page in a different web browser to see the embedded QuickTime Player from the nested object

8. Disable the QuickTime Player plugin to see the alternative text from the nested object

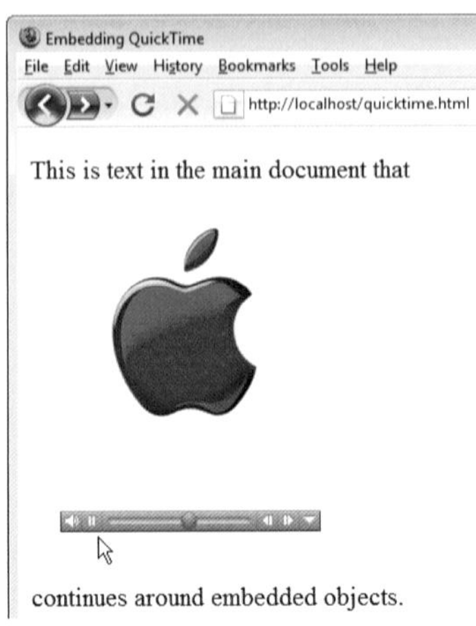

Beware

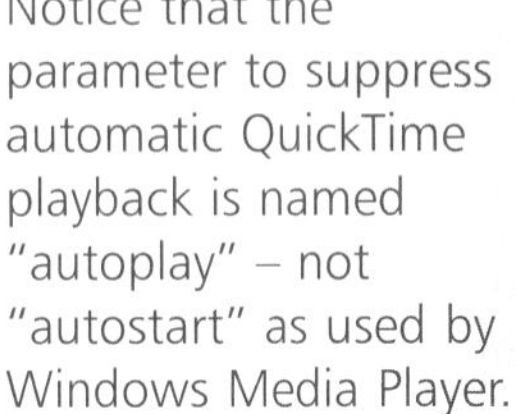

Notice that the parameter to suppress automatic QuickTime playback is named "autoplay" – not "autostart" as used by Windows Media Player.

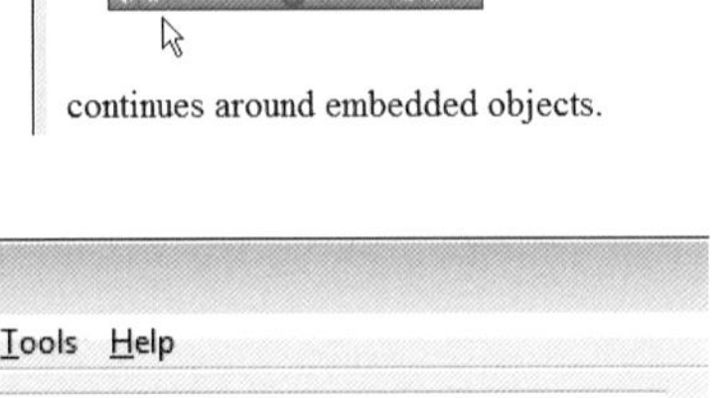

Embedding RealPlayer

You can discover more about RealPlayer online at **www.realplayer.com**.

The Real Networks RealPlayer can be embedded into a HTML document as an **<object>** element to play multi-media, with **width** and **height** attributes to specify its size on the web page. Sadly the technique to embed the RealPlayer plugin is not consistent among browsers. Internet Explorer requires the **<object>** tag to include a **classid** attribute specifying a lengthy ActiveX component identifier with the precise value of "CLSID:CFCDAA03-8BE4-11CF-B84B-0020AFBBCCFA". Other browsers require the tag to include a **type** attribute specifying a MIME type of "audio/x-pn-realaudio-plugin", a **data** attribute specifying the media path, and a **controls** attribute specifying "ImageWindow,ControlPanel,StatusBar" components. This means that cross-browser support requires two **<object>** elements – nesting one **<object>** element within another allows the browser to apply the appropriate technique while ignoring that which is inappropriate.

The **<object>** element can enclose **<param>** elements to specify parameters for the plugin with **name** and **value** attributes. The path to the media is specified to a parameter named "src" and an "autostart" parameter may be given a "false" value to prevent automatic playback – unless that is desirable.

real.html

1. Start a new HTML document with the Strict DTD

```
<!DOCTYPE HTML PUBLIC "-//W3C//DTD HTML 4.01//EN"
          "http://www.w3.org/TR/html4/strict.dtd">
```

2. Add a root element containing a head and body section

```
<html> <head>
<title>Embedding RealPlayer</title>
<meta http-equiv="Content-type"
  content="text/html; charset=ISO-8859-1"></head>
<body><!-- Content goes here. --></body> </html>
```

3. Within the body section, insert a paragraph

```
<p>This is text in the main document that<br>

<br>continues around embedded objects.</p>
```

4. Between the line breaks in the paragraph, insert a RealPlayer object for Internet Explorer

```
<object height="180" width="240"
classid="CLSID:CFCDAA03-8BE4-11CF-B84B-0020AFBBCCFA">
<param name="src" value="real.rm">
<param name="controls"
        value="ImageWindow, ControlPanel, StatusBar">
<param name="autostart" value="false">
<!-- Nested object to go here. --> </object>
```

5. Now insert a nested RealPlayer object for other browsers

```
<object type="audio/x-pn-realaudio-plugin"
        data="real.rm" height="180" width="240" >
  <param name="controls"
        value="ImageWindow, ControlPanel, StatusBar">
 <param name="autostart" value="false">
[Real Media @ http://localhost/real.rm] </object>
```

6. Save the HTML document alongside the Real media file then open the web page in Internet Explorer to see the embedded RealPlayer from the outer object

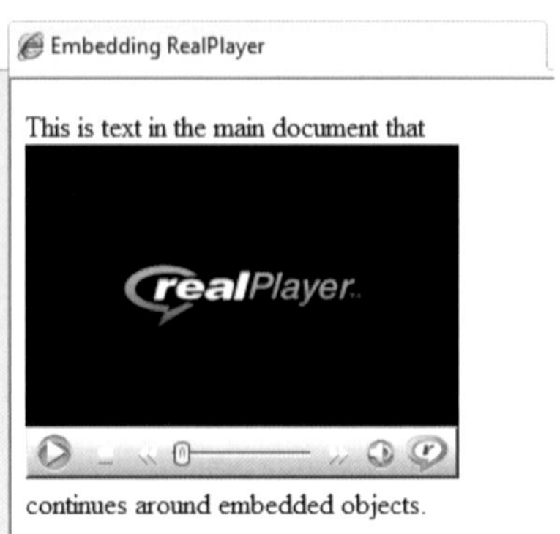

7. Open the web page in a different web browser to see the embedded RealPlayer from the nested object

8. Disable the RealPlayer plugin to see the alternative descriptive text from the nested object

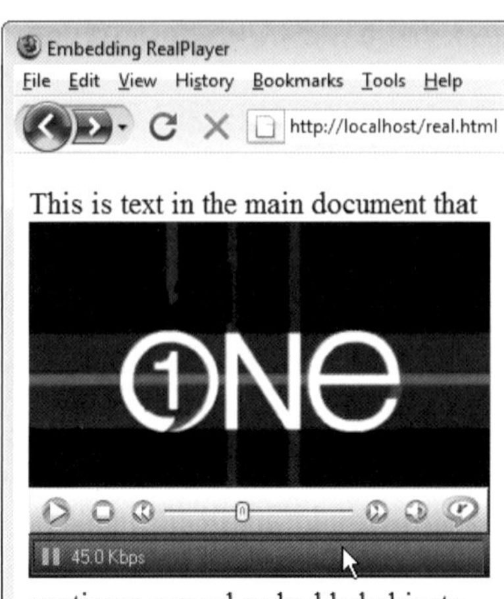

Beware

This example embeds RealPlayer version 11. Earlier versions were embedded using the, now deprecated, HTML **<embed>** tag.

Hot tip

Change the **controls** attribute value to "ImageWindow" and the **autostart** attribute value to "true" to automatically play the media file once – without visible controls.

Summary

- The HTML **<object> </object>** tags are used to embed external resources within a HTML document
- An **<object>** tag can include **width** and **height** attributes to specify the size of a display area on the web page, a **data** attribute to specify the path to the resource, and a **type** attribute to describe the type of resource to embed
- MIME types are the standard descriptions of web resources
- Each **<object>** element can include alternative text to be displayed when the resource cannot be embedded
- Multiple **<param>** elements can be enclosed within an **<object>** element to specify object parameters using their **name** and **value** attributes
- For Internet Explorer the Windows Media Player, QuickTime, and RealPlayer plugins are all ActiveX components specified by the **classid** attribute of the **<object>** element
- For Firefox the Windows Media Player, QuickTime, and RealPlayer plugins are all specified by their MIME type to the **type** attribute of an **<object>** element
- The ability to nest an **<object>** element within another **<object>** element allows cross-browser support of different plugins within the same part of the web page
- When an **<object>** element contains a **classid** attribute the resource path is specified by a parameter, not its **data** attribute
- Visibility of Windows Media Player controls is specified by the parameter named "uiMode", and the "autostart" parameter can prevent automatic playback when its value is "false"
- To display all three components of the RealPlayer interface a parameter named "controls" must specify the value of "ImageWindow, ControlPanel,StatusBar"

8 Inserting hyperlinks

This chapter demonstrates how to insert hyperlinks in a HTML document so the user can easily access related documents and resources.

Creating hyperlinks

When the internet carried only text content "hypertext" provided the ability to easily access related documents and was fundamental to the creation of the world wide web. Today images can also be used for this purpose so any navigational element of a web page is now referred to as a "hyperlink".

Hyperlinks are enclosed within **<a> </a>** anchor tags, which specify the target path to an **href** attribute in the opening tag. The web browser will display a hyperlink in a manner that distinguishes it from regular text – typically hypertext gains an underline and image-based hyperlinks gain a colored border.

Each web page hyperlink is sensitive to three interactive states:

- **Hover** – gaining focus, the cursor is placed over the hyperlink
- **Active** – retrieving the linked resource, the user clicks the link
- **Visited** – the linked resource has previously been retrieved

Style rules can be used to emphasize each hyperlink state:

hyper-1.html

1. Start a new HTML document with the Strict DTD
```
<!DOCTYPE HTML PUBLIC "-//W3C//DTD HTML 4.01//EN"
          "http://www.w3.org/TR/html4/strict.dtd">
```

2. Add a root element containing a head section incorporating a style sheet, and a body section
```
<html> <head> <title>Creating Hyperlinks</title>
<meta http-equiv="Content-type"
      content="text/html; charset=ISO-8859-1">
<link rel="stylesheet" type="text/css" href="hyper.css">
</head>
<body><!-- Content goes here. --></body> </html>
```

3. In the body section, insert a large heading
```
<h1>Page One</h1>
```

4. Now insert a paragraph containing a hyperlink
```
<p>
<a href="hyper-2.html" title="A hyperlink to page two.">
Read More on Page Two</a>
</p>
```

5. Save the HTML document then create a second document containing a hyperlink targetting the first document

```
<p>
<a href="hyper-1.html" title="A hyperlink to page one.">
Read Origin on Page One</a>
</p>
```

hyper-2.html

6. Save the HTML document then open a text editor and add style rules for each hyperlink state

```
a:hover { background: yellow ; color: red ; }
a:active { background: red ; color: white ; }
a:visited { background: blue ; color: white ; }
```

hyper.css

7. Save the Cascading Style Sheet alongside the HTML documents then open the first web page in your browser to see the hyperlink

8. Hover the cursor over the hyperlink then hold down the left mouse button to activate the hyperlink

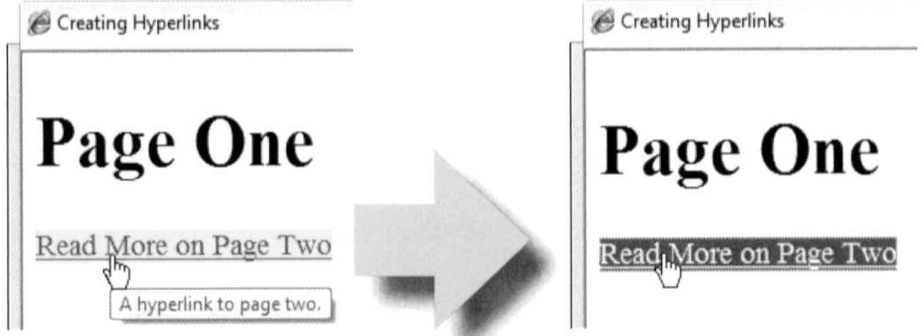

9. Release the mouse button to load the linked document then click its hyperlink to reload the first document

Don't forget

The hyperlink on the second page instantly appears in the visited state because the browser recognizes its target as previously read.

Accessing links via keys

There are three different ways to access the target of a hyperlink:

- **Pointer** – a mouse, trackball, or similar device places a screen pointer over a hyperlink then the user clicks to access its target
- **Tab** – repeatedly hit the Tab key to successively focus on each hyperlink in turn, then hit Return to access the target of the current selected hyperlink
- **Access Key** – hit a designated character key to focus on a particular hyperlink, then hit Return to access its target

Hot tip

The **accesskey** attribute may also be used in **<area>**, **<label>**, **<textarea>**, **<input>**, **<legend>**, and **<button>** tags.

A designated character key is specified for a hyperlink by the **accesskey** attribute of an **<a>** anchor tag. The method to utilize the designated key varies across platforms – Windows users must press Alt+*accesskey* while Mac users must press Cmd+*accesskey* :

access-1.html

1. Start a new HTML document with the Strict DTD

```
<!DOCTYPE HTML PUBLIC "-//W3C//DTD HTML 4.01//EN"
               "http://www.w3.org/TR/html4/strict.dtd">
```

2. Add a root element containing a head section incorporating a style sheet, and a body section

```
<html> <head> <title>Following Hyperlinks</title>
<meta http-equiv="Content-type"
        content="text/html; charset=ISO-8859-1">
<link rel="stylesheet" type="text/css" href="access.css">
</head>
<body><!-- Content goes here. --></body> </html>
```

Don't forget

The closing **</li>** tags are optional but clearly denote the end of each item in a list.

3. In the body section, insert a large heading

```
<h1>Home</h1>
```

4. Now insert an ordered list of three hyperlinks, which each include an accesskey attribute

```
<ol>
<li>
<a href="access-1.html" accesskey="1">Home Page</a></li>
<li>
<a href="access-2.html" accesskey="2">Detail Page</a></li>
<li>
<a href="access-3.html" accesskey="3">Index</a></li>
</ol>
```

5. Save the HTML document then copy'n'paste it to create two more similar documents and edit their headings
   <h1>**Detail**</h1>
   <h1>**Index**</h1>

6. Save the HTML documents then open a text editor and add style rules to remove the default hyperlink styles and to highlight hyperlinks when they receive focus

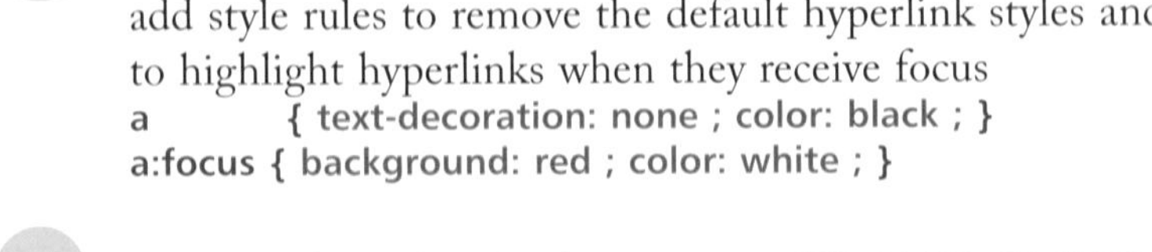

```
a       { text-decoration: none ; color: black ; }
a:focus { background: red ; color: white ; }
```

7. Save the Cascading Style Sheet alongside the HTML documents then open the first web page to see the links

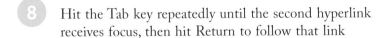

8. Hit the Tab key repeatedly until the second hyperlink receives focus, then hit Return to follow that link

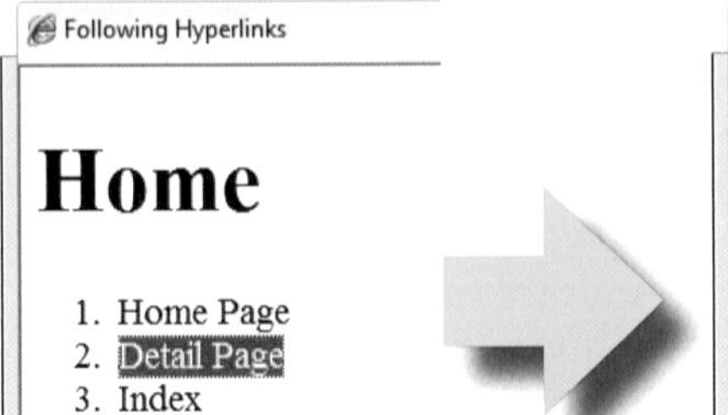

9. Press the Alt key and number three key to focus on the third hyperlink, then hit Return to follow that link

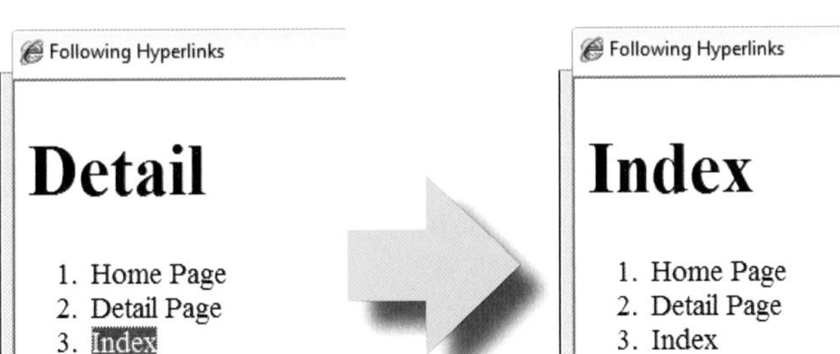

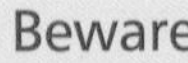

Beware

Removing the default hyperlink styles means they are no longer instantly recognizable as links – so should be avoided unless some other indication makes the user aware they can be used for navigation.

Linking to page fragments

Hyperlinks can target a specific point in a document that has been created as a "fragment" anchor – an **<a>** anchor tag that includes a **name** attribute to which is assigned a unique name. Within the hyperlink the fragment anchor's name is specified to the **href** attribute prefixed by a # hash character.

Following a hyperlink to a fragment anchor displays the document from the point where the fragment anchor is located:

frag-1.html

1. Start a new HTML document with the Strict DTD

```
<!DOCTYPE HTML PUBLIC "-//W3C//DTD HTML 4.01//EN"
            "http://www.w3.org/TR/html4/strict.dtd">
```

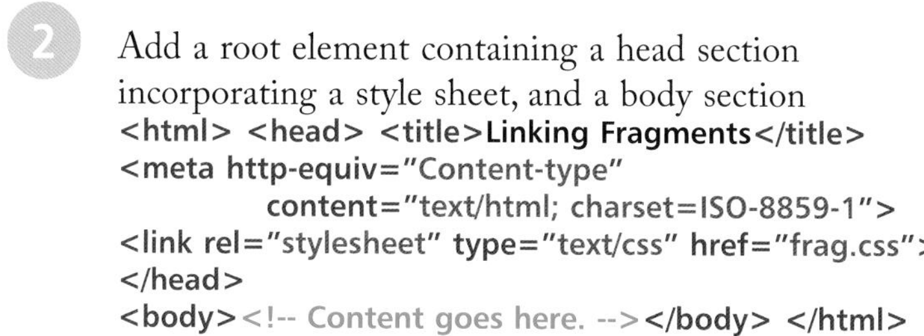

2. Add a root element containing a head section incorporating a style sheet, and a body section

```
<html> <head> <title>Linking Fragments</title>
<meta http-equiv="Content-type"
        content="text/html; charset=ISO-8859-1">
<link rel="stylesheet" type="text/css" href="frag.css">
</head>
<body><!-- Content goes here. --></body> </html>
```

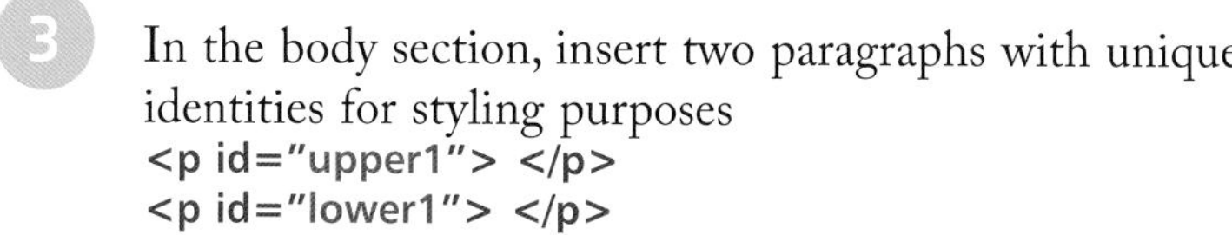

3. In the body section, insert two paragraphs with unique identities for styling purposes

```
<p id="upper1"> </p>
<p id="lower1"> </p>
```

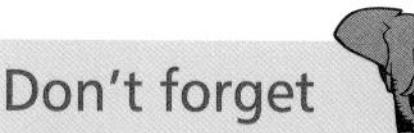

Don't forget

The **#** hash character is used to target fragment names, to specify hexadecimal color values, and to select **id** attributes in style rules.

4. Within the first paragraph, insert a fragment anchor that is a hyperlink to another fragment anchor

```
<a name="upper" href="#lower">
        Skip to the lower section.</a>
```

5. Within the second paragraph, insert a fragment anchor that is a hyperlink to the previous fragment anchor

```
<a name="lower" href="#upper">
        Back to the upper section.</a>
```

frag-2.html

6. Save the HTML document then copy'n'paste it to create a second document and edit its paragraph identities

```
<p id="upper2"> </p>
<p id="lower2"> </p>
```

7. Now within the first paragraph of the first document, insert a hyperlink to the fragment anchor in the second paragraph of the second document

```
<br><a href="frag-2.html#lower">
        Skip to the next page lower section.</a>
```

8. Save the HTML documents then open a text editor and add style rules to create a border, background color, and a standard height for each paragraph

```
p       { height: 100px ; border: 1px solid black ; }
#upper1 { background: #FEEDB7 ; }
#lower1 { background: #C9E5FC ; }
#upper2 { background: #84C984 ; }
#lower2 { background: #FFBF23 ; }
```

frag.css

9. Save the Cascading Style Sheet alongside the HTML documents then open the first web page to see the links

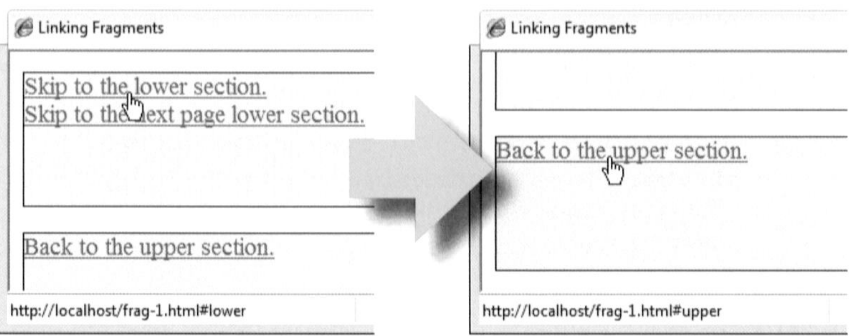

10. Click on the first hyperlink in each paragraph, to move between the fragment anchors in the first page, then click on the second link in the first paragraph to access the second paragraph on the second page

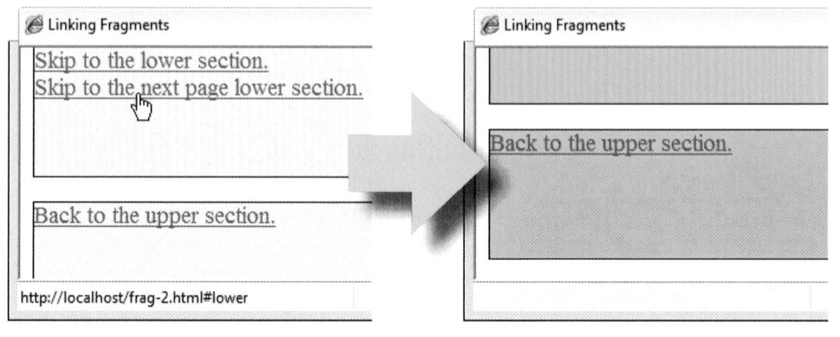

Hot tip

At the end of long HTML documents, include a hyperlink to a fragment anchor at the start of the document – so the user need not scroll back up.

Linking to protocols

The **href** attribute of a hyperlink will typically target a resource using the HyperText Transfer Protocol **http**: but it may also target resources using other protocols. Script functions can be called with the **javascript**: protocol and email clients can be invoked by the **mailto**: protocol.

protocol.html

1. Start a new HTML document with the Strict DTD

```
<!DOCTYPE HTML PUBLIC "-//W3C//DTD HTML 4.01//EN"
                "http://www.w3.org/TR/html4/strict.dtd">
```

2. Add a root element containing a head section, incorporating a style sheet and script, and a body section

```
<html>
<head>
<title>Linking Protocols</title>
<meta http-equiv="Content-type"
        content="text/html; charset=ISO-8859-1">
<link rel="stylesheet" type="text/css" href="protocol.css">
<script type="text/javascript" src="protocol.js"></script>
</head>
<body><!-- Content goes here. --></body> </html>
```

3. In the body section, insert a small heading and an unordered list with an identity for scripting

```
<h3>Functional Hyperlinks</p>
<ul id="topics">
<li>Topic 1.1</li>
<li>Topic 1.2</li>
<li>Topic 1.3</li>
</ul>
```

4. Next insert an element containing three hyperlinks

```
<div>
<a href="javascript:topics(1)">Show Topics</a><br>
<a href="javascript:topics(0)">Hide Topics</a><br>
<a href="mailto:wendy@example.com">
                Send Wendy a Message</a>
</div>
```

protocol.css

5. Save the HTML document then open a text editor and add style rules for the list and links container

```
ul { visibility: hidden ; height: 0px ; color: #FF6600 ; }
div { width: 200px ; border: 3px double #FF6600 ;
      background: #FEEDB7 ; color: #FF6600 ; }
```

6 Save the Cascading Style Sheet alongside the HTML document then open a text editor and carefully copy this script – exactly as it is listed

```
function topics(n)
{
  var tag = document.getElementById("topics");
  tag.style.visibility = (n) ? "visible" : "hidden" ;
  tag.style.height = (n) ? "auto" : "0px" ;
}
```

protocol.js

7 Save the script as "protocol.js" alongside the HTML document then open the web page in your browser and activate the first hyperlink to reveal the unordered list

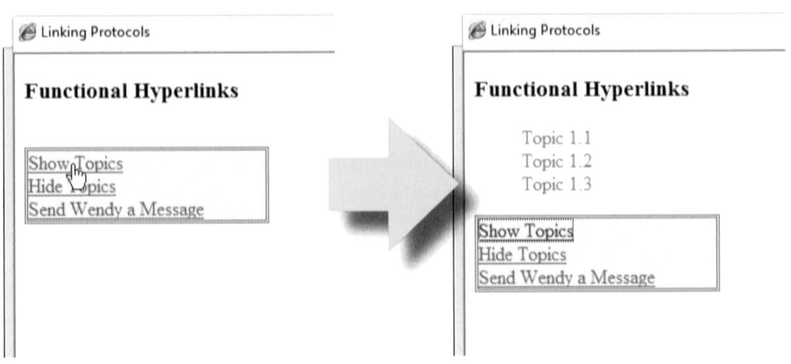

Hot tip

The parameters in the function call represent **true** (1) and **false** (0) – the unordered list is only visible when true.

8 Activate the second hyperlink to hide the unordered list once more then activate the third hyperlink to invoke the email client on your system

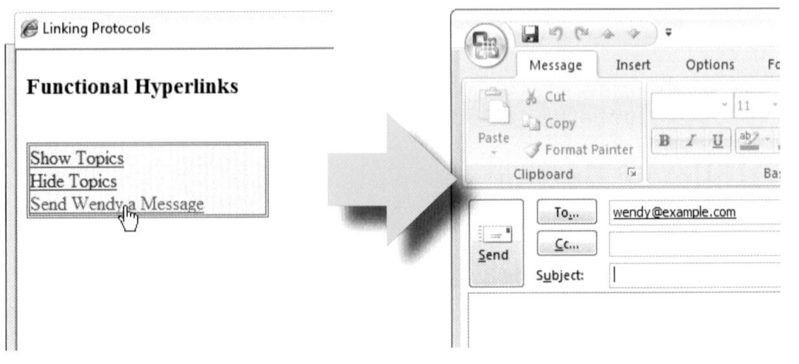

Don't forget

The **mailto:** protocol automatically adds the email address of the recipient in the "To" field of the email client.

Using images as hyperlinks

To make the navigational features of a HTML document more visually appealing images can be used as hyperlinks – simply by nesting an **<img>** image element within an **<a>** anchor element.

rollover.html

1. Start a new HTML document with the Strict DTD

```
<!DOCTYPE HTML PUBLIC "-//W3C//DTD HTML 4.01//EN"
                "http://www.w3.org/TR/html4/strict.dtd">
```

2. Add a root element containing a head section incorporating a style sheet, and a body section

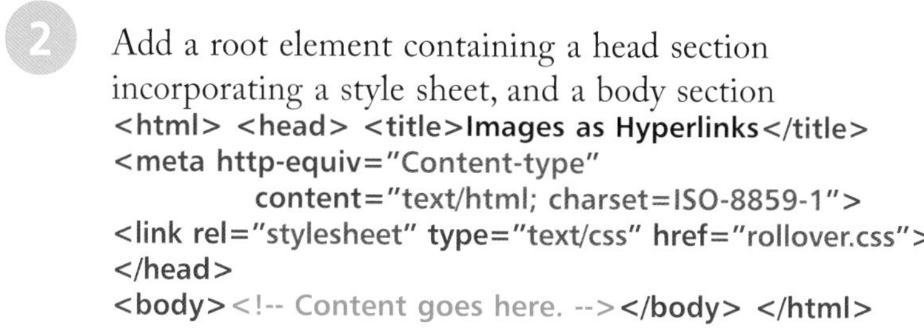

```
<html> <head> <title>Images as Hyperlinks</title>
<meta http-equiv="Content-type"
        content="text/html; charset=ISO-8859-1">
<link rel="stylesheet" type="text/css" href="rollover.css">
</head>
<body><!-- Content goes here. --></body> </html>
```

3. In the body section, insert a heading and a container element with a class for styling

```
<h2>Rollover Button</h2>
<div class="btn">        </div>
```

4. Within the container element, insert a hyperlink with a nested image

```
<a href="http://www.youtube.com">
<img src="rollover-btn" width="192" height="67"
      alt="Hyperlink to the YouTube website.">
</a>
```

5. Save the HTML document then open the web page in your browser and follow the hyperlink

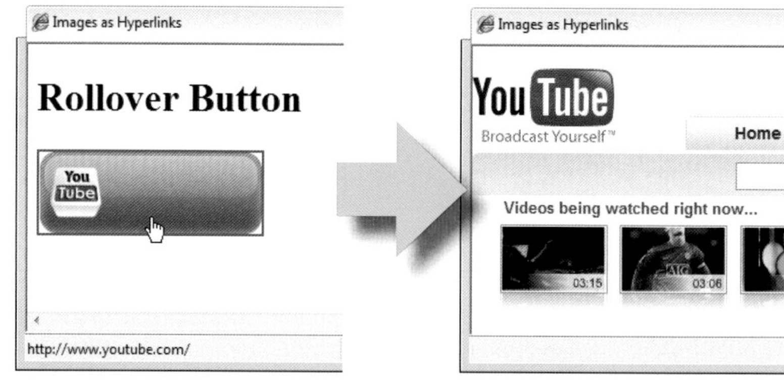

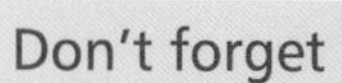

The dimensions of the images in this example create a large button for illustration purposes – actual web page buttons are typically smaller.

Browsers usually add a border around an image when it is nested within a hyperlink to indicate that it is not merely an illustration. Style rules can remove the image border and can also swap the image when the cursor is placed over it to perform a "rollover". There are several ways to achieve this effect – the technique described below hides the image when the cursor is placed over it to reveal the background image on the container element behind:

6. Open a text editor and add a style rule to set the container element the same size as the button image and to specify a background image for the container

```
.btn { width: 192px ; height: 67px ;
        background: url(rollover-bg.png) ; }
```

rollover.css

7. Next add a style rule to set the anchor element the same size as the button image

```
.btn a { display: block ; width: 192px ; height: 67px ; }
```

8. Now add a style rule to remove the default border from around the button image

```
.btn a img { border: 0px ; }
```

9. Finally add a style rule to hide the button image when the cursor is placed over it

```
.btn a:hover img { visibility: hidden ; }
```

10. Save the Cascading Style Sheet alongside the HTML document then open the web page in your browser to see the border is removed and the rollover effect performs

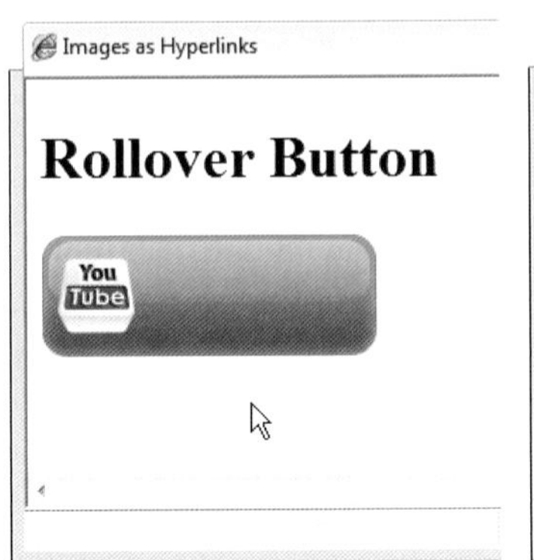

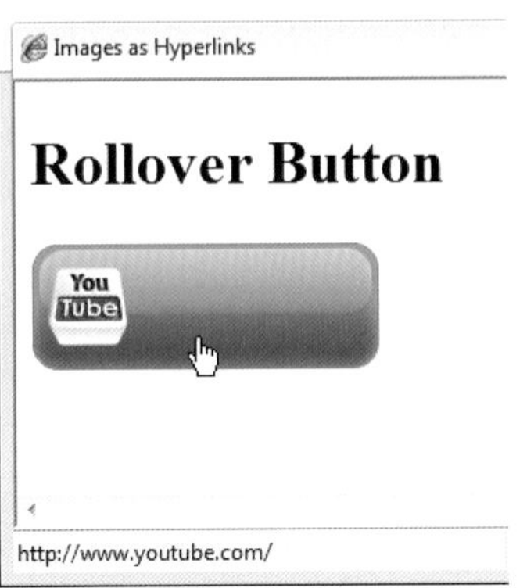

Hot tip

Unlike some other rollover techniques here both images are already loaded, so the rollover performs instantly, and the **<img>** tag provides alternative text when images are not enabled.

Producing image map links

A single image can target multiple hyperlink resources if an image "map" is added to define "hot spot" areas for each hyperlink. To use an image map the **<img>** tag must include a **usemap** attribute to specify a map name, prefixed by a hash # character. The image map is contained within **<map> </map>** tags and its name is specified by a **name** attribute in the opening **<map>** tag.

Each area of the image that is to become a hyperlink hot spot is defined by four attributes of an **<area>** tag within the **<map>** element. The **shape** attribute specifies its shape as **rect** (rectangle), **circle**, or **poly** (polygon) and the **coords** attribute specifies a comma-separated list of its x-axis and y-axis coordinates:

Shape	Coordinates
rect	left-x, top-y, right-x, bottom-y
circle	center-x, center-y, radius
poly	x1,y1, x2,y2, x3,y3, etc. – one pair for each point. The first point and the final point must have identical coordinates to join up the shape

Additionally, each **<area>** tag must have an **href** attribute, to specify the hyperlink's target, and an **alt** attribute to specify alternative text to be displayed when images are not enabled.

map.html

1. Start a new HTML document with the Strict DTD

```
<!DOCTYPE HTML PUBLIC "-//W3C//DTD HTML 4.01//EN"
                "http://www.w3.org/TR/html4/strict.dtd">
```

2. Add a root element containing head and body sections

```
<html> <head> <title>Image Map Hyperlinks</title>
<meta http-equiv="Content-type"
   content="text/html; charset=ISO-8859-1"></head>
<body><!-- Content goes here. --></body> </html>
```

map.png

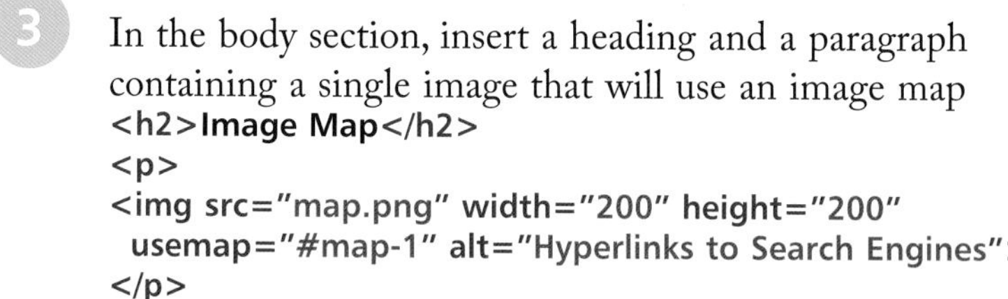

3. In the body section, insert a heading and a paragraph containing a single image that will use an image map

```
<h2>Image Map</h2>
<p>
<img src="map.png" width="200" height="200"
  usemap="#map-1" alt="Hyperlinks to Search Engines">
</p>
```

4. Next in the paragraph, insert a map element with a name matching that specified by the image's **usemap** attribute

```
<map name="map-1">          </map>
```

5. Within the map element, define a rectangular hot spot area covering the top left quarter of the image

```
<area   shape="rect" coords="0,0,100,100"
        href="http://www.yahoo.com"
        alt="Yahoo! Panel" title="Link to Yahoo!" >
```

6. Now define three more hot spots of the same size, covering the other three quarters of the image, then save the HTML document and open it in your web browser

```
<area   shape="rect" coords="100,0,200,100"
        href="http://www.ask.com"
        alt="Ask Panel" title="Link to Ask" >

<area   shape="rect" coords="0,100,100,200"
        href="http://www.google.com"
        alt="Google Panel" title="Link to Google" >

<area   shape="rect" coords="100,100,200,200"
        href="http://www.altavista.com"
        alt="AltaVista Panel" title="Link to AltaVista" >
```

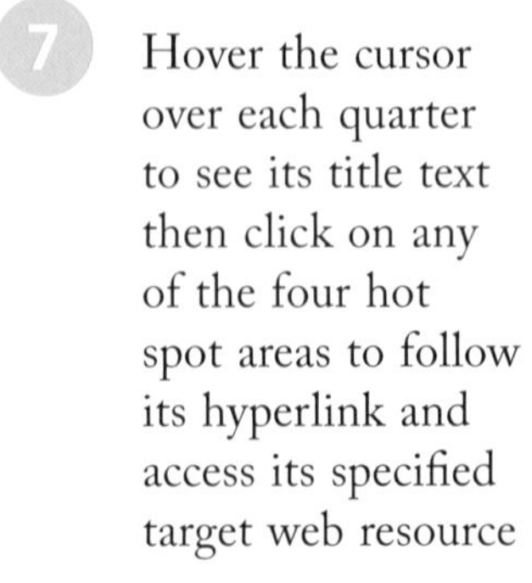

7. Hover the cursor over each quarter to see its title text then click on any of the four hot spot areas to follow its hyperlink and access its specified target web resource

Beware

Validation will fail unless an **alt** attribute is included in all **<img>** tags and all **<area>** tags.

Generating popups

Hyperlinks can be used without an actual target resource to perform CSS rollovers and "popup" effects. Typically the **<a>** anchor tag's **href** attribute is assigned a **#null** value in this case. The CSS **a:hover** pseudo-class can create hot spots – much like the image map hot spots in the previous example. In response the style rules can reveal previously hidden HTML elements to display as popups in front of other content. These are useful to display additional graphical or textual content:

popup.html

1. Start a new HTML document with the Strict DTD

```
<!DOCTYPE HTML PUBLIC "-//W3C//DTD HTML 4.01//EN"
                  "http://www.w3.org/TR/html4/strict.dtd">
```

2. Add a root element containing a head section incorporating a style sheet, and a body section

```
<html> <head> <title>Linking Popups</title>
<meta http-equiv="Content-type"
   content="text/html; charset=ISO-8859-1"></head>
<link rel="stylesheet" type="text/css" href="popup.css">
<body><!-- Content goes here. --></body> </html>
```

3. In the body section, insert a heading and a paragraph within a container element

```
<div id="content">
<h2>The Porsche Principle</h2>
<p>Porsche doesn't simply build sports cars. Porsche is
more. Much more. And Porsche is different.</p>
</div>
```

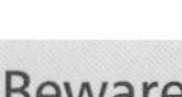

Beware

Ensure there are no fragment anchors named "null" in the document.

4. Add another container enclosing three hyperlinks with both text and image content

```
<div class="links">

<a href="#null">Boxster <span class="pop">
<img src="popup-1.png" width="151" height="87"
        alt="Boxster Image"><br>Boxster</span> </a>

<a href="#null">Cayman <span class="pop">
<img src="popup-2.png" width="151" height="87"
        alt="Cayman Image"><br>Cayman</span> </a>

<a href="#null">911 <span class="pop">
<img src="popup-3.png" width="151" height="87"
        alt="911 Image"><br>911</span> </a>
</div>
```

5. Save the HTML document then open a text editor and add a style rule for the content container

```
#content { position: absolute; left: 120px; width: 380px;
                  font-size: small ; z-index: 0;                  }
```

popup.css

6. Next add style rules for the links container

```
.links { width: 100px ; float: left; }
.links a { display: block; padding: 5px;
          margin-bottom: 15px; text-decoration: none;
          color: #002E92; background: #C9E5FC;               }
.links a:hover { color: # FFF; background: #F00;  }
```

7. Now add style rules for hidden content and to popup the hidden content in response to the cursor position

```
.pop { display: block; position: absolute; top: auto; left:
120px; width: 200px; color: #FFF; background: #F00;
padding: 5px; visibility: hidden ; z-index: 10; }
.links a:hover .pop { visibility: visible; }
```

8. Save the Cascading Style Sheet alongside the HTML document then open the web page in your browser and roll the cursor over the hyperlinks to see the popups

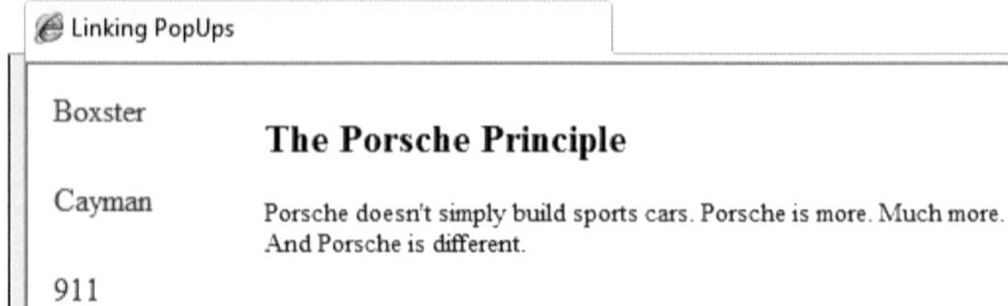

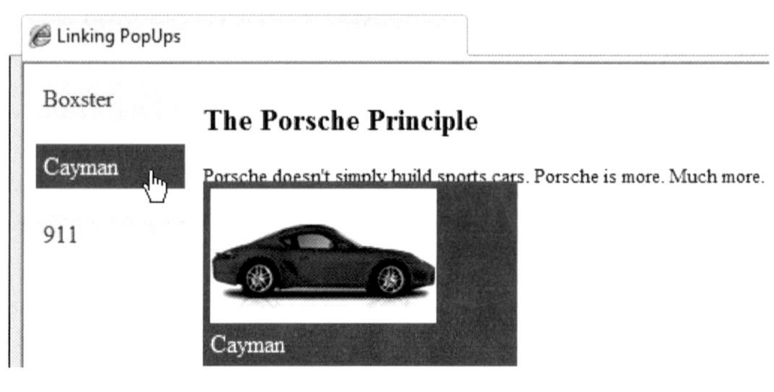

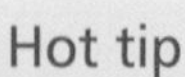

Hot tip

Assigning a value of "#" to an anchor's **href** attribute targets the top of that document.

Summary

- The HTML **<a> </a>** anchor tags are used to enclose hyperlinks within a HTML document
- A **href** attribute can be included in an **<a>** anchor tag to specify the target resource of that hyperlink
- Each hyperlink is sensitive to hover, active, and visited states
- Hyperlinks can be accessed by a pointer, the tab key, or a designated key specified to the **<a>** tag's **accesskey** attribute
- A **name** attribute can be included in an **<a>** anchor tag to create a fragment anchor
- When targeting a fragment anchor the **href** attribute must specify the fragment's name prefixed by a **#** hash character
- A hyperlink may target a resource via the **http:** protocol, or with other protocols such as **javascript:** and **mailto:**
- Rollover effects are performed by the CSS **a:hover** pseudo-class to swap images in response to the cursor position
- A single image can target multiple hyperlink resources by adding an image map to specify an area for each hyperlink
- The **<map> </map>** tags enclose **<area>** elements, to define the areas of an image map, and a **name** attribute must be included in the **<map>** tag to specify a name for that map
- To use an image map the **<img>** tag must include a **usemap** attribute specifying the map's name prefixed by a **#** hash character
- Each **<area>** tag must include **shape**, **coords**, **href**, and **alt** attributes and the shape may be a value of **rect**, **circle**, or **poly**
- Hyperlinks can be used without a target to perform CSS effects by assigning a **#null** value to the **<a>** tag's **href** attribute
- Popup effects are performed by the CSS **a:hover** pseudo-class to reveal hidden content in response to the cursor position

9 Using frames

This chapter demonstrates how to simultaneously display multiple framed HTML documents in a single browser window.

Framing in columns

A single browser window can be divided into "frames" that each display a different HTML document. The layout of the frames is determined by a "frameset" document that specifies the size and position of each frame using **<frameset> </frameset>** tags.

Discover more on the frameset specifications online at **www.w3.org**.

The opening **<frameset>** tag can include a **cols** attribute to specify the horizontal allocation of frame width, expressed in pixels or percentage of the total width, to display documents in columns. Values are assigned to the **cols** attribute as a comma-separated list to be applied from left to right. Alternatively a * wildcard value can be assigned to specify that the frame should occupy the available remaining width.

Each **<frameset>** element encloses **<frame>** elements that include a **src** attribute specifying the path to a HTML document to be loaded into that frame.

Unlike other HTML documents, each frameset document must begin with the special frameset DTD described on page 12. Additionally you should note that a frameset document contains a head section and a frameset section – but there is no body section:

column.html

1. Start a new HTML document with the Frameset DTD

```
<!DOCTYPE HTML PUBLIC
        "-//W3C//DTD HTML 4.01 Frameset//EN"
        "http://www.w3.org/TR/html4/frameset.dtd" >
```

2. After the Document Type Definition add a root element

```
<html>
<!-- Head and Frameset sections to go here. -->
</html>
```

3. In the root element, insert a head section specifying a frameset title and a character set

```
<head>
<title>Three Column Frameset</title>
<meta http-equiv="Content-type"
        content="text/html; charset=ISO-8859-1">
</head>
```

4. Next insert a frameset section creating three columns

```
<frameset cols="30%, 30%, *">
<!-- Frames to go here. -->
</frameset>
```

5. In the frameset section, insert frame elements specifying the path to HTML documents for each column
```
<frame src="column-1.html">
<frame src="column-2.html">
<frame src="column-3.html">
```

6. Save the HTML frameset document then create the three documents to appear in each frame – each containing a heading and a column of numbers

7. Save the documents for each frame alongside the frameset HTML document then open the frameset document in your browser to see the column documents appear in each frame of the browser window

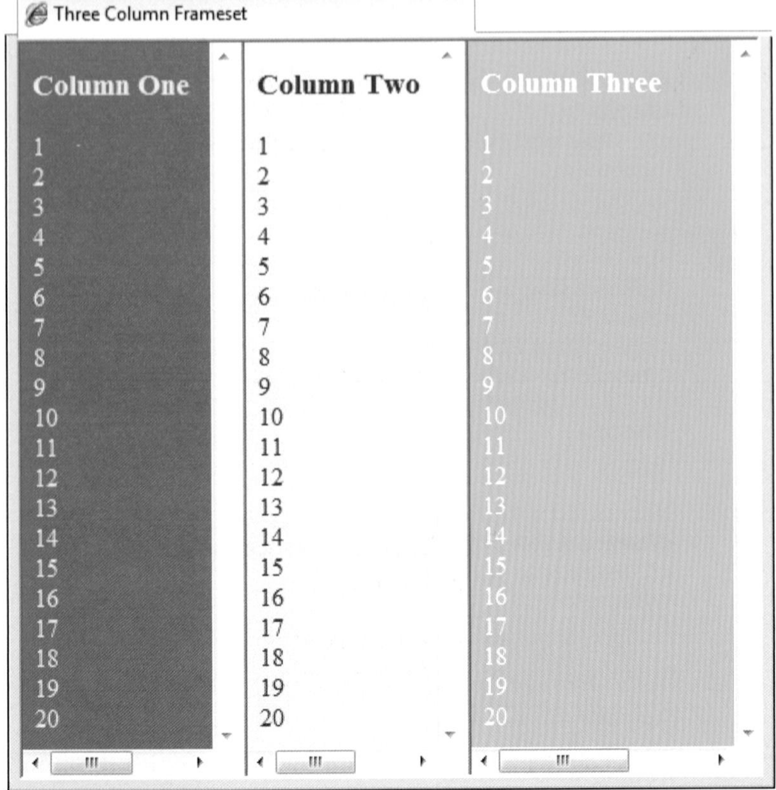

Don't forget

The **<frame>** tag is a single tag that does not require a closing tag.

Framing in rows

Just as a single browser window can be divided into "frames" that each display a different HTML document in columns, as described in the previous example, a "frameset" document can specify the size and position of each frame in rows.

The opening **<frameset>** tag can include a **rows** attribute to specify the vertical allocation of frame width, expressed in pixels or percentage of the total height, to display documents in rows. Values are assigned to the **rows** attribute as a comma-separated list to be applied from top to bottom. Alternatively a * wildcard value can be assigned to specify that the frame should occupy the available remaining height.

row.html

1. Start a new HTML document with the Frameset DTD

```
<!DOCTYPE HTML PUBLIC
        "-//W3C//DTD HTML 4.01 Frameset//EN"
        "http://www.w3.org/TR/html4/frameset.dtd" >
```

2. After the Document Type Definition add a root element

```
<html>
<!-- Head and Frameset sections to go here. -->
</html>
```

3. In the root element, insert a head section specifying a frameset title and a character set

```
<head>
<title>Three Row Frameset</title>
<meta http-equiv="Content-type"
        content="text/html; charset=ISO-8859-1">
</head>
```

4. Next insert a frameset section creating three rows

```
<frameset rows="30%, 30%, *">
<!-- Frames to go here. -->
</frameset>
```

5. In the frameset section, insert frame elements specifying the path to HTML documents for each row

```
<frame src="row-1.html">
<frame src="row-2.html">
<frame src="row-3.html">
```

6. Save the HTML frameset document then create the three documents to appear in each frame – each containing a heading and a row of numbers

7. Save the documents for each frame alongside the frameset HTML document then open the frameset document in your browser to see the row documents appear in each frame of the browser window

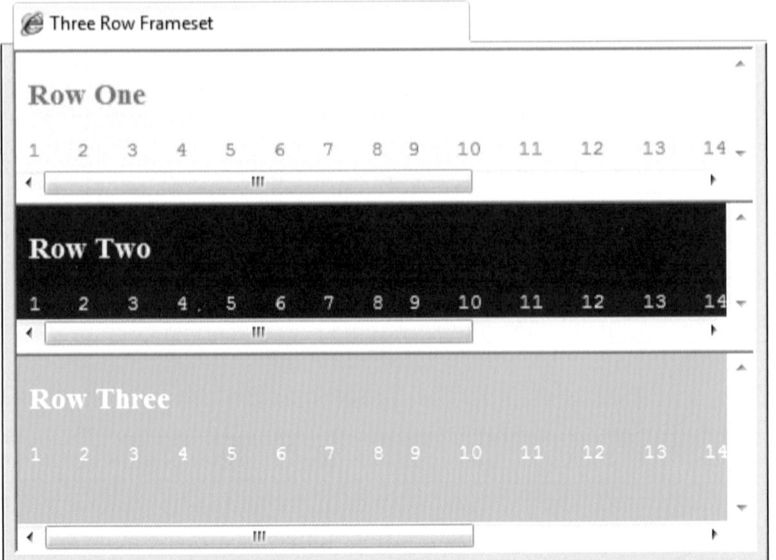

8. Use the scroll bars to view content that overflows the browser window

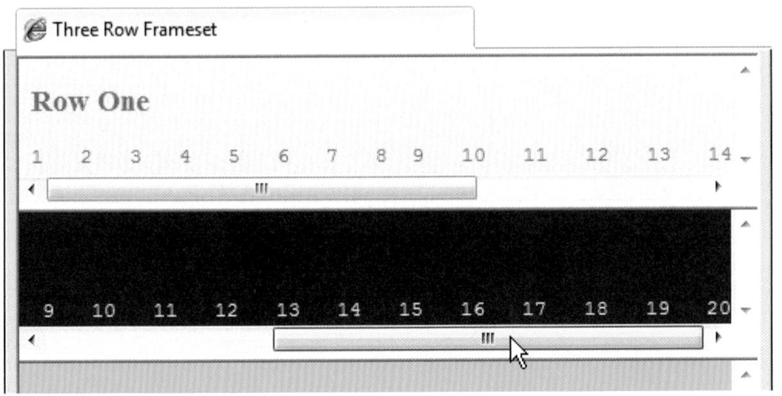

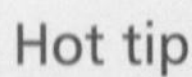

Hot tip

Create the number rows within a **<pre>** element to preserve the spacing.

Don't forget

By default each frame is provided with horizontal and vertical scroll bars so the user can view any overflowing content.

Creating a nested frameset

Frameset documents can contain nested framesets to describe a more elaborate arrangement of both rows and columns. For example, a frameset containing two columns could replace the second column with a nested frameset containing two rows. If that column occupies 80% of the available width and its first row occupies a height of 120 pixels the frames are arranged like this:

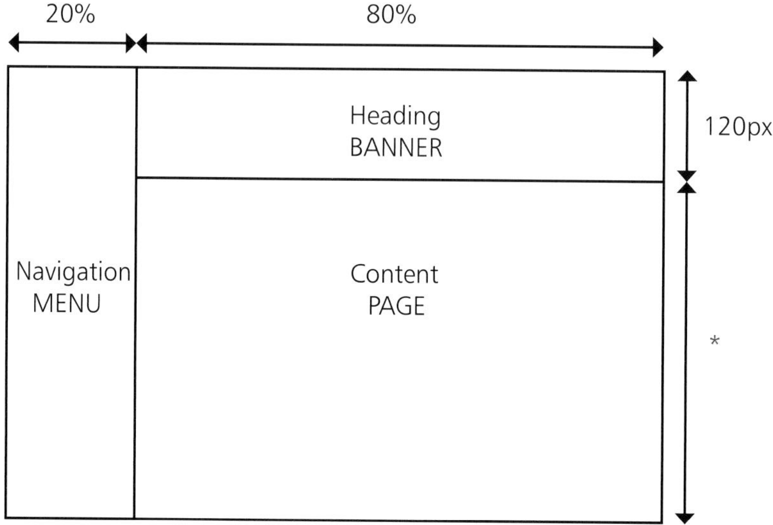

The illustration labels suggest how each frame might create a web page that has a static navigation panel, a banner that may be occasionally changed, and a main page area containing content:

1. Start a new HTML document with the Frameset DTD

```
<!DOCTYPE HTML PUBLIC
        "-//W3C//DTD HTML 4.01 Frameset//EN"
        "http://www.w3.org/TR/html4/frameset.dtd" >
```

2. After the Document Type Definition add a root element containing a head section

```
<html>
<head>
<title>Nested Frameset</title>
<meta http-equiv="Content-type"
        content="text/html; charset=ISO-8859-1">
</head>
<!-- Frameset section to go here. -->
</html>
```

3. Next insert a frameset section creating two columns

```
<frameset cols="20%, 80%">
<!-- Frames to go here. -->
</frameset>
```

4. In the frameset section, insert frame elements specifying the path to HTML documents for each column

```
<frame src="column-1.html">
<frame src="column-2.html">
```

5. Now in the frameset section, replace the second column frame with a nested frameset creating two rows

```
<frameset rows="120, *">
<frame src="row-1.html">
<frame src="row-2.html">
</frameset>
```

6. Save the HTML frameset document then create the three documents to appear in each frame

7. Save the documents for each frame alongside the frameset HTML document then open the frameset document in your browser to see the documents appear in each frame of the browser window

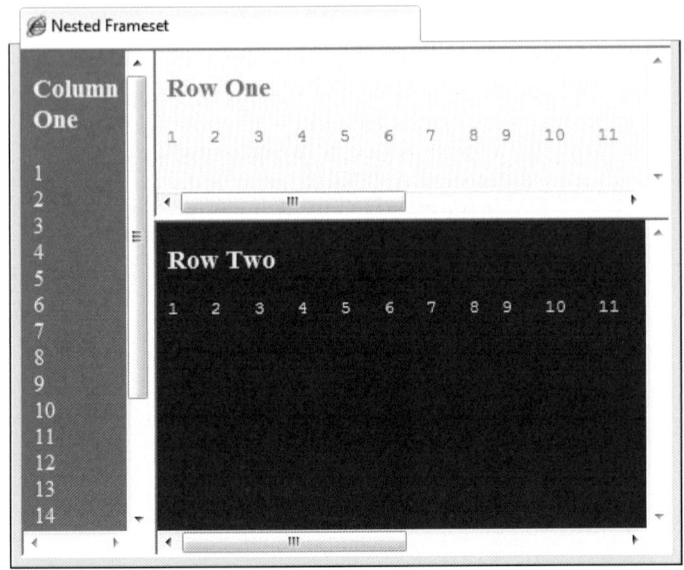

Don't forget

The **<title>** element of the frameset document appears on the browser tab – not those of the frame documents.

Hot tip

Specify a fixed pixel value for each frame to prevent the scrollbar position changing when the browser window gets resized.

Hiding scroll bars

The automatic inclusion of scroll bars for each frame in a frameset creates a cluttered appearance in the browser window so web page authors will often want to remove them where not essential. This simply requires a **scrolling** attribute to be included in each **<frame>** tag specifying a "no" value.

Additionally the individual frame borders can be removed to create a flatter "single page" appearance by including a **frameborder** attribute in each **<frame>** tag specifying a zero value:

1. Make a copy of the **nest.html document** from the previous example and rename it "nobars.html"

2. Open the HTML document in your web browser and examine the frame edges to identify their components

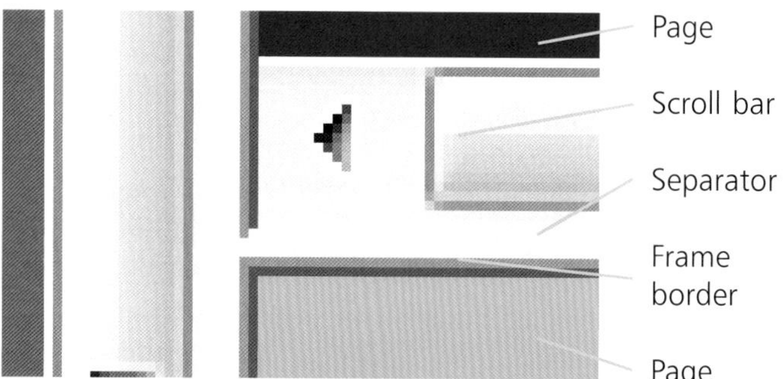

3. Open the HTML document in a text editor then insert attributes to remove the scroll bars from each frame

```
<frameset cols="20%, 80%">
  <frame src="column-1.html" scrolling="no">
  <frameset rows="120,*">
        <frame src="row-2.html" scrolling="no">
        <frame src="row-2.html" scrolling="no">
  </frameset>
</frameset>
```

4. Save the amended HTML document then open it in your web browser to see the scroll bars have been removed – but the frame borders still remain

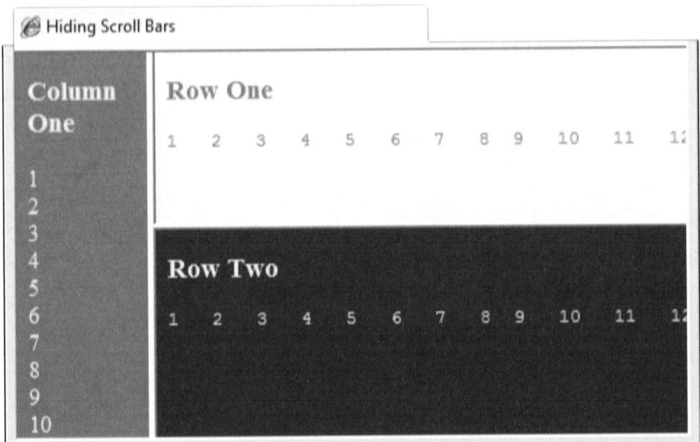

Don't forget

The value assigned to the **frameborder** attribute is a boolean value not a width value – it may be either 0 (off) or 1 (on).

5. Reopen the HTML document in a text editor then insert attributes to remove the frame border from each frame

```
<frameset cols="20%, 80%">
<frame src="column-1.html"
                scrolling="no" frameborder="0">
<frameset rows="120,*">
<frame src="row-2.html" scrolling="no" frameborder="0">
<frame src="row-2.html" scrolling="no" frameborder="0">
</frameset>
</frameset>
```

6. Save the amended HTML document then open it in your web browser once more to see the frame borders have been removed – leaving just the separators to indicate this is a frameset rather than a single document

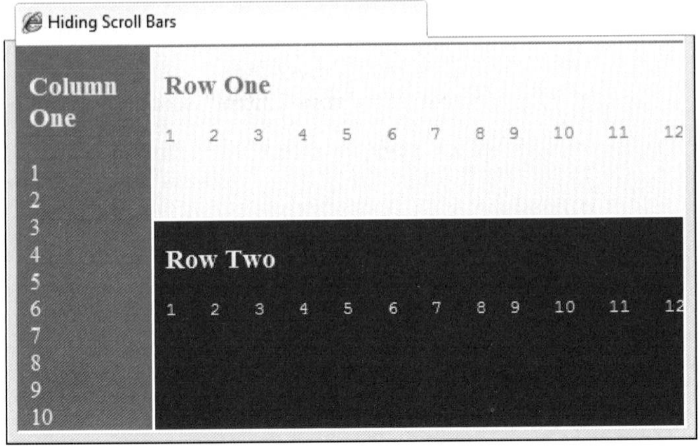

Hot tip

You can remove the separators by adding a **border="0"** attribute to each **<frameset>** tag. This is widely supported by browsers but is not part of the W3C HTML 4 specifications.

Changing frame content

Hyperlinks regard the frame in which they appear as a separate browser window so will load their target resource into that frame when the link is followed.

Previously a **target** attribute could be included in an **<a>** anchor tag to specify a different frame to load a target resource but this attribute has been deliberately omitted from the Strict HTML 4 specifications to discourage the use of frames.

Scripting can now be used to specify which frame should load a hyperlink target resource – so hyperlinks in a "Navigation Menu" frame can load new documents into a "Content Page" frame, or even into a "Heading Banner" frame:

change.html

1. Make a copy of the **nobars.html document** from the previous example and rename it "change.html"

2. Open the frameset document in a text editor then edit the attribute values to fix the menu frame width and assign a new source document for the menu frame

```
<frameset cols="120,*">
<frame src="menu.html"
        scrolling="no" frameborder="0">
```

menu.html

3. Save the modified frameset document then start a new HTML document with the Strict DTD

```
<!DOCTYPE HTML PUBLIC "-//W3C//DTD HTML 4.01//EN"
                "http://www.w3.org/TR/html4/strict.dtd">
```

4. Add a root element containing a head section incorporating a script and a style sheet, and a body section

```
<html> <head> <title>Navigation Menu</title>
<meta http-equiv="Content-type"
          content="text/html; charset=ISO-8859-1">
<script type="text/javascript" src="menu.js"></script>
<link rel="stylesheet" type="text/css" href="frame.css">
</head>
<body><!-- Content goes here. --></body> </html>
```

5. In the body section, insert a heading and a paragaph containing a hyperlink to a script function

```
<h3>Menu</h3>
<p><a href="javascript:next('row-3.html',1)">
                                Change Banner</a> </p>
```

6 Now insert a ruled line followed by another paragraph containing a hyperlink to a script function

```
<hr><p><a href="javascript:next('column-1.html',2)">
                                        Change Page</a> </p>
```

7 Save the HTML document alongside the frameset document then open a text editor and copy this script

```
function next( url, n )
{ parent.window.frames[n].location=url; }
```

menu.js

8 Save the script as "menu.js" alongside the HTML documents then open the frameset document in your web browser and use the hyperlinks to change frame contents

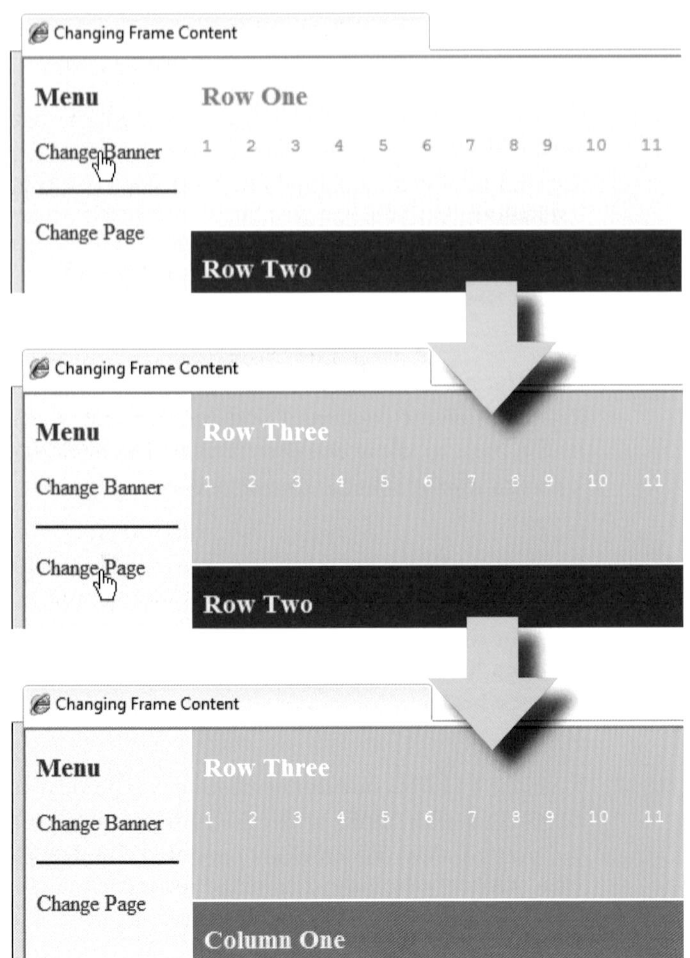

Hot tip

These hyperlinks pass the script the name of the document to load and the number of the frame in which to load it. Each frame is numbered, starting at zero, in the order the **<frame>** tags are listed in the source frameset document's HTML source code.

Don't forget

The contents of the style sheet used by this HTML document, and all others in this chapter, is not listed as it merely styles colors for contrast and removes the default hyperlink features in the navigation menu.

Providing frame alternatives

Using frames to simultaneously display multiple HTML documents is considered to be bad practice by many web developers as some browsers, such as those on handheld devices, may be unable to accommodate frames. Consequently it is prudent to provide an alternative means to view the content.

The HTML **<noframes> </noframes>** tags can be added to a frameset document to enclose content to be displayed when frames are not supported and must be contained at the end of a **<frameset>** element.

The **<noframes>** element can usefully include a hyperlink to the HTML document in the main frame, which can provide an alternative means of navigation through the content pages:

noframes.html

1. Make a copy of the **change.html document** from the previous example and rename it "noframes.html"

2. Open the frameset document in a text editor then insert alternative text for browsers that cannot view frames
**<noframes>! The page you are trying to view uses frames <br>... but frame support is not enabled or is unavailable in your browser.
<a href="column-1.html"> You can view a frameless version with this link.</a></noframes>**

3. Save the modified frameset document then open the hyperlink target document and insert a link at the bottom of the page to allow the user to view the next page
<p> <a href="column-2.html">Next Page</a> </p>

4. Save the HTML document then open the next hyperlink target and insert links at the bottom of the page to allow the user to view the next page and the previous page
<p> <a href="column-1.html">Previous Page</a> |
<a href="column-3.html">Next Page</a> </p>

5. Save the HTML document then open the next hyperlink target and insert links at the bottom of the page to allow the user to view the previous page and the first page
<p> <a href="column-2.html">Previous Page</a> |
<a href="column-1.html">Home Page</a> </p>

6. Save the HTML document then open the frameset document in a browser that cannot view frames and follow the hyperlinks to view the website content

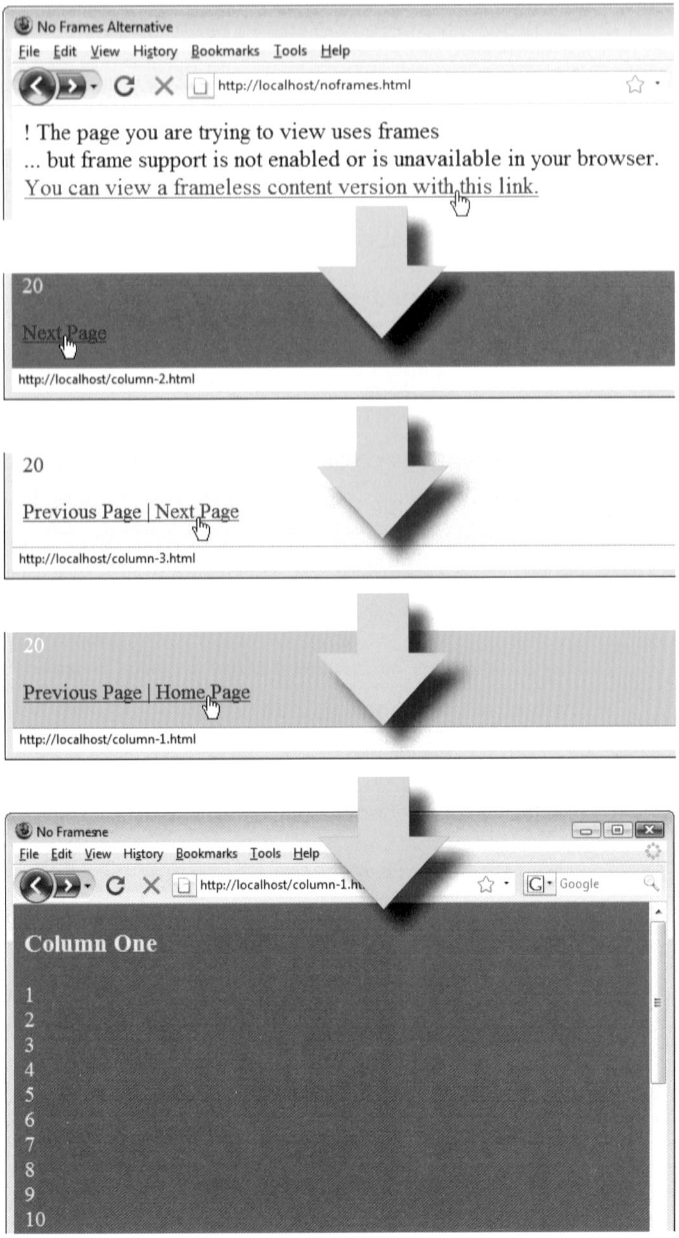

To disable frame support in Mozilla Firefox type **about:config** in the address field, hit Return then double-click on the item **browser.frames. enabled** to change its value from **true** to **false**.

Summary

- A single browser window can be divided into frames that each display a different HTML document
- The **<frameset> </frameset>** tags contain **<frame>** elements that define each division of the browser window
- A **cols** attribute can be included in the **<frameset>** tag to specify the horizontal allocation of frame width
- A **rows** attribute can be included in the **<frameset>** tag to specify the vertical allocation of frame height
- Each frameset document must begin with the frameset DTD
- Framesets can be nested to describe an arrangement of both rows and columns
- A frameset contains no body section but its **<title>** element specifies the web page title that the browser displays
- By default the web browser will automatically display scroll bars, a separator, and a frame border for each frame
- The scroll bars can be removed from a frame by assigning a "no" value to a **scrolling** attribute within its **<frame>** tag
- The frame borders can be removed from a frame by assigning a "0" value to a **frameborders** attribute within its **<frame>** tag
- The separators can be removed from a frameset by assigning a "0" value to a non-standard **borders** attribute within its **<frameset>** tag
- A script function can be used to change frame content from a hyperlink in another frame
- The **<noframes> </noframes>** tags allow alternative text to be provided for browsers that do not support frames
- Hyperlinks can usefully be added to frame content pages to provide an independent means of page navigation

10 Building forms

This chapter demonstrates how to build form components into the body section of a HTML document for submission of data to a web server.

Submitting forms

Web page forms are built from a number of HTML elements that submit data to a web server for processing. Each one of these elements include a **name** attribute and a **value** attribute so the data assigned to these attributes can be processed by the associated name=value pairs. For example, where a **name** attribute is assigned "Brand" and a **value** attribute is assigned "Dodge" the name=value pair represents the data as Brand=Dodge.

The examples in this chapter use the free Abyss Personal Edition web server available from **www.aprelium.com**.

All form components are enclosed within **<form> </form>** tags. Each opening **<form>** tag must include a **method** attribute, specifying which HTTP method should be used to submit the form, and an **action** attribute specifying the URL of a web server script that should be used to process the submitted data.

The **method** attribute can be assigned values of "GET" or "POST". Submission via the preferred GET method appends the data to the URL, whereas submission via the POST method encodes the data differently and can be used when the GET method fails.

Typically a HTML form will have a "Submit" button that the user clicks to submit data for processing. This is created by assigning the value "submit" to the **type** attribute of an **<input>** tag. Additionally this tag may include **name** and **value** attributes to submit data assigned to them as a name=value pair.

The server-side script used throughout this chapter is written in the Perl language and requires the installation of ActivePerl support on Windows systems. This can be freely downloaded from **www.activestate.com**.

In order to demonstrate form submission and web server response the examples throughout this chapter use a personal web server. This emulates submission of data to an external web server but is installed locally on the host computer. Like many web servers it has a directory named "htdocs" in which to deposit web pages and can be addressed by the domain name "localhost", or alternatively by the IP address 127.0.0.1. For example, to view the default page entitled "index.html" web page with the server running enter **http://localhost/index.html** in the browser address field, or alternatively enter **http://127.0.0.1/index.html**.

To provide a response from the web server the **htdocs** directory contains a custom server-side script named "echo.pl" that echos the submitted name=value data in a HTML document – in each example its URL is assigned to the form's **action** attribute. The web server's response displays the values in a **<div>** container with "rounded" corners, using the technique described on page 72.

submit.html

1. Start a new HTML document with the Strict DTD

```
<!DOCTYPE HTML PUBLIC "-//W3C//DTD HTML 4.01//EN"
                    "http://www.w3.org/TR/html4/strict.dtd">
```

2. Add a root element containing head and body sections

```
<html> <head> <title>Form Submission</title>
<meta http-equiv="Content-type"
          content="text/html; charset=ISO-8859-1">
</head>
<body><!-- Content goes here. --></body> </html>
```

3. In the body section, insert a HTML form element

```
<form method="GET" action="http://localhost/echo.pl">

</form>
```

4. In the form element, insert a paragraph containing a submit button

```
<p> <input type="submit" name="Submit Button"
        value="My Form Submission" > </p>
```

5. Save the HTML document then open it in your browser, via a web server, then click the button to submit the data assigned to its name=value pair, and to see the response

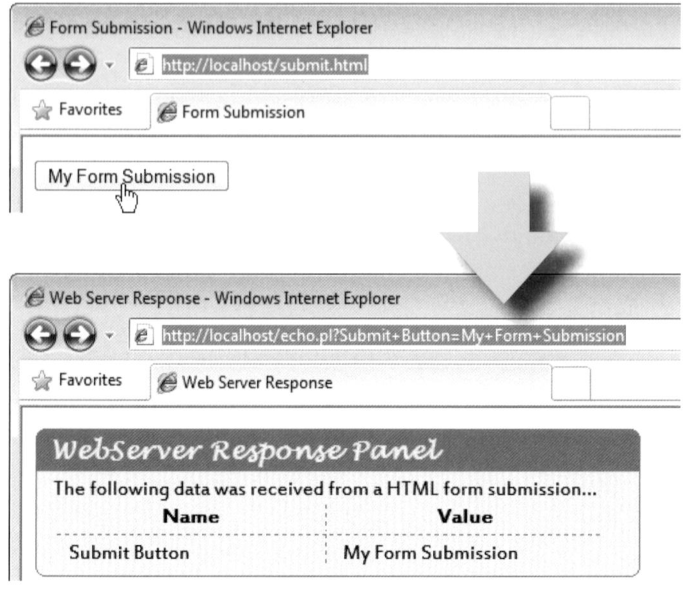

Beware

Examples in this chapter must be opened via a web server domain, such as localhost – you cannot send data to the server if they are opened by simply clicking on the HTML file icon.

Don't forget

Notice the data appended in the browser's address field by the GET method – you can submit via the POST method to prevent this for sensitive data.

Gathering text input

A HTML form can provide text boxes where the user can input data for submission to the web server for processing. These are created by assigning the value "text" to the **type** attribute of an **<input>** tag and a name to its **name** attribute. Upon submission the data in the text box is sent as the value associated with the given name as a name=value pair. Optionally the **<input>** tag can include a **value** attribute to specify a default value.

A text box for the input of a password is created by assigning the value "password" to the **type** attribute of an **<input>** tag. This functions like any other text box except it does not display its contents as readable text.

Both password and regular text **<input>** elements can optionally include a number of other attributes to control their performance:

- **size** – the width of the text box in average character widths
- **maxlength** – the maximum number of characters
- **readonly** – the default value in the text box cannot be changed
- **disabled** – the text box is grayed out and will not be submitted

text.html

1. Start a new HTML document with the Strict DTD

```
<!DOCTYPE HTML PUBLIC "-//W3C//DTD HTML 4.01//EN"
              "http://www.w3.org/TR/html4/strict.dtd">
```

2. Add a root element containing head and body sections

```
<html> <head> <title>Text Submission</title>
<meta http-equiv="Content-type"
        content="text/html; charset=ISO-8859-1">
</head>
<body><!-- Content goes here. --></body> </html>
```

3. In the body section, insert a HTML form element containing a submit button for the GET method

```
<form method="GET" action="http://localhost/echo.pl">
<!-- Text input elements to go here. -->
<p><input type="submit" value="Submit Form"></p>
</form>
```

4. Within the form element, insert a definition list element

```
<dl>   </dl>
```

5. In the definition list, insert labels and text field elements

```
<dt>User Name :
<dd><input type="text" name="1. Name">
<dt>Password :
<dd><input type="password" name="2. Password">
<dt>City :
<dd><input type="text" name="3. City" value="Dallas">
<dt>Area :
<dd><input type="text" name="4. Area"
                        value="Downtown" disabled>
<dt>State :
<dd><input type="text" name="5. State"
                        value="Texas" readonly>
<dt>Zip Code :
<dd><input type="text" name="6. Zip Code"
                        size="5" maxlength="5">
```

Don't forget

The optional closing **</dt>** and **</dd>** tags are best included but are omitted here for brevity.

6. Save the HTML document then open it in your browser via a web server, enter some data, and submit the form

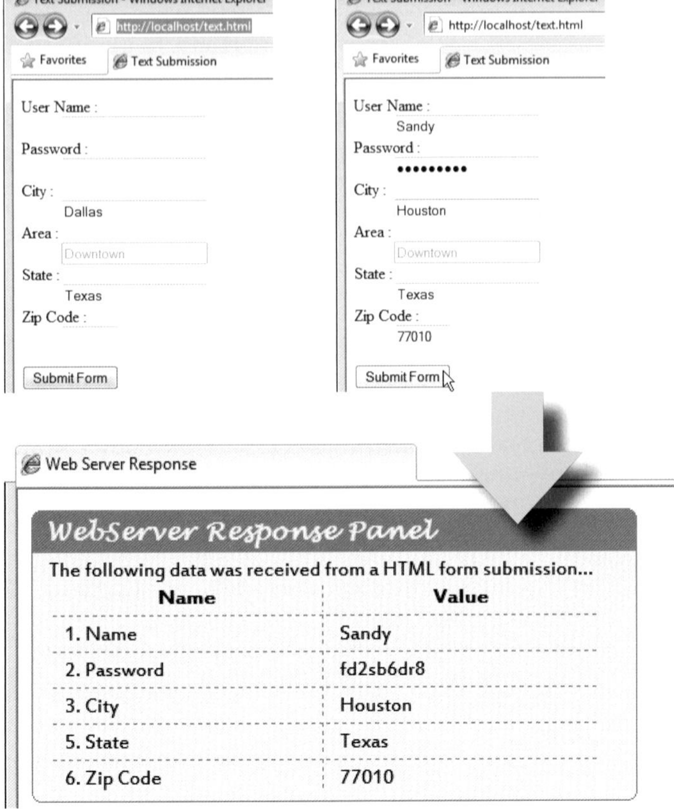

The server-side script returns the submitted data sorted in alphanumeric name order – notice that field #4 is disabled so its data was not submitted.

Providing text areas

A HTML form can provide a multi-line text field where the user can input data for submission to the web server for processing. These are created by **<textarea> </textarea>** tags that may enclose default text content. The **<textarea>** tag should include a **name** attribute that will be associated with the element's content upon submission as a name=value pair. Additionally this tag must include a **rows** attribute, to specify the number of visible text lines, and a **cols** attribute to specify its width in average character widths. Optionally it may also include a **readonly** attribute to prevent the user editing its content.

When submitting large bodies of text you must be aware of some capacity limitations of the GET method. This varies by browser but Internet Explorer typically allows the URL to contain up to approximately 2000 characters. The POST method provides much larger capacity as the text is sent in the HTTP header, not appended to the URL:

Beware

The average character width may vary between browsers – so the size of a **<textarea>** field may appear differently.

textarea.html

1. Start a new HTML document with the Strict DTD

```
<!DOCTYPE HTML PUBLIC "-//W3C//DTD HTML 4.01//EN"
                  "http://www.w3.org/TR/html4/strict.dtd">
```

2. Add a root element containing head and body sections

```
<html> <head> <title>Text Area Submission</title>
<meta http-equiv="Content-type"
          content="text/html; charset=ISO-8859-1">
</head>
<body><!-- Content goes here. --></body> </html>
```

3. In the body section, insert a HTML form element containing a submit button for the POST method

```
<form method="POST" action="http://localhost/echo.pl">
<!-- Text area element to go here. -->
<p><input type="submit" value="Submit Form"></p>
</form>
```

4. Within the form element, insert a paragraph containing an empty text area

```
<p>
<textarea name="The Future Web" rows="10" cols="50">
</textarea>
</p>
```

Don't forget

Unlike a text **<input>** element the **<textarea>** element has no **value** attribute – as its content is treated as its value.

5. Save the HTML document then open it in your browser via a web server, enter some data, and submit the form

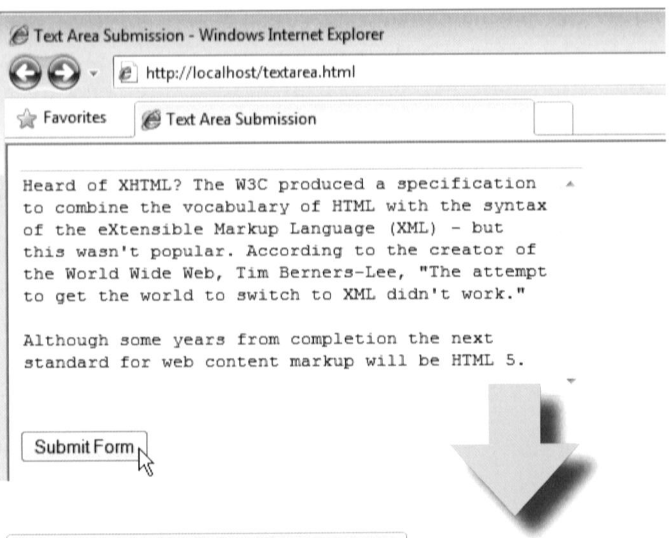

Web Server Response

WebServer Response Panel

The following data was received from a HTML form submission...

Name	Value
The Future Web	Heard of XHTML? The W3C produced a specification to combine the vocabulary of HTML with the syntax of the eXtensible Markup Language (XML) - but this wasn't popular. According to the creator of the World Wide Web, Tim Berners-Lee, "The attempt to get the world to switch to XML didn't work." Although some years from completion the next standard for web content markup will be HTML 5.

ieHTTPHeaders

Host: localhost
Content-Length: 428

The+Future+Web=Heard+of+XHTML%
3F+The+W3C+produced+a+specification+to+combine+the+vocabulary+of+HTML+with+the
+syntax+of+the+eXtensible+Markup+Language+%28XML%29+-+but+this+wasn%
27t+popular.+According+to+the+creator+of+the+World+Wide+Web%2C+Tim+Berners-
Lee%2C+%22The+attempt+to+get+the+world+to+switch+to+XML+didn%27t+work.%22%
0D%0A%0D%
0AAlthough+some+years+from+completion+the+next+standard+for+web+content+markup+
will+be+HTML+5.

Hot tip

The ieHTTPHeaders plugin for Internet Explorer, introduced back on page 11, can be used to see the **<textarea>** value embedded in the response header with spaces and punctuation replaced by escape codes.

Checking boxes

A HTML form can provide a visual checkbox "on/off switch" that the user can toggle to include or exclude its associated data for submission to the server. When the box is checked the switch is set to "on" and its name=value pair will be submitted, but when the box is unchecked the switch is set to "off" and its name=value pair is not submitted.

Beware

The <fieldset> element only groups the related elements it encloses for visual presentation – it does not associate them programatically.

A checkbox is created by assigning the value "checkbox" to the **type** attribute of an **<input>** tag. This tag must also include a **name** attribute and a **value** attribute to specify the name=value pair values. Optionally this tag may also include a **checked** attribute to set the initial state of the switch to "on" – so a check mark will automatically appear in the checkbox.

Checkbox names may be individually unique or several checkboxes can share a common name to allow the user to select multiple values for the same named property. In this case the selected values are returned by the web server as a comma-separated list where name=value,value,value.

Multiple checkboxes that share a common name can be visually grouped by surrounding their **<input>** elements by **<fieldset> </fieldset>** tags. These may also contain **<legend> </legend>** tags to contain a group name:

checkbox.html

1. Start a new HTML document with the Strict DTD

```
<!DOCTYPE HTML PUBLIC "-//W3C//DTD HTML 4.01//EN"
                "http://www.w3.org/TR/html4/strict.dtd">
```

2. Add a root element containing head and body sections

```
<html> <head> <title>Checkbox Submission</title>
<meta http-equiv="Content-type"
        content="text/html; charset=ISO-8859-1">
</head>
<body><!-- Content goes here. --></body> </html>
```

3. In the body section, insert a HTML form element containing a submit button for the GET method

```
<form method="GET" action="http://localhost/echo.pl">
<!-- Checkbox elements to go here. -->
<p><input type="submit" value="Submit Form"></p>
</form>
```

4. Within the form element, insert a paragraph containing an automatically checked checkbox

```
<p> Yes, I would like to receive details
<input type="checkbox" name="Ask For"
                              value="Details" checked> </p>
```

5. Next in the form element, insert a fieldset containing a legend and five unchecked checkboxes

```
<fieldset>
<legend>Activities of Interest...</legend>
Sailing<input type="checkbox" name="Do" value="Sail">
Walking<input type="checkbox" name="Do" value="Walk">
Driving<input type="checkbox" name="Do" value="Drive">
Ski-ing<input type="checkbox" name="Do" value="Ski">
Jogging<input type="checkbox" name="Do" value="Jog">
</fieldset>
```

6. Save the HTML document then open it in your browser via a web server, check some boxes, and submit the form to see the response

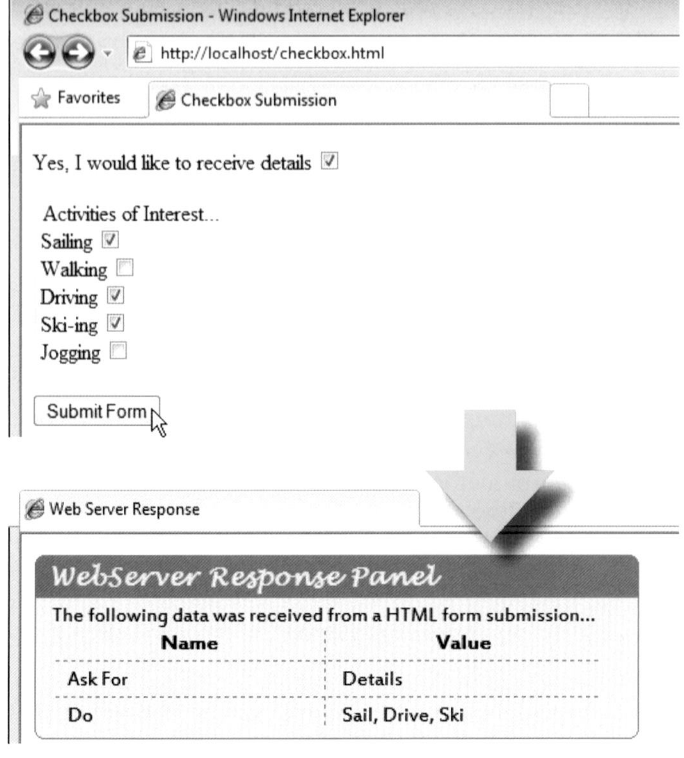

Hot tip

Notice that the **checked** attribute is not assigned a value – its mere presence sets the checkbox switch to "on" and its absence leaves the switch in its default "off" state.

Don't forget

With the illustrated boxes checked the name=value pairs are not sent for the Walking and Jogging activities.

Choosing radio buttons

A HTML form can provide visual "radio button" groups, from which the user can select one button to include its associated data for submission to the server. When the button is selected its switch is set to "on" and its name=value pair will be submitted, otherwise its switch is set to "off" and its name=value pair is not submitted. Unlike checkboxes, radio buttons that share a common name are mutually exclusive, so when one radio button is selected all others in that group are automatically switched off.

A radio button is created by assigning the value "radio" to the **type** attribute of an **<input>** tag. This tag must also include a **name** attribute and a **value** attribute to specify the name=value pair values. Optionally this tag may also include a **checked** attribute to set the initial state of the switch to "on" – so the button will automatically appear selected.

Radio button groups that share a common name can be visually grouped by surrounding their **<input>** elements by **<fieldset> </fieldset>** tags. These may also contain **<legend> </legend>** tags to contain a group name:

radio.html

1. Start a new HTML document with the Strict DTD

```
<!DOCTYPE HTML PUBLIC "-//W3C//DTD HTML 4.01//EN"
                 "http://www.w3.org/TR/html4/strict.dtd">
```

2. Add a root element containing head and body sections

```
<html> <head> <title>Radio Button Submission</title>
<meta http-equiv="Content-type"
        content="text/html; charset=ISO-8859-1">
</head>
<body><!-- Content goes here. --></body> </html>
```

3. In the body section, insert a HTML form element containing a fieldset with a legend and a submit button for the GET method

```
<form method="GET" action="http://localhost/echo.pl">
<p>Choose only one answer...</p>
<fieldset>
<legend>What kind of language is HTML?</legend>

<!-- Radio button elements to go here. -->

</fieldset>
<p><input type="submit" value="Submit Form"></p>
</form>
```

4. Within the form's fieldset element, insert three radio buttons, with one selected

```
Scripting <input type="radio"
                    name="Definition" value="Scripting">
Markup <input type="radio"
                    name="Definition" value="Markup">
Programming <input type="radio"
          name="Definition" value="Programming" checked>
```

5. Save the HTML document then open it in your browser via a web server, select the radio button associated with the correct answer, and submit the form to see the response

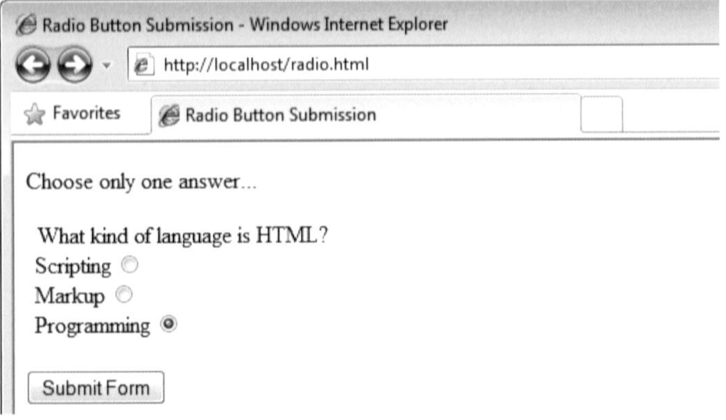

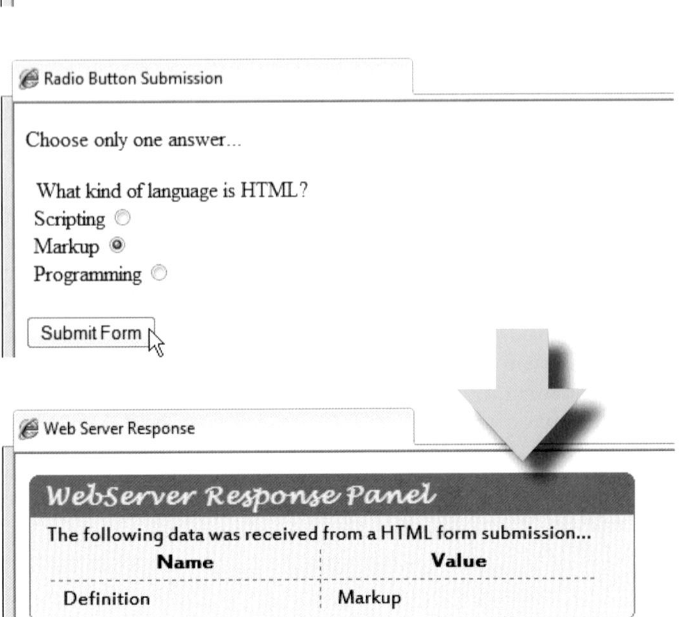

Don't forget

Radio button elements resemble the buttons on old radios where each button selected a particular radio station.

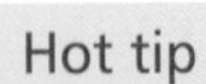

Hot tip

Always include a **checked** attribute to automatically select one button in each radio button group – to provide a default choice.

Selecting options

A HTML form can provide a select option list, from which the user can select one option to include its associated data for submission to the server.

A select option list is created using **<select> </select>** tags. The opening **<select>** tag must include a **name** attribute specifying a list name. The **<select>** element encloses **<option> </option>** tags that define each option. Each opening **<option>** tag must include a **value** attribute specifying an option value. When the form is submitted the list name and the selected option value are sent to the web server as a name=value pair.

Optionally one **<option>** tag may also include a **selected** attribute to automatically select that option and the **<option>** elements may be visually grouped by enclosure in **<optgroup> </optgroup>** tags. The opening **<optgroup>** tag may specify an option group name to a **label** attribute.

A select option list will normally appear as a single-line dropdown list unless a **size** attribute is included in the **<select>** tag to specify the number of rows to be visible:

select.html

1. Start a new HTML document with the Strict DTD

```
<!DOCTYPE HTML PUBLIC "-//W3C//DTD HTML 4.01//EN"
                "http://www.w3.org/TR/html4/strict.dtd">
```

2. Add a root element containing head and body sections

```
<html> <head> <title>Select Option Submission</title>
<meta http-equiv="Content-type"
          content="text/html; charset=ISO-8859-1">
</head>
<body><!-- Content goes here. --></body> </html>
```

3. In the body section, insert a HTML form element containing an empty paragraph element and a submit button for the GET method

```
<form method="GET" action="http://localhost/echo.pl">
<p>

<!-- Select option elements to go here. -->

</p>
<p><input type="submit" value="Submit Form"></p>
</form>
```

4. Within the form element, insert a fixed height select option list with one option selected

```
<select name="HTML List Type Selector One" size="4" >
<optgroup label="List Type 1">
<option value="UL">Unordered List</option>
<option value="OL" selected>Ordered List</option>
<option value="DL">Definition List</option>
</optgroup>
</select>
```

5. Next within the form element, insert a dropdown select option list with one option selected

```
<select name="HTML List Type Selector Two">
<optgroup label="List Type 2">
<option value="UL">Unordered List</option>
<option value="OL">Ordered List</option>
<option value="DL" selected>Definition List</option>
</optgroup>
</select>
```

6. Save the HTML document then open it in your browser via a web server and open the dropdown list, then submit the default selected options to see the response

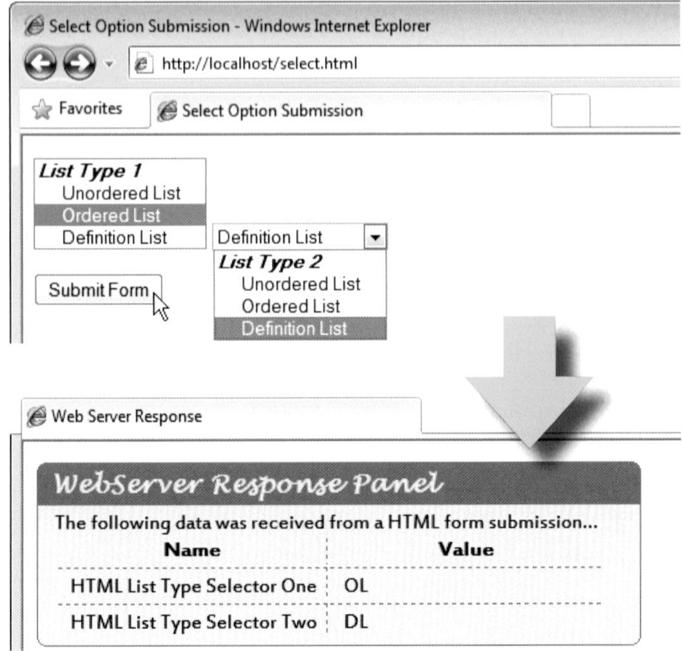

Beware

Notice that both select option lists must be enclosed within a block-level element.

Hot tip

Always include a **selected** attribute to automatically select one option in each option group – to provide a default choice.

Uploading files

A HTML form can provide a file selection facility, which calls upon the operating system's "Choose File" dialog to allow the user to browse their local filesystem and select a file.

A file selection facility is created by assigning the value "file" to the **type** attribute of an **<input>** tag and a name to its **name** attribute. This element produces a text field and a "Browse" button to launch the Choose File dialog. After a file has been selected its full path appears in the text field. Optionally the **<input>** tag can also include a **size** attribute to specify the text field size in average character widths. When the form is submitted the element name and the selected file's name are sent to the web server as a name=value pair.

Where a selected file is to be uploaded to the web server the **<form>** tag must include an **enctype** attribute specifying a value of "multipart/formdata" and its **method** attribute specify POST:

upload.html

1. Start a new HTML document with the Strict DTD

```
<!DOCTYPE HTML PUBLIC "-//W3C//DTD HTML 4.01//EN"
                "http://www.w3.org/TR/html4/strict.dtd">
```

2. Add a root element containing head and body sections

```
<html> <head> <title>File Upload</title>
<meta http-equiv="Content-type"
        content="text/html; charset=ISO-8859-1">
</head>
<body><!-- Content goes here. --></body> </html>
```

3. In the body section, insert a HTML form element containing a submit button for the POST method

```
<form method="POST" action="http://localhost/echo.pl"
        enctype="multipart/formdata">
<p>
<!-- File input element to go here. -->

<input type="submit" value="Submit Form"></p>
</form>
```

4. Within the form paragraph, insert a file input element and a line break

```
<input type="file" name="File" size="50"> <br>
```

5. Save the HTML document then open it in your browser via a web server and Browse to select a local file

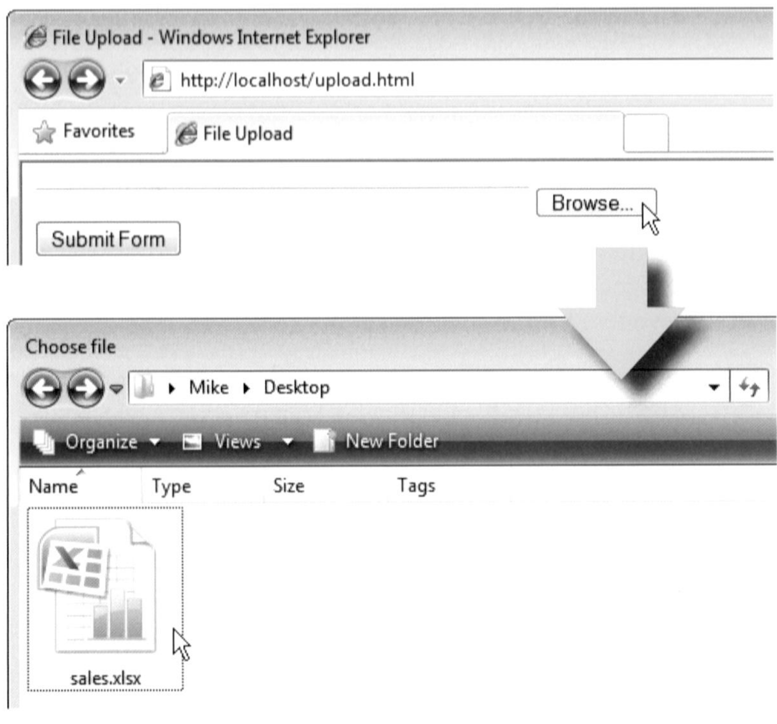

Notice that only the file name is submitted to the web server – the browser knows its full path.

6. Once a file has been selected, submit the form to see the web server's response

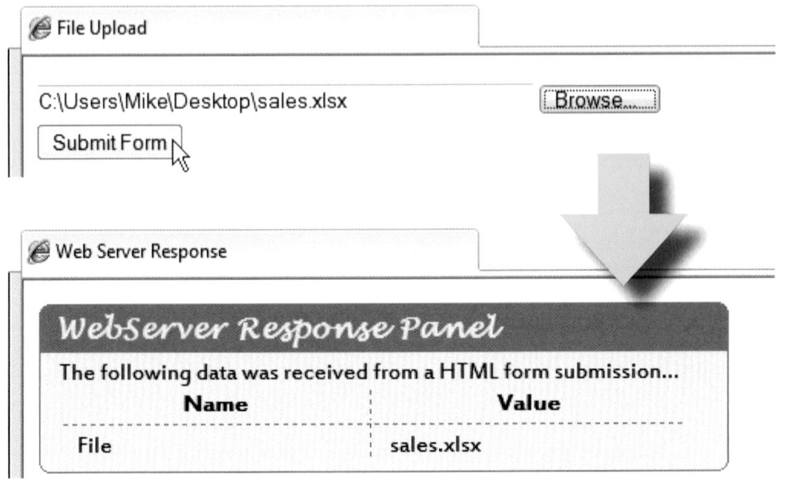

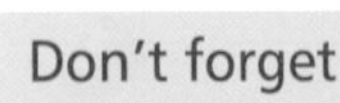

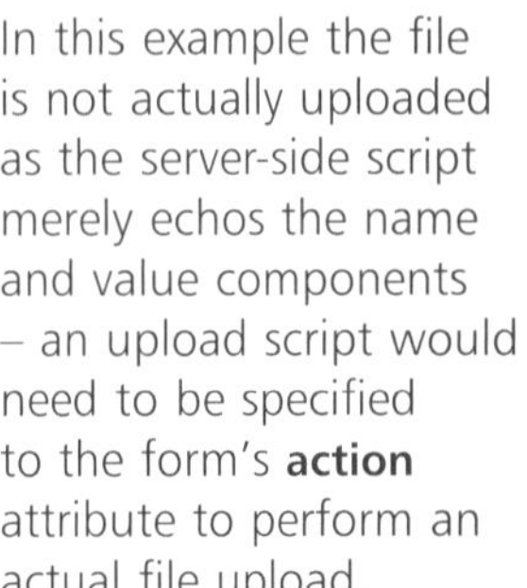

In this example the file is not actually uploaded as the server-side script merely echos the name and value components – an upload script would need to be specified to the form's **action** attribute to perform an actual file upload.

Utilizing hidden data

The HTML form components introduced previously in this chapter enable the user to enter data for submission to a web server but HTML also provides form components to submit hidden data to the web server – both static and scripted data.

Hidden form data is created by assigning the value "hidden" to the **type** attribute of an **<input>** tag. This tag must also include a **name** attribute and may include a **value** attribute to specify static data that will be submitted as a name=value pair. Optionally the **<input>** tag may include an **id** attribute and omit the **value** attribute so its value can be specified by script. For example, static data could identify a form number and scripting could identify the user's browser and submission date:

hidden.html

1. Start a new HTML document with the Strict DTD

```
<!DOCTYPE HTML PUBLIC "-//W3C//DTD HTML 4.01//EN"
                     "http://www.w3.org/TR/html4/strict.dtd">
```

2. Add a root element containing a head section incorporating a script, and a body section

```
<html> <head> <title>Hidden Data Submission</title>
<meta http-equiv="Content-Type"
          content="text/html; charset=ISO-8859-1">
<script type="text/javascript" src="hidden.js"></script>
</head>
<body><!-- Content goes here. --></body> </html>
```

3. In the body section, insert a HTML form element containing a submit button for the GET method

```
<form method="GET" action="http://localhost/echo.pl">
<p>
<!-- Hidden and User input elements to go here. -->

<input type="submit" value="Submit Form"></p>
</form>
```

4. Within the form paragraph, insert an input element for user data

```
User Name: <input type="text" name="Name" >
```

5. Next within the form paragraph, insert a hidden input element for static data

```
<input type="hidden" name="Form No." value="257">
```

Hot tip

Hidden data elements are useful to maintain user data across a website – a user name input on the first page can be recalled on any other page.

6. Now within the form paragraph, insert hidden inputs with identities for scripting but without value attributes

```
<input type="hidden" id="Browser" name="Browser">
<input type="hidden" id="Date" name="Date">
```

7. Save the HTML document then open a text editor and precisely copy this small script to set hidden input values

hidden.js

```
function init()
{
  document.getElementById("Browser").value=
                                      navigator.appName;
  document.getElementById("Date").value=new Date();
}
window.onload=init;
```

8. Save the script as "hidden.js" alongside the HTML document then open the web page in your browser via a web server and submit the form to see the hidden data

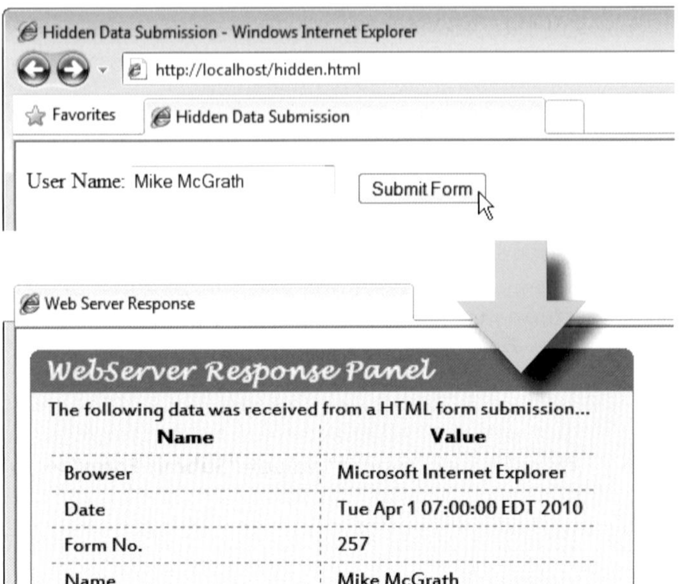

JavaScript is case-sensitive so you must use the correct case when copying scripts.

Pushing buttons

A HTML form can provide a push button for scripting purposes. When the user pushes a button a "click event" occurs to which a script function can respond. This allows the user to dynamically interact with the form and can be used to set attribute values. A push button is created by specifying a "button" value to the **type** attribute of an **<input>** tag and should include an **id** attribute so the script can easily identify that element.

A HTML form can be returned to its original state by pushing a Reset button that is created by specifying a "reset" value to the **type** attribute of an **<input>** tag:

button.html

1. Start a new HTML document with the Strict DTD

```
<!DOCTYPE HTML PUBLIC "-//W3C//DTD HTML 4.01//EN"
                "http://www.w3.org/TR/html4/strict.dtd">
```

2. Add a root element containing a head section incorporating a script, and a body section

```
<html> <head> <title>Push Buttons</title>
<meta http-equiv="Content-Type"
          content="text/html; charset=ISO-8859-1">
<script type="text/javascript" src="button.js"></script>
</head>
<body><!-- Content goes here. --></body> </html>
```

3. In the body section, insert a HTML form element containing a Reset button, a push button, and a submit button for the GET method

```
<form method="GET" action="http://localhost/echo.pl">
 <!-- Fieldset to go here. -->
<p><input type="reset" value="Reset Form" >
<input id="btn" type="button" value="Choose For Me">
<input type="submit" value="Submit Form"></p>
</form>
```

4. Within the form element, insert a fieldset containing a checkbox group

```
<fieldset> <legend>Pizza Toppings</legend>
<input id="pepperoni" type="checkbox"
  name="Toppings" value="Pepperoni"> Pepperoni |
<input id="mushroom" type="checkbox"
  name="Toppings" value="Mushroom"> Mushroom |
<input id="bbqsauce" type="checkbox"
  name="Toppings" value="BBQ Sauce"> BBQ Sauce
</fieldset>
```

5. Save the HTML document then open a text editor and copy this script to respond to the push button click event

```
function init()
{ document.getElementById("btn").onclick=choose; }

function choose()
{ document.getElementById("pepperoni").checked=true; }

window.onload=init;
```

button.js

6. Save the script as "button.js" alongside the HTML document then open the web page in your browser via a web server and click the push button to check a box

7. Click the Reset button to clear the form then check other boxes and submit the form

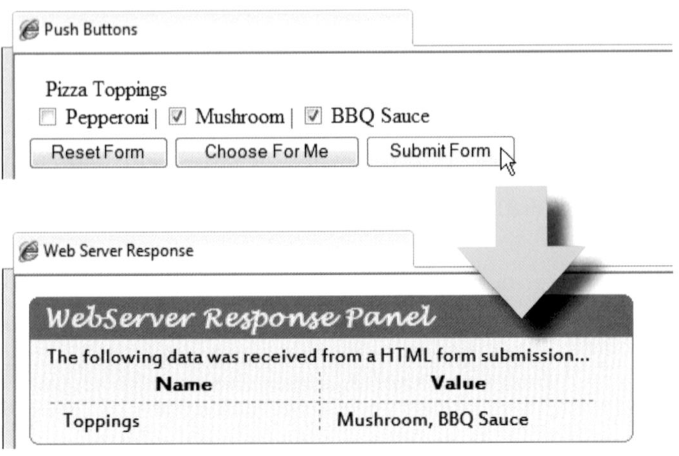

Hot tip

When the document has loaded this script nominates a function for the push button's **onclick** property that will check a checkbox when the button gets pushed.

Using images for submission

A HTML form can use an image to submit form data, in place of a regular submit button, by specifying an "image" value to the **type** attribute of an **<input>** tag and including an **alt** attribute. When a pointing device clicks on the image the form data is submitted along with the X and Y coordinates where the click occurred:

ibutton.html

1. Start a new HTML document with the Strict DTD

```
<!DOCTYPE HTML PUBLIC "-//W3C//DTD HTML 4.01//EN"
                 "http://www.w3.org/TR/html4/strict.dtd">
```

2. Add a root element containing head and body sections

```
<html> <head> <title>Image Submission</title>
<meta http-equiv="Content-Type"
        content="text/html; charset=ISO-8859-1">
</head><body><!-- Content here. --></body> </html>
```

3. In the body section, insert a HTML form element containing a text input and an image for form submission

```
<form method="GET" action="http://localhost/echo.pl">
 <p>Email Address:<input type="text" name="address">
<input type="image" src="ibutton.png" alt="Submit">
</p></form>
```

4. Save the HTML document then open it in your browser via a web server, enter data and click the image

Don't forget

The X,Y coordinates are measured across the image area – so at its top left corner X=0, Y=0.

A regular <img> tag can also be used to submit a form by including an **onclick** attribute to call a script function. This is often useful to implement validation of form data before submission:

5. In the head section, insert an element to incorporate a script

```
<script type="text/javascript" src="ibutton.js"></script>
```

6. Edit the form to replace the image input by a regular image and to add two element identities for scripting

```
<form id="form1"
        method="GET" action="http://localhost/echo.pl">
 <p>Enter Your Email Address:
<input id="adr" type="text" name="address" size="40">
<image src="ibutton.png" alt="Submit"
        width="130" height="45" onclick="send()">
</p></form>
```

7. Save the amended HTML document then open a text editor and precisely copy this script function

```
function send()
{
 var address=document.getElementById("adr").value;
 var pattern=
/^([a-zA-Z0-9_.-])+@([a-zA-Z0-9_.-])+\.([a-zA-Z])+([a-zA-Z])+/;
 if( ! pattern.test(address) ) alert( "Invalid Email Address" );
 else document.getElementById("form1").submit();
}
```

ibutton.js

8. Save the script alongside the HTML document as "ibutton.js" then open the web page and submit the form with any invalid email address to see an error message

9. Correct the error and submit the form once more

Hot tip

The script in this example checks the input text against a regular expression pattern that describes the format of any valid email address. The pattern must appear on a single line – exactly as it is listed here.

Adding images to buttons

HTML 4 can create push buttons that display small "logo" images using **<button> </button>** tags to enclose an **<img>** element. Each **<button>** tag should include a **type** attribute to specify whether the button is simply a scripting "button" or if it should "submit" or "reset" the form. Scripting buttons can include an **onclick** attribute to call a script function or specify a script action. Text within the **<button>** element will appear on the button face:

logo.html

1. Start a new HTML document with the Strict DTD

```
<!DOCTYPE HTML PUBLIC "-//W3C//DTD HTML 4.01//EN"
                "http://www.w3.org/TR/html4/strict.dtd">
```

2. Add a root element containing head and body sections

```
<html> <head> <title>Logo Buttons</title>
<meta http-equiv="Content-Type"
        content="text/html; charset=ISO-8859-1">
</head><body><!-- Content here. --></body> </html>
```

3. In the body section, insert a HTML form element containing a fieldset with a legend and a text input

```
<form method="GET" action="http://localhost/echo.pl">
 <fieldset>
<legend>Favorite Color</legend>
<input type="text" name="Color">
<!-- Button elements to go here. -->
</fieldset>
</form>
```

4. In the fieldset, insert a scripting button element specifying a script action for when it gets clicked

```
<button type="button"
onclick="alert('Enter your favorite color in the text box')">
<!-- Image and face text to go here. -->
</button>
```

5. In the button element, insert an image element and text to appear on the face of the button

```
<img src="logo-q.png"
        width="32" height="32" alt="Help">Help
```

6. Next add a button element to submit the form

```
<button type="submit">
<img src="logo-s.png" width="32" height="32"
        alt="Submit">Submit</button>
```

7. Now add a button element to reset the form

```
<button type="reset">
<img src="logo-x.png" width="32" height="32"
        alt="Reset">Reset</button>
```

8. Save the HTML document then open it in your browser via a web server and click the Help button for information

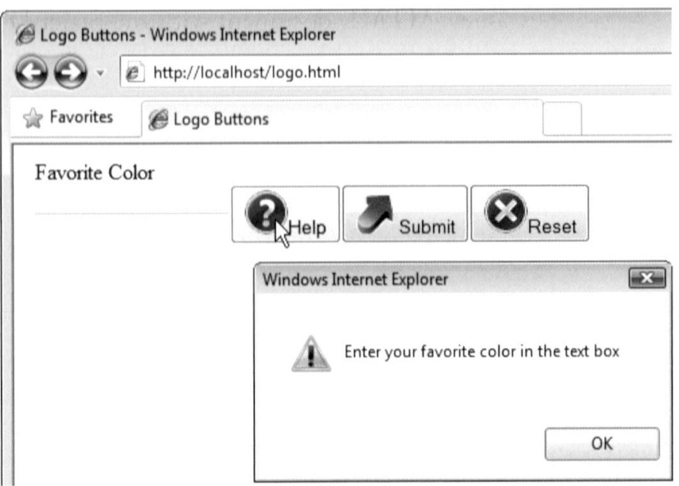

9. Enter a color and click the Reset button to clear the text box, then enter a different color and click the Submit button to submit the form to the web server

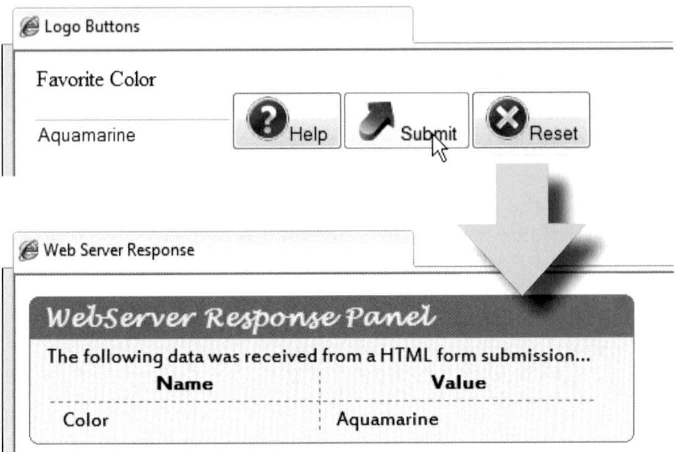

You can specify a default value for a text input to the **value** attribute of its **<input>** tag.

Labeling form controls

Text that is to be associated with a HTML form control can be enclosed within **<label> </label>** tags. The opening **<label>** tag can include a **for** attribute to specify the value assigned to the control's **id** attribute to make the association. Alternatively the **<label>** element can simply enclose both the text and the control element to make the association. This allows styling to be applied to the entire label – including the text and the control. Often this is useful to distinguish the control associated with particular text.

Additionally each form control element may include a **tabindex** attribute to specify its tabbing order within the document as a unique value between 0 and 32,767. Using the tab key the user can then navigate through the document starting at the lowest **tabindex** value and proceeding through successively higher values:

label.html

1. Start a new HTML document with the Strict DTD

```
<!DOCTYPE HTML PUBLIC "-//W3C//DTD HTML 4.01//EN"
                  "http://www.w3.org/TR/html4/strict.dtd">
```

2. Add a root element containing head and body sections

```
<html> <head> <title>Form Labels</title>
<meta http-equiv="Content-Type"
          content="text/html; charset=ISO-8859-1">
</head><body><!-- Content here. --></body> </html>
```

3. In the body section, insert a HTML form element containing a submit button – to be first in the tab order

```
<form method="GET" action="http://localhost/echo.pl">
<!-- Fieldset to go here. -->
<p>
<input type="submit" value="Submit Form" tabindex="1">
</p>
</form>
```

4. In the form element, insert a fieldset containing a legend

```
<fieldset> <legend>Tools</legend>
<!-- Form control elements to go here. -->
</fieldset>
```

5. In the fieldset, insert a label containing a checkbox control and associated text – to be second in the tab order

```
<label>Hammer
<input type="checkbox" name="Tools"
       value="Hammer" tabindex="2"> </label>
```

Hot tip

A form "control" is any **<input>**, **<button>** or **<textarea>** element. A **tabindex** attribute can be included in these tags and also in any **<a>**, **<area>**, **<object>**, or **<select>** tag.

6. Repeat step five to insert five more labelled checkbox controls with various values, in successive tab order, then save the HTML document and open it in your browser

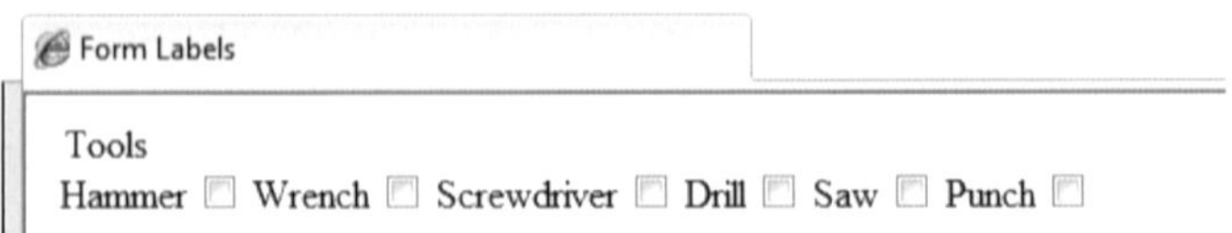

7. To visually identify labels and controls incorporate a style sheet by adding an element in the document head section
<link rel="stylesheet" type="text/css" href="label.css">

8. Insert an attribute in each alternate label tag
<label class="hilite">

9. Save the HTML document once more then open a text editor and create a style rule
label.hilite { background : red ; color: white ; }

label.css

10. Save the Cascading Style Sheet alongside the HTML document then open the web page via a web server – use the tab key to check some boxes, then submit the form

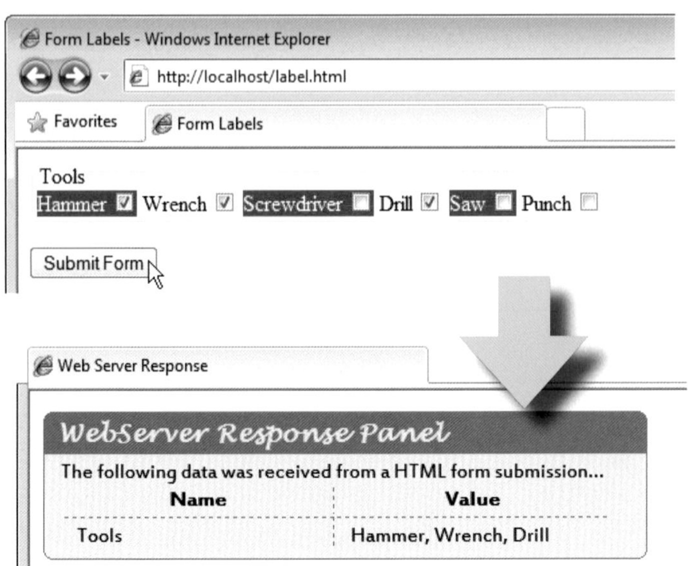

Hot tip

Use the tab key to navigate between form controls and use the space bar to check, uncheck, and submit.

Scripting event attributes

HTML provides a number of attributes to respond to "events" that are "fired" as the user interacts with the elements of a document. These attributes can specify a line of script code or nominate a script function to handle the event. Typically the "event-handler" function will dynamically change one or more element properties. Form controls can be used for scripting purposes without a **<form>** element if not for submission.

The table below lists all the scripting event attributes together with a brief description and the elements where they may be used:

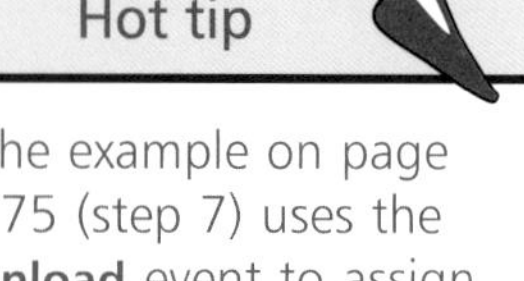

The example on page 175 (step 7) uses the **onload** event to assign values to hidden form elements. The example on page 177 (step 5) uses the **onload** event to nominate an event-handler function for a button's **onclick** event. The example on page 179 (step 6) uses the **onclick** attribute to submit a form.

Attribute	Event fires when	Available in
onload	document has loaded	**body, frameset**
onunload	document unloads	
onclick	mouse button clicked	**[most elements]**
ondblclick	mouse double-clicked	
onmousedown	mouse button pressed	
onmouseup	mouse button released	
onmouseover	cursor moves on	
onmousemove	cursor moves across	
onmouseout	cursor moves off	
onkeypress	key pressed & released	
onkeydown	key pressed down	
onkeyup	key released	
onfocus	focus is gained	**a, area, label, input, select, textarea, button**
onblur	focus is lost	
onsubmit	form is submitted	**form**
onreset	form is reset	
onselect	text is selected	**input, textarea**
onchange	focus is lost after the value is changed	**input, select, textarea**

Hot tip

The ability to dynamically change document content in response to user actions is also known as "Dynamic HTML" or just "DHTML".

1. Start a new HTML document with the Strict DTD

```
<!DOCTYPE HTML PUBLIC "-//W3C//DTD HTML 4.01//EN"
                    "http://www.w3.org/TR/html4/strict.dtd">
```

event.html

2. Add a root element containing head and body sections

```
<html> <head> <title>Handling Events</title>
<meta http-equiv="Content-Type"
            content="text/html; charset=ISO-8859-1">
</head><body><!-- Content here. --></body> </html>
```

Beware

Notice that outer quote marks are double quote characters but inner nested quote marks are single quote characters.

3. In the body section, insert a paragraph containing a form control with two event attributes for scripting

```
<p> <input type="text" value="Click Here to Focus"
onfocus="value='Focus Received';style.color='red';"
onblur = "value='Focus Lost';style.color='blue';">
</p>
```

4. Next in the paragraph, insert a span with one event attribute for scripting

```
<span
onclick="innerHTML='Mouse Clicked'; style.color='blue';">
 ... then Click Here to Move Focus</span>
```

5. Save the HTML document then open it in your browser and follow the on-page instructions to fire the events

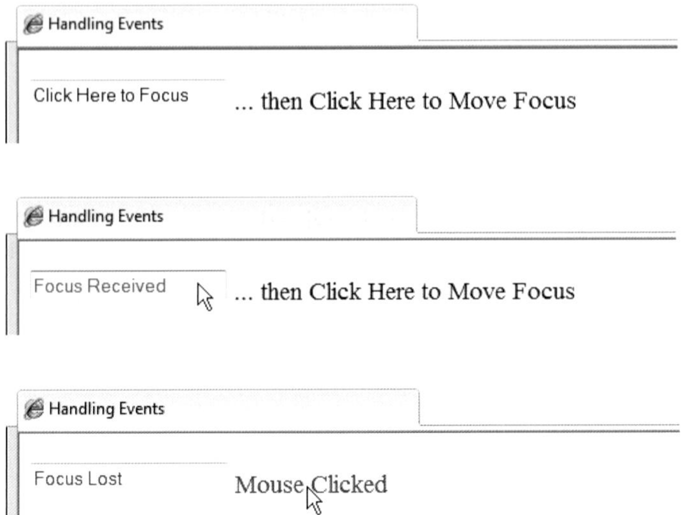

Don't forget

The **onmouseover**, **onmousedown**, and **onmouseout** attributes can be used to represent an element's state – in a similar manner to the CSS **hover**, **active**, and **visited** pseudo-classes.

Summary

- A HTML form submits data to a web server as a name=value pair for processing by a server-side script
- Form controls can be contained within **<p> </p>** paragraph or **<fieldset> </fieldset>** tags, between **<form> </form>** tags
- The opening **<form>** tag must include an **action** attribute, to specify the URL of the processing script to process, and can include a **method** attribute to specify the submission method
- Each **<input>** tag should contain a **type** attribute to specify the control type as "text", "password", "checkbox", "radio", "submit", "image", "reset", "button", "hidden", or "file"
- An **<input>** tag can include **name** and **value** attributes to specify data for submission as a name=value pair
- A multi-line text field is created by **<textarea> </textarea>** tags and requires **rows** and **cols** attributes to specify its size
- Radio button and checkbox inputs only submit their **name** and **value** attribute values if they are checked
- An option list is created by enclosing a number of **<option>** elements within **<select> </select>** tags
- When creating a form to upload files an **enctype** attribute must be included within the **<form>** tag
- A form may be submitted by a regular submit **<input>** element, by an image **<input>** element, or by a **<button>** element
- Each form control can be enclosed within **<label> </label>** tags to visually group them with text for styling purposes
- Hidden and button form controls are often used for scripting
- HTML elements can include event attributes that allow script to dynamically respond to user actions
- Form controls can be used for scripting without a **<form>** element if their data is not for submission to the web server

Index

A

B

C

D

E

F

G

H

I

J

K

L

M

N

O

P

Q

R

S

T

U

V

W